GENDER AND AMERICAN HISTORY SINCE 1890

D1056690

REWRITING HISTORIES
Series editor: Jack R. Censer

Already published
THE INDUSTRIAL REVOLUTION AND WORK IN
NINETEENTH-CENTURY EUROPE
Edited by Lenard R. Berlanstein

SOCIETY AND CULTURE IN THE SLAVE SOUTH
Edited by J. William Harris

ATLANTIC AMERICAN SOCIETIES
From Columbus Through Abolition 1492–1888
Edited by Alan Karras and John McNeill

Forthcoming
DIVERSITY AND UNITY IN EARLY NORTH AMERICA
Edited by P. Morgan

NAZISM AND GERMAN SOCIETY 1933–1945
Edited by David Crew

GENDER AND AMERICAN HISTORY SINCE 1890

Edited by
Barbara Melosh

London and New York

First published 1993
by Routledge
11 New Fetter Lane, London EC4P 4EE

Simultaneously published in the USA and Canada
by Routledge
29 West 35th Street, New York, NY 10001

Editorial contribution © 1992 Barbara Melosh
Individual contributions © 1992 individual contributors

Typeset in 10 on 12 point Palatino by
Florencetype Ltd
Printed in Great Britain by
T.J. Press (Padstow) Ltd, Padstow, Cornwall

British Library Cataloguing in Publication Data

A catalogue record for this book is available from the
British Library

Library of Congress Cataloguing in Publication Data

Gender and American History since 1890 / edited by
Barbara Melosh.
p. cm. — (Rewriting histories)
Includes bibliographical references and index.
1. Sex role–United States–Historiography. 2. Sex
customs–United States Historiography. I. Melosh,
Barbara. II. Series.
305.30973

ISBN 0-415-07675-7   ISBN 0-415-07676-5 (pbk)

CONTENTS

CONTENTS

ILLUSTRATIONS

EDITOR'S PREFACE

Rewriting history, or revisionism, has always followed closely in the tow of history writing. In their efforts to re-evaluate the past, professional as well as amateur scholars have followed many approaches, most commonly as empiricists, uncovering new information to challenge earlier accounts. Historians have also revised previous versions by adopting new perspectives, usually fortified by new research, which overturn received views.

Even though rewriting is constantly taking place, historians' attitudes toward using new interpretations have been anything but settled. For most, the validity of revisionism lies in providing a stronger, more convincing account that better captures the objective truth of the matter. Although such historians might agree that we never finally arrive at the "truth," they believe it exists and over time may be better and better approximated. At the other extreme stand scholars who believe that each generation or even each cultural group or subgroup necessarily regards the past differently, each creating for itself a more usable history. Although these latter scholars do not reject the possibility of demonstrating empirically that some contentions are better than others, they focus upon generating new views based upon different life experiences. Different truths exist for different groups. Surely such an understanding, by emphasizing subjectivity, further encourages rewriting history. Between these two groups are those historians who wish to borrow from both sides. This third group, while accepting that every congeries of individuals sees matters differently, still wishes somewhat contradictorily to fashion a broader history that incorporates both of these particular visions. Revisionists who stress empiricism fall into the first of the three camps, while others spread out across the board.

Today the rewriting of history seems to have accelerated to a blinding speed as a consequence of the evolution of revisionism. A variety of approaches has emerged. A major factor in this process has been the enormous increase in the number of researchers. This explosion has reinforced and enabled the retesting of many assertions. Significant ideological shifts have also played a major part in the growth of revisionism. First, the crisis of Marxism, culminating in the events in Eastern Europe in 1989, has given rise to doubts about explicitly Marxist accounts. Such doubts have spilled over into the entire field of social history which has been a dominant subfield of the discipline for several decades. Focusing on society and its class divisions implied that these are the most important elements in historical analysis. Because Marxism was built on the same claim, the whole basis of social history has been questioned, despite the very many studies that had little directly to do with Marxism. Disillusionment with social history simultaneously opened the door to cultural and linguistic approaches largely developed in anthropology and literature. Multiculturalism and feminism further generated revisionism. By claiming that scholars had, wittingly or not, operated from a white European/American male point of view, newer researchers argued other approaches had been neglected or misunderstood. Not surprisingly, these last historians are the most likely to envision each subgroup rewriting its own usable history, while other scholars incline toward revisionism as part of the search for some stable truth.

Rewriting Histories will make these new approaches available to the student population. Often new scholarly debates take place in the scattered issues of journals which are sometimes difficult to find. Furthermore, in these first interactions, historians tend to address one another, leaving out the evidence that would make their arguments more accessible to the uninitiated. This series of books will collect in one place a strong group of the major articles in selected fields, adding notes and introductions conducive to improved understanding. Editors will select articles containing substantial historical data, so that students – at the least those who approach the subject as an objective phenomenon – can advance not only their comprehension of debated points but also their grasp of substantive aspects of the subject.

The works on gender included in this volume represent a first generation of studies in a field which itself sprang from the most recent wave of rethinking historical accounts. When writing the history of women, scholars challenged a record based primarily on men's experiences. The history of gender – definitions of masculinity and femininity and their change over time – developed in this process, urged on by influences including feminism and increasing interest in language. Although originally based in women's history, this new subject also emphasizes that men are gendered historical subjects; a history of men and masculinity has begun to emerge. Such work has uncovered rich and varied definitions of masculinity and femininity, complicating our view of what is "natural" and suggesting that society and culture, not biology, determine gender identities.

Jack R. Censer

1

INTRODUCTION

Barbara Melosh

Sex is announced in the first sentence of our social lives. As a baby is born under the bright lights of a twentieth-century American delivery room, the physician declares, "It's a boy!" or "It's a girl!" With recent advances in prenatal testing, some expectant parents can even identify the sex of their growing fetuses. As adults, we experience gender as a fundamental part of identity, inseparable from the self. In much contemporary science, biological determinism is gradually replacing an older emphasis on environment, giving new weight to the view of sexual difference as natural, as proceeding from immutable biological difference.

The authors represented in this anthology reject that view. Even the title proclaims a critical stance, for if sexual difference is natural, it can have no history and requires no explanation. The term "gender," used by every author in this volume, itself signals a certain position in contemporary debates about sexual difference. In 1975, Gayle Rubin's influential essay "The Traffic in Women" proposed a usage that has been widely adopted.[1] "Sex," she argued, should indicate the biological fact of difference: the chromosomes, hormones, and characteristic anatomical differences associated with male and female. "Gender," by contrast, would signify the cultural elaborations upon sexual difference, "a socially imposed division of the sexes" (Rubin, p. 179). Rubin viewed biological sexual differences as real and necessary, but she argued that cultural interpretations of these differences exaggerated the extent of difference (pp. 178–80). Her distinction at once conceded sexual difference and rejected it as a sufficient explanation for the sexual inequality and female subordination observable in virtually every human society.

1

Following Rubin, women's historians have adopted the term to signal a view of sexual difference as simultaneously arbitrary and deeply embedded – not grounded in the facts of biology, but nonetheless rooted in history and social structure. Though feminists do not share any single view of the relationship of sex and gender, most reject an *essentialist* position – the view that biology imposes fixed boundaries on male and female behavior, potential, or aspiration. The question of biological difference may never be fully answered, given the complex intertwining of nature and nurture in human development. Meanwhile, it seems reasonable to assume that sexual inequality (readily observable) rather than biological difference accounts for women's subordinate position in social life.

To the general reader, "gender" might seem to fit easily within the concerns and vocabulary of women's history, and indeed, for many of the authors in this volume, a focus on gender proceeds from within a commitment to the field of women's history. But "gender" has also come to connote a departure from women's history and a searching critique of its politics and intellectual rationale. Historian Joan Wallach Scott has argued that women's history risks undermining its own political commitments to sexual equality.[2] Ironically, the demonstration of women's historical "otherness," Scott argues, ultimately reinforces a sense of sexual difference as fixed and immutable. Acknowledging the tremendous vigor and productivity of women's history, such critics have also noted its relative isolation. Though women's historians have taken up interpretive issues and evidence of related fields such as labor history or political history, the transmission has seldom worked the other way: women's history itself remains "other," defined as marginal in relation to a partial history that still claims a more universal status for itself.

It is not enough simply to add women's history to the burgeoning specialties of the historical profession, most women's historians would agree. Scott argues further that it is not enough to rewrite history by considering the evidence of women's lives. Instead, we must recognize the defining role of gender as a historical category: a powerful construction about difference that not only shapes sexual division of labor but also deeply informs how historical subjects have imagined politics and society at every level. For Scott, the very language of "women's

2

and create what it means to be male and female. Following this post-structuralist argument, most of the authors in this volume use the term "social construction." That usage takes Rubin's formulation of sex and gender another step, implying a categorical rejection of any argument that would concede a "natural" distinction between the sexes. For post-structuralists, all of social life is understood through and defined by language; there can be no appeal to "realities" that bypass systems of interpretation.

Historians of gender have pushed against the boundaries of women's history to argue that cultural constructions of sexual difference fundamentally inform history. Thus the discourses of gender not only regulate the social behavior of men and women in sexuality, family, and work, but they also become ways of ordering politics and of maintaining hierarchies of all kinds. "Gender" describes a fundamental understanding of difference that organizes and produces other relationships of difference – and of power and inequality.[6]

Post-structuralist assumptions about knowledge and its construction also imply the need for a new kind of historical writing, done in a self-critical voice that would acknowledge the partiality of historical knowledge and the historian's own implication in the construction of gender. Many of these essays demonstrate the search for new ways of writing history as the authors ponder the problems of evidence and historical interpretation and seek to convey the multiplicity of positions from which historical subjects understood and enacted their lives. As historian Nancy Hewitt and others have pointed out, a critical history of gender must also scrutinize its own claims about the priority of gender.[7] Even as the authors represented here consider the weight of gender in American history, they also take account of other significant differences – such as race, class, and sexual orientation – as categories and cultural identities that inform gender and social life.

Post-structuralism supports feminist challenges to the disciplines, and its theories have touched most of the authors represented here. Most notably, these essays demonstrate the influence of post-structuralist attention to language; the authors develop new insights about their subjects through close readings of many kinds of cultural texts, from sex manuals to paintings to symbolic action on the picket line. However, the common vocabulary of terms such as "discourse" and "social construction" is slightly misleading. Few of these authors, and few historians working today, have followed post-structuralist theory to its limit. They have borrowed some ideas from post-structuralist theory, or found it congenial with earlier commitments to interdisciplinary scholarship, but they do not share its ultimate skepticism about historical knowledge. Most would also reject the post-structuralist premise that there can be no distinction between discourse and social experience.

Christina Simmons focuses on the discourses of sexuality in the early twentieth century, but she explains the discourse itself as a *response* to women's changing social positions in the early twentieth century and as an effort to name and control changes in sexual practices that predated the articulation of new sexual ideology. Joanne Meyerowitz maintains the same distinction between ideology and experience; indeed, she finds patterns in working-class women's lives that suggest the limited reach of a middle-class discourse of sexuality. George Chauncey, Jr., and Donna Penn couch their arguments more fully within social constructionist frames, examining competing discourses of sexuality in gay and lesbian history. Ellen Wiley Todd, Melissa Dabakis and I take visual representation as one aspect of the construction of gender, but all probe the relationship of such images to social experience as well as to other texts; discourse is not all. Gail Bederman's essay represents perhaps the fullest realization of a post-structuralist historical method, for she analyzes gender as it is implicated in and fundamentally shapes the discourses of race and of political power. Jacquelyn Dowd Hall and Linda Gordon have called for revisions of labor history and social welfare history that would recognize the profound significance of gender, but both find their intellectual homes within social and women's history. Gordon, in addition, has been a vigorous and trenchant critic of Scott and of the uses of post-structuralist theory.[8]

These essays suggest the outlines of an emerging history of gender in the twentieth-century United States, and they illustrate some of the questions and kinds of evidence that are currently shaping this work. Building on the social and women's history of the past twenty years, the authors explore twentieth-century constructions of gender as aspects of post-Freudian culture and the changing structure of capitalism.

Nineteenth-century Victorian culture described sexual difference in terms of the duties and obligations that followed from men's and women's inherent characteristics. Women's moral superiority made them ideal wives and mothers, charged with the solemn responsibility of guiding errant children and men. Manly character derived from the stern masculine control of sexual impulses and emotion and from steady and resolute application to work. This formulation provided ideological support for an economic structure that increasingly relied on wage work done outside the home and that celebrated striving and unrestrained competition in the quest for profit and productivity.

By the early twentieth century, discernibly different conceptions of gender had begun to displace Victorian manhood and womanhood. With popularizations of Freud, psychoanalysts, medical practitioners, sexual theorists and a broad range of middle-class commentators criticized what they portrayed as Victorian repression and affirmed sexual expression as part of modern marriage. In contrast to Victorian images of women (or at least ladies) as passionless, twentieth-century pundits acknowledged female sexuality and approved women's sexual expression within marriage. Freudian views of sexuality bolstered emerging homosexual identities: Freudian paradigms for psychosexual development placed new emphasis on object choice (the sex of one's sexual partner) as a central category of sexuality. Within a burgeoning consumer economy, nineteenth-century ideas of character, demonstrated through hard work, discipline, and restraint, yielded to twentieth-century versions of self-fulfillment through sexuality, family, leisure, and consumption. Paid work, a predominantly masculine realm in the nineteenth century, became increasingly "feminized," both as more women entered the labor force and as new managerial and sales jobs required men to practice traditionally feminine strategies of persuasion.

In addition to uncovering historical changes in ideas of sexual difference, historians of gender have also emphasized the wide reach of such paradigms of difference. Formulations of difference not only shape historical experiences of maleness and femaleness, but they also inflect economic and political structures. Historians of gender have begun to investigate the gendered meanings of consumption, work, reform, and war. In the expansion and promotion of a consumer economy, gender meanings shift as work takes on "feminine" characteristics and consumption is often linked to sensual and erotic images.[9] Women's historians have redrawn the boundaries of labor history with investigations of women's work and have argued the importance of gender in understanding the work and resistance of both men and women.[10] In a sweeping revision of the history of reform, women's historians have recast the Progressive era and are now undertaking to rewrite the history of the welfare state more broadly. A focus on female reformers, for example, radically expands our ideas of the historical boundaries of the Progressive era, for their activism outlasted that of their male counterparts whose waning idealism was once taken to signal the end of that reform era. Overturning an older view of the 1920s as a hiatus in reform, these historians suggest a continuity of reform that extended to the New Deal and shaped its agenda.[11] Historians are also exploring the expanding state apparatus of the twentieth century as it is implicated in the construction of gender. Prescriptions for men's and women's proper places are embedded in the twentieth-century welfare state.[12] At the same time, rhetorics of gender have also provided justifications for nationalism and war; attention to the gendering of political language enables new historical insights about the exercise of state power.[13]

Historians of gender have yet to produce an overarching new synthesis of twentieth-century history, and indeed some would object that such a "master narrative" is neither possible nor desirable. At the least, such a synthesis is premature, as many subjects have yet to be explored. The essays in this volume reproduce the imbalance of coverage in existing historiography; we know much more about female gender than male, and we know more about the first half of this century than about the years since 1950. The strongest contribution of this work so far has been methodological: as these essays demonstrate, a focus on gender offers questions and approaches that open up new ways of seeing the past.

Part I takes up the history of sexuality and the redrawing of the cultural boundaries of gender. Considered historically, sexuality – seemingly straightforward and commonsensical – becomes complicated and elusive. These essays pose fascinating questions about gender and the construction of sexual identities. Examining the broad diversity of sexual ideologies and practices that have existed even in our own century, historians have argued that culture, not biology, fundamentally defines sexual experience. Christina Simmons's "Modern Sexuality and the Myth of Victorian Repression" sets the stage with an interpretation of the new sexual ideologies of the early twentieth century as "a cultural adjustment of male power to women's departure from the Victorian order" – the remaking of discourse, not the liberation of innate sexuality. Simmons challenges the history-of-progress notions that dominate our understanding of changing sexual ideologies in an argument that shows how a broadening acceptance of female heterosexual expression also meant a suppression of women's social and erotic connections to one another.

In "Sexual Geography and Gender Economy," Joanne Meyerowitz examines working-class single women in Chicago and their participation in "sexually unconventional subcultures" that refused the constraints of middle-class sexual prescriptions. In these communities, not only in the manuals of sex theorists, Meyerowitz argues, we see the emergence of twentieth-century forms of sexual expression. Even as she reveals the evidence of working-class women's experience, Meyerowitz also discusses the shifting representations of this experience, whether in the images of contemporary reformers, urban sociologists, and moviemakers, or in the interpretive frames of historians.

George Chauncey, Jr., uses the records of a 1919 Navy investigation to examine the prevailing construction of homosexuality and its relationship to changing masculine identities. His evidence reveals a view of homosexuality radically different from current constructions. Rather than considering homosexuality as a relatively fixed (for some, even genetically determined) sexual orientation, defined by one's erotic feelings, sexual behaviour, and choice of sexual partners, Chauncey's historical subjects defined as homosexual only those men who assumed the "female" or passive role in their sexual practices.

In "The Meanings of Lesbianism in Postwar America," Donna Penn considers the weight of gender roles and choice of sexual partners in the historical definition and experiences of lesbianism. Responding to Chauncey and others, Penn argues that gender roles persist as an important marker even after they have faded in discourses of male homosexuality. She traces the butch, or mannish woman, within lesbian communities and in discourses about lesbianism. If these women share the difference of same-sex sexuality with gay men, Penn argues, nonetheless they inhabit a different history, shaped by their particular experience as women.

In Part II, "Work and consumption in visual representations," three essays interpret gendered images of shoppers, sirens, and workers in easel paintings, New Deal murals and sculpture, and graphics. The politics of looking have played a prominent part in feminist critiques, from protest against images in advertising, fashion, and mass media to challenges of street harassment and the debate over pornography. Feminist art historians have recognized the place of art in celebrating and securing a social elite and have analyzed how visual representations contribute to the construction of gender. John Berger's influential *Ways of Seeing*[14] portrayed the tradition of the nude as the expression and reproduction of male domination, as the male artist looks at the female model to paint her nude image for the consumption of a male buyer. In theories of "the gaze," art historians have focused on issues of display and spectatorship in the production and circulation of art.[15]

Ellen Wiley Todd's "Art, the 'New Woman,' and Consumer Culture" examines the shopper and the siren in the works of two American painters, Kenneth Hayes Miller and Reginald Marsh. Todd explores such diverse sources as Old Master painting, contemporary photographs of New York City, advertising, film posters, and artists' letters and diaries to interpret these representations of gender and consumption. Miller and Marsh, she finds, incorporated images of "new women" into their paintings, registering and revising contemporary cultural constructions of gender; we can read their works as evidence of that shifting discourse. "Manly Work," by Barbara Melosh, analyzes images of manhood in New Deal public art as responses to a perceived crisis of masculinity between the wars. Widely used elements like the brawny arms and independent labor of the manly worker suggest a coherent discourse of masculinity. At the same time, evidence from New Deal-era audiences of these works reveals diverse and often conflicting interpretations of the image, complicating our view of the cultural work of art. Melissa

Dabakis's "Gendered Labor" takes a close look at the familiar Norman Rockwell image of Rosie the Riveter, reading "Rosie" as an emblem of the contradictions of gender and class in wartime constructions of women as paid workers.

Part III provides examples of political uses of the language of gender. Every author in this volume would protest that gender and language are always political: I use the term here to identify the uses of gender in discourse that is explicitly political, self-consciously deployed in social negotiations of power and inequality. Gail Bederman shows how Ida B. Wells mobilized a range of contemporary representations of masculinity in her campaign to confront Northern whites' complicity with lynching. Wells turned ideologies of manhood to her own use, challenging white men's ideals of manhood and civilization with stark evidence of the barbarism of lynching. Bederman's analysis discloses the complex operations of gender in a rhetoric that made manhood a trope for civilization and a code for white superiority. Jacquelyn Dowd Hall's "Disorderly Women" begins by challenging the categories of labor historians who have focused primarily on union organization and conventional politics and have therefore underestimated women workers' activism. Hall examines defiant women workers who manipulated cultural ideologies of gender to display their resistance to the authority of bosses and police during a tense strike. In the last essay, Linda Gordon criticizes a historiography of reform and the welfare state that has largely ignored the crucial category of gender. Gordon repudiates the post-structuralist claim for the defining power of discourse in her analysis of the clients of reform agencies, who sometimes resisted the agencies and sometimes sought help from them without necessarily surrendering to middle-class constructions of their needs. Her essay also demonstrates the reflective presentation of some current historical writing; Gordon describes the successive interpretive frames and questions that guided her own analysis.

A final word. Some readers may be discomfited by the openly political commitments of the historians represented in this volume, all of whom have framed their questions in response to one or more of the social movements of the last twenty-five years: the New Left, the women's movement and the varieties of feminism that it inspired, the gay and lesbian movements. All interpretation is political, we would respond. Take the measure

11

of these authors' interpretations by asking how their questions and commitments enhance or limit our understanding of the past. Ask whether the premises of these essays serve to open up new ways of thinking about history. And, of course, hold these works to the standards we would apply to any historical interpretation: consider the thoroughness of the research, the use of evidence, the strength and logic of the argument, the significance of the conclusions.

NOTES

1 Gayle Rubin, "The Traffic in Women," in *Toward an Anthropology of Women*, ed. Rayna Rapp Reiter (New York: 1975), 157–210.
2 Joan Wallach Scott, "Women's History," in *Gender and the Politics of History* (New York: 1988), 15–27.
3 See, for example, "Gender Histories and Heresies," special issue of *Radical History Review* 52 (Winter 1992); and 1991 conference program of the American Studies Association, Baltimore, MD.
4 For a good introduction to Foucault's work, consult Michel Foucault, *Language, Counter-Memory, Practice: Selected Essays and Interviews*, trans. Donald F. Bouchard and Sherry Simon (Ithaca, NY: 1977).
5 See Scott, *Gender and the Politics of History*.
6 Ibid., 44–5.
7 For a broad review of the literature of women's history and an astute analysis of the problem of differences among women, see Nancy A. Hewitt, "Beyond the Search for Sisterhood: American Women's History in the 1980s," in *Unequal Sisters: A Multicultural Reader in Women's History*, ed. Ellen Carol DuBois and Vicki L. Ruiz (New York and London: 1990), 1–14. This collection itself attests to women's historians' current commitment to this question of recognizing and theorizing difference.
8 See the debate between Joan W. Scott and Linda Gordon as articulated in Scott's review of Gordon's *Heroes of Their Own Lives*, Gordon's response to Scott, Gordon's review of Scott's *Gender and the Politics of History*, and Scott's response, all in *Signs* 15, 4 (Summer 1990): 848–60.
9 See, for example, Roland Marchand, *Advertising the American Dream: Making Way for Modernity, 1920–1940* (Berkeley: 1985).
10 See, for example, Ruth Milkman, *Women, Work, and Protest: A Century of U.S. Women's Labor History* (London and New York: 1985). For a recent collection of articles on gender and labor, see Ava Baron, ed., *Work Engendered: Toward a New History of American Labor* (Ithaca, NY: 1991), especially Baron's illuminating review of the literature and agenda for research, "Gender and Labor History: Learning from the Past, Looking to the Future," 1–46.
11 An early statement of this position was J. Stanley Lemons, *The*

Woman Citizen: Social Feminism in the 1920s (1973; reprint, Charlottesville, VA: 1990). The argument has been expanded and developed in subsequent work, including Susan Ware, *Beyond Suffrage: Women in the New Deal* (Cambridge: 1981); Ellen F. Fitzpatrick, *Endless Crusade: Women Social Scientists and Progressive Reform* (New York: 1990); Robyn Muncy, *Creating a Female Dominion in American Reform, 1890–1935* (New York: 1991); and Noralee Frankel and Nancy S. Dye, eds, *Gender, Class, Race, and Reform in the Progressive Era* (Lexington, KY: 1991).

12 Linda Gordon leads a rich field of feminist revisions of the US welfare state; see *Women, the State, and Welfare*, ed. Linda Gordon (Madison, WI: 1990) and Gordon, *Heroes of Their Own Lives: The Politics and History of Family Violence* (New York: 1988). See also Mimi Abramovitz, *Regulating the Lives of Women: Social Welfare Policy from Colonial Times to the Present* (Boston: 1988). For a useful overview of feminist investigations of the state in Western Europe and the US, see Seth Koven and Sonya Michel, "Gender and the Origins of the Welfare State," *Radical History Review* 43 (Winter 1989): 112–19.

13 See, for example, Margaret Randolph Higonnet *et al.*, eds, *Behind the Lines: Gender and Two World Wars* (New Haven, CT: 1987).

14 John Berger, *Ways of Seeing* (New York: 1973).

15 Many art historians have taken up Laura Mulvey's argument on the politics of looking in film; see her "Visual Pleasure and the Narrative Cinema," *Screen* 16, 3 (Autumn 1975): 6–18, and "Afterthoughts on 'Visual Pleasure and Narrative Cinema' Inspired by *Duel in the Sun*," reprinted in *Feminism and Film Theory*, ed. Constance Penley (New York and London: 1988), 69–79.

Part I
SEXUALITY AND GENDER

2

MODERN SEXUALITY AND THE MYTH OF VICTORIAN REPRESSION

Christina Simmons

Christina Simmons's essay on changing ideas about sexuality in the 1920s and 1930s shows the intricate relationship of new sexual theory and contemporary discourses of gender. In the wake of Freud, many doctors, psychologists, and other contemporary commentators repudiated the excessive sexual control that they associated with the Victorians and endorsed sexual expression as a crucial part of modern marriage. Their prescriptions for sexual behavior were also prescriptions for masculinity and femininity more generally. Simmons mines popular fiction, advice manuals, and professional literature to discover a colourful lexicon of types. Appropriate models for masculinity emerge in the "healthy male animal," even as the image of the "poor worm" and the "blunderer" provide cautionary tales about men who were too weak or too forceful. In recurring female types – the Victorian matriarch, the complaining wife, the career woman, and the flapper – commentators carved out an ideal that rejected the strictures of the past, yet they did so without offering unqualified approval to female independence either. The so-called sexual revolution had mixed implications for women, Simmons shows us – indeed, she concludes that "the new sexual discourse of the 1920s and 1930s represented not 'liberation' but a new form of regulation."

* * *

For twentieth-century Americans the first sexual revolution popularized the image of the flapper, an ideal of youth, beauty, and freedom of action for women, but also one of sexual vitality. "The emancipated flapper is just plain female under her paint and outside her cocktails," explains a flapper's father in

17

Gertrude Atherton's best-selling novel of 1923, *Black Oxen*. "More so for she's more stimulated. Where girls used to be merely romantic, she's romantic. . .plus sex instinct rampant." But in the shadows stands another figure, the authority against whom the flapper had rebelled – a stern and asexual matron, representative of outmoded Victorianism. "She believed in purity," wrote Sinclair Lewis, describing one such lady, Mrs. Keast, in *Ann Vickers* (1932): "She had, possibly as a result of fifty-five years complete abstinence from tobacco, alcohol, laughter, sexual excitement, and novels, a dark bagginess under her eyes, and twitching fingers." These contrasting images represent two elements in a new discourse on sexuality that appeared in the writings of white liberal commentators on sexual life in the 1920s and 1930s.[1]

This group of thinkers created what I call the myth of Victorian repression to describe and condemn old patterns of sexual behavior and shape new ones. Through this device they interpreted and codified for white middle-class Americans the new morality that had emerged in the 1910s. By proclaiming the existence and legitimacy of female sexual desire, the new morality undermined the basis of the Victorian sexual code and encouraged some women's sexual assertiveness. Other women clung to the influence gained through sexual restraint. The myth of Victorian repression constituted a response to both forms of women's power.

These sexual revisionists proclaimed a modernist liberation from a repressive Victorian past, and subsequent historiography has tended to accept that frame of reference. Michel Foucault has astutely criticized this paradigm, arguing that the supposed repression of the nineteenth century can better be seen as a "deployment of sexuality," the creation of new bourgeois discourses about sexuality, which in fact "incited" a greater intensity of consciousness about and desire for a "truth" of sex than had existed in earlier historical times. Hence, the Victorian prescription of restrained sexual activity and modest sexual speech did not mean the absence or "repression" of sexuality but rather focused psychic attention on it. At the heart of the knowledge produced by such discourses were shifting relations of power between parents and children, women and the male medical establishment, the state and fertile couples, and psychiatry and sexual "deviants." Foucault sees the early twentieth-century sexual revolution, the so-called antirepressive struggle, as "a tactical shift and reversal" in the deployment of sexuality but not a fundamental break with the past.[2]

Analysis of liberal American discourse on sexuality in this period reveals both genuine changes in sexual prescriptions and important continuities with the past. I shall argue here that the myth of Victorian repression represented a cultural adjustment of male power to women's departure from the Victorian order. It constituted a strategic modification rather than a decline of male dominance. Although the new morality was made possible above all by women's greater political and economic activity – suffrage and reform work, college education, labor force participation – the new sexual discourse of the 1920s and 1930s attacked women's increased power. The myth of Victorian repression rehabilitated male sexuality and cast women as villains if they refused to respond to, nurture, or support it. And by identifying women with Victorianism and men with a progressive and realistic understanding of sex, it confirmed men's sexual dominance as normative in modern marriage.

Intellectuals, bohemians, and radicals attacked Victorian middle-class sexual mores in the first two decades of the century at the same time that sexual behavior seems to have been changing. Long-standing demands for female-controlled contraception – through voluntary motherhood* and the right to say no – shifted toward a new demand for artificial means of birth control to facilitate female sexual pleasure as well as fertility control. Public discussion of these ideas signaled to both critics and proponents that more sexual activity was taking place inside and outside marriage, an increase precipitated by changes in women's sexual attitudes and behavior.[3]

Women had been key figures in the Victorian ideology of sexual control. Nineteenth-century middle-class men and women, whether feminists, free lovers,** or conservative moralists, had

---

* Voluntary motherhood was a nineteenth-century movement that defended women's right to control sexual contact within marriage and thus to exert some control over their childbearing.
** Nineteenth-century advocates of free love, such as Victoria Woodhull and Tennessee Claflin, rejected the authority of the state and the church in controlling marriage. They defended women's free choice of sexual partners and their right to control sexuality. However, the term did not have the later twentieth-century connotation of unrestrained sexual expressiveness or endorsement of sex with many partners.

all feared sexual excess and called for moderation. By the 1850s sexual continence, limiting sexual activity to legal marriage and a reproductive goal, had become the dominant cultural ideal. Allowing women to set the pace in sexual activity was commonly seen as a means to the ideal. Women were thought to be characterized by "passionlessness" and to be guided more by maternal instinct than sexual desire *per se*. Hence, they were expected to dampen men's unnatural obsession with sex. Although contradicted by women's legal obligation to submit sexually to their husbands, the image of women as upholders of sexual restraint was a powerful element in Victorian culture.[4] Pursuing it, women mounted active campaigns for social purity, including attacks on prostitution and indecency in theater and literature. Victorian men took an equally substantive part in sexual control, however, in their own purity reform work. The YMCA contributed to the enactment in 1873 of the Comstock Act outlawing obscenity, including birth control and abortion devices and information. Federal Agent Anthony Comstock, enforcer of the law named for him, survived into the twentieth century to be mocked by sexual radicals for his efforts to ferret out vice wherever it lurked. While many people's actual behavior or feelings contradicted these prescriptions, the cultural power of this discourse on sexuality was pervasive and long-lasting.[5]

By the early twentieth century, however, Victorian conventions based on these sexual concepts were breaking down. Young women and men in the cities forged a new comradeship in a world of heterosocial* leisure sharply different from what Victorian manners had prescribed. In large cities new forms of amusement for unchaperoned couples challenged the sex-segregated or family-controlled recreation of Victorian middle-class life. Mixed-sex restaurants and cabarets, for example, appeared as part of New York nightlife in the 1890s. Men brought respectable women to establishments where men had previously gone alone or with prostitutes. In movie theaters and dance halls working-class couples set an example of sexually integrated amusement followed quickly by middle-class youth. "Good" and "bad" women now dressed similarly and frequented the same clubs.[6]

* "Heterosocial" pertains to activities and associations that included both men and women; it connotes an attitude that affirms camaraderie between the sexes.

For both sexes changing social realities laid the basis for a critique of Victorianism. By the 1910s young middle-class women's foothold in higher education, the labor force, and feminist and reform politics and institutions gave them an increasingly critical perspective on the old sexual order. Wifehood and motherhood no longer formed so exclusively the basis of their social power, and they could press demands for equality beyond suffrage. Many rejected self-restriction and declined to take responsibility for male sexual behavior. They explored female sexuality and espoused a positive romantic outlook on heterosexual relationships. As one feminist noted: "Of late there has been much public discussion of the wantonness of our modern youth; which, being interpreted, means the disposition of our girls to take the same liberty of indulgence in prenuptial sexual affairs that has always been countenanced in boys."[7]

Some young middle-class men also evinced alienation from nineteenth-century mores. Male white-collar workers in large industrial corporations faced more specialized and routinized tasks; the self-control and autonomy of the self-made man seemed less relevant or possible. Traditional politics seemed futile and corrupt. Many men turned to women, leisure, art, or radical politics for the fulfillment old masculine roles did not provide. One man, who had quit a demanding office job to spend more time with his wife, wrote in *The Masses* in 1914, "I had begun to feel that the one-sexed world in which I had been living was inadequate to human needs, that life ought to be lived and shared by men and women together."[8] Both women and men, then, looked for greater equality and companionship, including sexual companionship.

Later sexual studies conducted by Alfred Kinsey and others confirm the impressions of social commentators in the 1910s and 1920s that new patterns of sexual behavior were emerging. Middle-class women born after 1900 were increasingly willing to engage in premarital petting and intercourse and, when married, reached orgasm more often than those born in the nineteenth century. One observer of youth claimed that middle-class high school boys visited prostitutes less often by 1920 because their social class peers were acting as sexual partners.[9] The guardians of purity were descending from their pedestals.

Writers of fiction, religious and moral commentators,

physicians, and, increasingly, academic social scientists published prolific responses to the sexual revolution. Like the nineteenth-century physicians Foucault credits with making sexuality a matter of medical knowledge, these thinkers were generating a new psychological and sociological discourse about sexual behavior and marriage. During the 1910s a conservative movement for sex education attempted to reverse the tide of change in sexual behavior while vociferous sexual radicals exposed Victorian hypocrisy. By the 1920s, however, except among fundamentalists and Catholics, the predominant tone was of liberal reform. Realizing the social changes they observed were irreversible, academics, reformers, and a few radicals explained, justified, or criticized prevailing patterns of sexual behavior and developed a modern sexual ideology to guide behavior. They frequently cited the writings of Sigmund Freud and British sexologist Havelock Ellis, whose ideas were being popularized in the United States in the 1910s, but they reshaped European ideas into a distinctively new American discourse on sexuality and marriage. These writers included, for example, Judge Ben B. Lindsey, author of *Companionate Marriage*, a major text outlining modern marriage; Ira S. Wile, child psychiatrist and sex educator; Lorine Pruette, a psychologist who specialized in women's conflicts between marriage and career; and sociologist Ernest Groves, founder of the field of marriage counseling. Floyd Dell and Margaret Sanger, radical before the First World War in their critique of Victorian morality, turned in the 1920s to the pursuit of happiness within a reformed marriage. Sinclair Lewis's and Fannie Hurst's novels offered extended commentaries on sexual relationships. Two radical voices were those of Samuel Schmalhausen and V. F. Calverton, who collaborated in producing the *Modern Quarterly*, a journal of liberal and socialist opinion, between 1925 and 1932. Schmalhausen was a psychoanalyst and Calverton a young radical critic interested in problems of sex.[10]

These thinkers differed in their evaluation of institutional marriage but held in common a revised assessment of the value of sexual activity and a set of male and female stereotypes that they used as positive and negative models of sexual behavior. With these sexual ideas and images, the commentators on sex in the 1920s constructed the myth of the Victorian repression, which demonstrated the errors of the earlier ideology of sexual restraint and attempted to shape an appropriate new dynamic for relations between the sexes.

A clamor against sexual repression marked liberal and radical opinion of the 1920s. Schmalhausen outlined the complaints most dramatically:

> If we survey traditional civilization, we are impressed by one fact as always conspicuously present: the vast array of machinery of intimidation (physical, emotional, intellectual, spiritual) used by the authoritative elders to prevent the free and easy expression of sex desire. The times waited for a Freud to come along and make clear to a blind mankind how tragic the costs of this civilized machinery of intimidation. This exposé of the staggering human cost of sexual frustration I look upon as the ultimate important contribution of Freud. Why were the authoritative elders so concerned with preventing nature from being natural?

Limiting sex expression to reproductive purposes now appeared cruel and arbitrary. Lindsey argued that continence was an idea perpetuated by religious fanatics who saw in sex only "ugliness, original sin, and fig leaves." Dell proclaimed grandly that the destruction of the patriarchal family "has laid the basis for a more biologically normal family life than has existed throughout the whole of the historical period." Thus nineteenth-century American culture appeared as a historical aberration that violated fundamental human nature.[11]

Not only was sex a natural part of life, it was a positive source of energy and creativity rather than a drain on individual powers, as the Victorians had asserted. As Sanger wrote, "To be strongly sexed means that the life force can suffuse and radiate through body and soul. It means radiant energy and force in every field of endeavor." Even rebellion against the code of monogamy, while it was "to be condemned from the higher social point of view," nevertheless "represents biological strength and urge," wrote Wile and Mary Winn. "It is the surplus creative force of the race."[12]

These thinkers felt that the Victorian distance between women and men created an unpleasant tension between husband and wife, especially in sexual interactions. Victorians had seen that tension as a way to limit sexual activity, part of an invigorating moral struggle, but thinkers of the 1920s found sexual conflict exhausting and dangerous. Permitting regular sexual activity was a lesser evil than repression, which seemed to lead to neuroses and weak, unhappy individuals. Groves hoped that asceticism had "passed forever from the category of ideals into that of mental abnormalities." Not only was repression harmful; it did not work. Although many sexual reformers still feared sex outside marriage, they argued that rigid controls exacerbated the danger. Sex could not simply be suppressed, for "futile repression ends in volcanic upheaval and a fresh outbreak of license." Furthermore, denying sexual urges made marriage itself less stable. A great many authors of works on sex and marriage claimed that divorce was caused by sexual maladjustments. Frigidity and impotence were said to result from the ascetic mentality. Hence, Victorian repression undermined the very institution it was supposed to protect.[13]

The hope of many of these critics was to save marriage by "sexualizing it," as Schmalhausen wrote. Companionate marriage represented the new cultural ideal developed during this period. It included birth control to accommodate the new woman's sexuality and to allow men to find sexual satisfaction inside marriage. Sexual and emotional comradeship formed the basis of union. Proponents of companionate marriage stressed early marriage and advocated divorce by mutual consent for the childless.[14] The companionate ideal epitomized twentieth-century liberal criticism of sexual repression.

The new marriage, with its ideal of sexual intimacy, required new behavior from both sexes. In tracts, exposés, and novels that examined heterosexual relations, a series of positive and negative images of men and women dramatized behavior and attitudes both to imitate and to avoid. The images conveyed three important themes of the sexual revisionism of the 1920s and 1930s: the rehabilitation of male sexuality, an attack on women's power to either control or withdraw from male sexual needs, and the creation of a new female ideal.

As part of the re-evaluation of male sexuality, sexual modernists modified an image of men used by Victorian moral reformers. The "sexual brute" became the "sexual blunderer." Symbolizing men's sexual power over women in the callous infliction of male desire on a passive and innocent wife, the Victorian image of the sexual brute had expressed women's protest against their lack of sexual knowledge and the legal rights husbands possessed over wives' bodies. Accounts of brutal rape on the wedding night demonstrated men's selfish and aggressive sexual impulses and women's victimization. The moral reformers who employed the image defended women's right to refuse intercourse and demanded improved control over male sexuality.[15]

Twentieth-century writers repeated wedding night stories but redefined the nature of the brutality to stress male ignorance of women's sexual needs rather than aggression or cruelty. Women would enjoy sex, it was asserted, if men learned to nurture feminine sexual feelings. Sanger, for example, recounted the story of a bride's disappointment with a husband whose approach on the wedding night "had been in the order of a hurried meal over a lunch counter." In another story a husband met friends in the hotel lobby on his wedding night and stayed up talking with the boys while his bride stewed. "The result was that she became a victim of a neurotic dissociation which completely ruined her marriage by producing a state of long-lasting asexuality."[16] Re-educating men constituted the central recommendation of those who used this image. Women's sexual interest, wrote Ellis, meant that "a new husband is required to meet the new wife." The sexual brute who tyrannized women had been transformed in the new thinking into a less awful personage, merely a blunderer who needed to learn consideration and fairness.[17]

The softening of the Victorian image of men indirectly acknowledged women's increased social power because in the new scenario women appeared less as pathetic victims than in the writings of Victorian reformers. Notions of "masculine supremacy or of female frailty and weakness" were no longer appropriate, wrote Wile and Winn. Yet the assumption in most writings that men had greater knowledge and sexual experience also showed an acceptance of continued male power. Even Sanger, who urged couples to read about and discuss sex and was concerned that women not be sexually coerced, assumed male sexual mastery. In order for the crucial initiation to go exactly right, she argued, the bridegroom must "dominate the whole situation."[18]

The idea that modern men must embrace and not suppress their sexual urges was even clearer in the image of the "poor worm," a repressed and fearful man unable to muster the sexual energy to master women. Far from showing character, a man who failed to pursue and obtain sexual satisfaction appeared unmanly. As one author put it sarcastically,

> Surely there is no sense in. . .ridiculing the activities of a man merely because his intentions chance to be honorable and his motives pure. It is carrying cynicism much too far to regard him as a hypocrite. Perhaps he prefers to manage his affairs in this strange manner. Perhaps he is fooling you.

Inadequate sexual energy was equated with lack of the appropriate aggressiveness: an impotent man might be "kind and gentle," "gentlemanly and refined," but he could not satisfy his wife and was not the man he should be. Created primarily by men, who seemed anxious about what it meant to be male in the modern world, this imagery evoked a sense that young women's sexual liberation required men to jettison Victorian habits in order to retain a dominant role. Acknowledging the existence of female sexuality called for a more vigorous male sexuality in response. Lack of the necessary vigor might hint of homosexuality, increasingly discussed and feared by the professionals producing this commentary.[19]

The sexual revisionists were redefining male sexuality as a less threatening or morally base element of male nature. They offered a positive image of the sexual male as the "healthy animal," responsive to women yet unafraid of his natural drives. Victorians, claimed the writers of the 1920s, had taught men to view sexuality as a "weakness," but modern thinkers realized that the sex drive was a man's "most dynamic urge," without which he would be "robbed of his manhood, an enfeebled weakling." The reformers denigrated those who feared aggression toward women as a dangerous part of male sexuality. Lindsey made this clearest when he revealed his admiration for the courage and spontaneity of young boys: " 'morality' doesn't play much part in the reactions of the normal lad – not if he is the healthy young animal he should be." As they grew up, the vitality was gradually crushed out of boys, and Lindsey believed women were the primary agents of this tragic maturation. The liberal view of sexuality in the 1920s sought to revise the negative evaluation of aggressive male sexuality and redirect cultural standards that accepted female control over men's energies.[20]

In the sexual revisionists' cautionary tale the blunderer and the poor worm warned men against both ignorant self-assertion in sex and excessive hesitation with women. The healthy animal, when he was sensitive and knowledgeable, made the best husband. He skillfully initiated his bride into sexual intimacy and, though he offered her respect and pleasure, he remained in charge. At the same time several recurrent female images warned readers of both sexes of the threat controlling, neglectful, or exploitative women posed to marriage. The stereotypes of the prudish Victorian matriarch, the demanding and burdensome wife, and the emotionally distant career woman represented caricatures of women who wielded excessive power and were not responsive to men's needs.

The image of the respectable married woman, especially as a mother, had epitomized the sexual purity and domesticity prescribed for bourgeois women in the nineteenth century. As purity became less of a concern, this ideal was rejected as sentimental at best. One reformer called for sociologists to carry on more "scientific" and "objective" discussions of sex without "the babbling of the term 'mother' with tearstained faces." Sexual reformers expressed both sympathy and impatience toward women raised with traditional modesty about sex. A young wife must "cease to take pride" in "outgrown maidenly reserve," warned Groves. She must abandon herself fully to the sexual embrace and accept the guidance of her husband because "his attitude toward sex is less likely to be warped."[21] Adhering to these outmoded ideas was a bad habit women had to give up to become mature modern adults.

The older woman who upheld Victorian values fared worse. Sexual commentators frequently used the image of the prudish Victorian matriarch, a woman who had the power but not the tenderness of the nineteenth-century mother yet demanded the customary deference from men for the sacrifices she made as a woman. In the novel *Love Without Money* Dell describes one such mother as "a natural-born policewoman." This woman, a former suffragist, finds even the mention of marriage unpleasant because it raises the topic of sex. She disciplines her children harshly and dominates her husband as well, hindering his career by demanding to stay in her home town, where her family is powerful. Sexual frigidity was central to this image. Lindsey created a vivid account of one such female character who told him, "Sex seems to me a horrible thing. It seemed so to my mother before me. She said the Bible teaches that it is evil, and that its only excuse is for propagating the race." This woman's prudish attitudes had alienated her husband, and he had found a mistress. While Lindsey criticized the husband, too, for his failure to deal more tactfully with his wife, he emphasized the woman's unnatural moral views and rigidity. Women like this were portrayed as attempting to control men by withholding sex. They ignored male sexual rights.[22]

The image of the burdensome and demanding wife provided a variation on the theme of the prudish and controlling one: both expressed the fear that women might use men to support them but then not be pliable and attentive to their husbands. The wife who was manipulative behind a front of feminine weakness, expected excessive male attention, and acted as a "noble martyr with unnamed ills" seemed to many modern writers to be taking advantage of men. The image was not of a sexually demanding woman but of a woman who might get her way by playing on men's sexual desires and the traditional conventions of deference to women. For example, in Fannie Hurst's novel *Back Street*, the protagonist's sister, a hypocritical and unattractive young woman, sleeps with her suitor, then uses a pregnancy scare to force him to marry her. Married, she becomes petty and morally conventional. Women's unfair privileges were manifest particularly when they spent money – that is, "men's" money. For an essay on fashion one woman reporter asked men why women spent more on clothes than men. "Because women dominate men in America," answered many of them who said they were "a shade weary of paying for all the whims of the middle-class woman." The gold-digger, or alimony-hunter, who actually married a man for money was an extreme case; the more common stereotype was of the woman who expected too much for what she gave.[23]

Interestingly, the image of the burdensome wife was the only one promulgated primarily by female sexual commentators. These writers sensed a shift in the nature of the exchange that constituted marriage and were critical of the dependent and inferior wife. Nineteenth-century homage to the wife and mother had been based on the idea of the tremendous sacrifices women made, especially in the suffering of childbirth and the general self-abnegation expected of them. But these commentators believed twentieth-century wives and mothers were spoiled and had easy lives. Psychologist Pruette observed, for example, a "tinge of glory" around the "countless greying men who plod to the offices and factories each morning" to feed their families. Women's tasks in the modern world, however, had been diminished in number and significance. Childbearing, for example, no longer required the great courage it once had. Instead, "pregnancy has become a period of neurotic fears and disabilities, ending undramatically in a whiff of anaesthetic." Without the dignity of such noble functions, the magisterial mother became a petty tyrant. These writers, "modern" career women, sensed that motherhood was no longer a source of real dignity and influence as it had been for their mothers and grandmothers. And in their own lives, seeking equality with men in careers and public life, they were no doubt sensitive to the ways dependency could undermine their autonomy. Hence, they sharply rejected Victorian deference and the kinds of women who still wanted it.[24]

A final unappealing character type was the career woman and feminist, often but not always single. Like the matriarch, she was hard, unsympathetic to men's needs, and hostile to sexuality. In the 1922 novel *Broken Barriers*, the male protagonist is married to such a woman. She is a writer and reformer who campaigns for birth control, equal pay for women, and an end to child labor, but who is personally cold and snobbish and who travels so much that she rarely lives with her husband. Her behavior justifies his affair with the young middle-class wage earner who is the heroine of the novel. Those who used this image often implied that single career women were actually disturbed by sex precisely because they suppressed it. Lindsey cited a liberal clergyman who claimed:

> I know women who have never married, and who ought to
> – who need marriage badly. They have the notion that they
> have sublimated all the sex they've got in feminist careers.
> But I've concluded with respect to such people that they
> either haven't got much, or else that there is an unused
> surplus of bottled-up sex inside of them that more than
> accounts for their nerves and their "peculiarities."

Authors pictured women like this as unattractive, unhappy, or personally inadequate.[25]

The career woman threatened men because her independence or her intellectual interests suggested she might refuse to take care of men or do without them altogether. Most of the writers on marriage, male and female, were uncomfortable with such an image of women. This discomfort led them to picture career women as overtly hostile to sexuality but secretly frustrated and desperate for male attention.[26] Other writers suggested that such women might be lesbians. The urgency of the sex instinct as it was now defined meant that when the "normal" channels for its expression were closed, it might emerge in homosexual relationships.[27]

Power and sexual independence from men were the charges leveled against women who resembled these types. The matriarch, the complaining wife, and the career woman gained power from adherence to Victorian conventions of respect for mothers and wives, from feminist activism, or from the economic independence of professional work. All were characterized by resistance to male power and none were marked by a strongly developed female sexuality except for the lesbian career woman. The danger implicit in these stereotypes, then, was not the sexual power of the nineteenth-century whore, potentially overwhelming to men, but the Victorian woman's sexual control. In *Back Street* Fannie Hurst dramatizes this reversal of Victorian images by portraying a kept woman sympathetically. The protagonist, Ray Schmidt, is completely devoted to her lover, Walter Saxel. Far from overpowering him, she has practically no self of her own and epitomizes the adoring, dependent, and subordinate woman. By contrast Saxel's wife is a powerful traditional woman. A respectable Jewish matron, she is spoiled by her husband and dominates his life almost totally by maintaining ties with her own strong family and promoting the interests of the Saxel children. In *Ann Vickers* Sinclair Lewis presents a sexually active single woman as an admirable heroine, not a threatening sexual figure. The only sexuality that appears dangerous and corrupt is lesbian sexuality, which leads to the psychic enslavement and suicide of one of Ann's closest friends. The negative images of women that appear in the writings of sexual revisionists, then, imply a strong fear of women's resistance to male sexuality. The sexual danger was not that women would overcome men but that they would deny male needs. The new, more aggressive male sexuality was required if men were to keep such women in line. As W. J. Robinson wrote in 1930, "militant feminism" would not appear in the women with a "normal, i.e. properly satisfied, sex life" with a potent man.[28]

The writers of the 1920s captured in the image of the flapper a more positive ideal for modern women. This figure both embodied the popular notion of the free woman and retained a softness that did not threaten men. The flapper participated in the male world, probably working at a job as well as leading an independent, sexually integrated social life. She found men exciting, interesting comrades and did not take a condescending or disapproving attitude toward their ways. Her combination of daring spirit and youthful innocence was precisely what made her attractive to men. As Pruette described her, the flapper "has laid aside many things that would have made life simpler for her: ideals of feminine constancy, of the sacredness of maternity, of her right to a living without working."[29] A vigorous, active companion of men, not a frail and dependent creature, she had given up some of the old claim to special consideration as a woman.

At the same time, the flapper cared more about men and babies than about her paid work or her development as an individual through work. She might be "torn between the desire to be tough-minded, aggressive and self-seeking, and the compulsion to be pleasing" but would probably give way to the latter wish as soon as a man became attentive. These young women saw jobs as necessary to their independence, but they did not want careers that required them to give up love and marriage. As one fictional heroine put it, she was more interested in "experience" than a career and vigorously denied being "cursed with ambitions." Dell particularly stressed the advantages of young women's jobs, which he said were the best way to meet husbands. He criticized "middle-class feminists" for accepting careers on male terms and not helping women adjust work to their inevitable roles as wives and mothers.[30] The flapper scorned the high-minded dedication that characterized the nineteenth-century settlement-house workers[*] and women professionals.

[*] Settlement-house workers were reformers, among them many of the first generation of college-educated women, who went to live in urban immigrant neighborhoods and who engaged in a wide array of reform activities – organizing day nurseries for working women, agitating for occupational safety and child labor laws, providing public health nursing services, supporting labor

Finally, the ideal flapper was not squeamish about sex. She accepted it as a normal part of human nature and did not condemn men for their desires. She stayed out late, danced close, and necked and petted without feeling imposed upon. One novelist demonstrated this new spirit when he described without condemnation a heroine who actually spends the night with her lover. She chooses freely to do so out of love and is not victimized by a lustful man. Yet the modern young woman was still quite romantic. Lindsey pictures a young woman named Millie, the daughter of the archetypal prude, who exemplified the flapper's virtues. Her father had told her straightforwardly about sex, and she pitied her mother for her antiquated attitudes. Millie had kissed a few boys but was discriminating, postponing further sexual involvement till she met a man she really loved. But, as she told Judge Lindsey, "when I fall in love I'm not going to be stingy."[31]

The flapper's romanticism and youth, however, connoted an innocence that contradicted women's full claim on human sexuality. The ambivalence of many sexual theorists appeared as they struggled to define women's new sexuality. Most asserted that women were not passive and asexual but did have some active interest in sexuality. Like Freud, however, these writers still postulated and, indeed, desired a conventional difference between male and female sexuality. Sanger wrote, for example, that "under stimulation the sexual nature of man asserts itself almost instantaneously ready for action," but that "the sex nature of woman is more deeply hidden in the mysterious recesses of her being. More deeply concealed, it is not so immediately susceptible to stimulation, is far slower in response and thus is not immediately ready for the act of love."[32] Ironically, like the Victorians, some thought women's true interest was in babies rather than sex. Lindsey urged less censure and more sympathy for the red-lipped, "apparently oversexed" flappers on grounds that they were not in fact "fresh bodies offered for the pleasure of men but bodies offered to the agony and bloody sweat of motherhood. That is what it really means with most of them, whether they and we are conscious of it or not."[33] It seemed impossible to deny that young women were exhibiting what by older standards was an immodest

unions. The first settlements were established in the 1890s; the most active era of settlement-house reform extended to about 1920.

interest in sex, but these definitions reassured apprehensive observers that young women were still guided more by traditional nurturing qualities than by an untamed sexuality. The lesbian was threatening precisely because she could enjoy a sexual life of intensity and self-interest unconnected to reproduction, and reproduction represented the payment, the sacrifice that symbolically drained female sexuality of its frightening powers.

A variety of male and female images, then, were used to develop the myth of Victorian repression. The myth criticized the old sexual ideas and roles and suggested alternatives more appropriate to a time when women had supposedly gained equality. The sexual ideologues who created the myth opposed the Victorian ideal of continence and favored more sexual activity. Many were tolerant of some premarital sexual activity; all favored more sexual contact within marriage. Some images reflected the greater social power and sexual demands of women during that time. Criticizing the insensitive blunderer and praising the flapper's adventurous spirit and sexual interest acknowledged women's rights to a fuller life. The ideal of the healthy male animal suggested that coping with women required more vigor, hence indirectly hinted that women were stronger than in the past. At the same time, however, the images served as warnings to men and women to avoid interactions involving equivalent or greater female power in any form. The image of the poor worm ridiculed timid or overly chivalrous men. The matriarch, complaining wife, and celibate or lesbian career woman served as negative models to warn self-important, willful, or independent women. The flapper figure proclaimed that a youthful and malleable adolescent was more attractive than a sexually experienced adult woman. The sexual revisionists, in short, recognized improvements in women's status and power, yet encouraged women not to go too far, not to abandon men, and not to try to control them.

The sexual commentators of the 1920s and 1930s reworked the sexual code in order to control behavior they feared in three ways: First, they increased the specifically sexual power normatively attributed to men before and within marriage. Men were to set the pace and energetically initiate women into sexual relations. Male deference to female passionlessness was gone.

Second, they severely criticized women's capacity to control or withdraw from men sexually. Sexually unresponsive women were caricatured. Victorian women's moral right and duty to limit sexual contact were overthrown. Third, they affirmed a new but still muted female sexuality. Women were supposed to desire and enjoy sexual relations but they were considered less lustful than men and their sexuality was still linked to maternal feeling. To replace the dignified Victorian matron with the youthful flapper as an ideal was to make female power taboo. Young and eager to please, the flapper lacked both the stature of the traditional wife and mother and a developed sexuality that could overpower men. These images attacked women's power and insisted upon men's power to control sexual interactions.

The new sexual discourse created by sexual revisionists had fundamentally altered Victorian ways of thinking. In some ways it was, as claimed, an attack on sexual "repression," if repression means a code of conduct limiting sexual activity. But it was, more specifically, an attack on *women's* control over *men's* sexuality. This control could come either from evasion of marriage (the career woman or lesbian) or from a Victorian sensibility exercised within marriage (the wife and mother figures). Certainly women's increased labor force participation and political activism, the winning of the suffrage, and the growing visibility and public discussion of lesbianism all made it clear that women could be free persons, not as coercively tied to men as in the past.[34]

Moreover, while some women adopted the new fun-loving flapper styles, traditional female expectations of marriage persisted among many women. Women's celebrated "new freedom" was most salient for single women since most white wives did not remain long in the labor force. Financially dependent wives might have been "complainers" because they still looked to men for material rewards they could not get for themselves. Elaine May's study of divorce in the early twentieth century shows that some wives adopted new and higher expectations of what men should provide and were willing to divorce when disappointed. And if young single women's sexual experimentation was based on their new public freedoms and jobs, then dependent wives lost the grounds for sexual assertiveness. Given the strength of persisting messages restricting female sexuality, it would not be surprising if many wives felt more at home looking for domestic influence based on the Victorian mode – by attempting to control male sexuality. May found more wives in her sample who were antipathetic to sexual relations than wives claiming unfulfilled desires. Within marriage, then, many women may have retained a Victorian sexual self-definition and may not have been ready for a sexual life that resembled traditional male preferences more than their own.[35] Such resistance might have been even more frustrating to men if public discussion of the new sexuality and women's freedom raised their expectations of sexual responsiveness from women. The myth of Victorian repression both reflected and helped perpetuate anxiety about women dominating men or eluding their control.

On the other hand, a fear of fully developed female sexuality, similar to the Victorian threat of the whore, continued more subtly in the new ideology as well. In this sense "repression" continued, limiting women more than men. The rudimentary revisionist acknowledgment of female sexuality (and its active expression by some young women) was disturbing to many Americans. The subordination and restriction of women had represented sexual control and stability for the whole culture. In this logic, Victorian women's adherence to continence within marriage disciplined men's economic and sexual energies by forcing them to support families. For women to abandon their modesty and follow men's lascivious behavior was to threaten the very basis of civilization. Catholics and fundamentalists argued this most cogently, but liberal reformers were also susceptible to this fear. Even the radicals, much more tolerant of potential disorder, expressed concern about the results of "the increasing subordination. . .of maternity to sexuality, of the mother ethic to the mistress ethic, of love to passion." One could only try to have faith, wrote Schmalhausen, that through the "peril of the sexual revolution" young people would find a balance between sexual impulse and the need for human harmony and stability.[36] That stability continued to be represented for many by women's domestic and maternal nurturance. Hence, sexual revisionists idealized the flapper, whose explorations of female sexuality remained relatively limited and were driven by romantic love. They condemned lesbians and by omission denied legitimacy to the heterosexually active and independent woman. The legacy of this omission is manifest in the difficulty some female adolescents have today in taking responsibility for their heterosexual activity.[37]

Rebellion against "Victorian repression," then, was much more complex than it appeared on the surface. Bourgeois women's role in sexual control, inherited from the nineteenth century, over-lapped in the early twentieth century with rising economic and social freedom of younger women. Whether sexually active or sexually controlling, women seemed to most liberal sexual theor-ists to have gained an improper advantage over men in modern life. The myth of Victorian repression conveyed a reaction against women's power in either form but particularly against passionless-ness and women's uses of it. The new sexual discourse of the 1920s and 1930s represented not "liberation" but a new form of regu-lation. The new rules were better adapted to a world where single women of the middle class were asserting a more active sexuality and where men pressed to legitimate theirs. Although some women participated in creating this discourse, it was grounded in a male perspective and reflected primarily fears of female power. The much vaunted new morality gestured in the direction of equality for women but effectively sustained the cultural power of men, focusing that power in the arena of sexuality.[38] Although women's social, political, and economic inequality remain perva-sive today, the continuing effects of the myth of Victorian repres-sion may help to account for many women's subjective perception that male sexual power is central to their oppression.

NOTES

First published in *Passion and Power*, ed. Kathy Peiss and Christina Simmons (Philadelphia: 1989), 157–77. Used by permission of MARHO, the Radical Historians' Organization.

Acknowledgments: I would like to thank Estelle Freedman, Joanne Meyerowitz, Kathy Peiss, and Bruce Tucker for comments on earlier drafts of this article and Kathy Peiss for very helpful editing.

1 Gertrude Atherton, *Black Oxen* (New York: 1923), 126; Sinclair Lewis, *Ann Vickers* (New York: 1932), 395.
2 For earlier historiography see, for example, Sidney Ditzion, *Marriage, Morals, and Sex in America* (1953; reprint, New York: 1969), 374–80; Henry May, *The End of American Innocence* (1959; reprint, Chicago: 1964), 338–47; Steven Marcus, *The Other Victorians* (1966; reprint, London: 1969), 287–8; James R. McGovern, "The American Woman's Pre-World War I Freedom in Manners and Morals,"

Journal of American History 55 (1968): 315–33; Michel Foucault, *The History of Sexuality*, vol. I, *An Introduction* (New York: 1978), trans. Robert Hurley, 69, 92–3, 103–5, 127–31.

3 McGovern, "The American Woman's Pre-World War I Freedom," 316–19; Barbara Epstein, "Family, Sexual Morality, and Popular Movements in Turn-of-the-Century America," 117–19, and Ellen Kay Trimberger, "Feminism, Men, and Modern Love: Greenwich Village, 1900–1925," 132, both in *Powers of Desire: The Politics of Sexuality*, ed. Ann Snitow, Christine Stansell, and Sharon Thompson (New York: 1983); Christina Simmons, " 'Marriage in the Modern Manner': Sexual Radicalism and Reform in America, 1914–1941" (Ph.D. dissertation, Brown University, 1982), 64–84.

Interestingly, the radicals of the 1910s, especially birth controllers, tended to attack male power over female sexuality, as is apparent in the cartoons in *The Masses* and the *Birth Control Review*. The mostly liberal group of thinkers discussed here shifted the focus to women's power over male sexuality.

4 See Michelle Zimbalist Rosaldo, "Woman, Culture, and Society: A Theoretical Overview," in *Woman, Culture, and Society*, ed. Michelle Zimbalist Rosaldo and Louise Lamphere (Stanford: 1974), 20–2, 31–4, for an account of women's special role in purity.

On fears of excess and on continence, see Charles E. Rosenberg, "Sexuality, Class and Role in 19th-Century America," *American Quarterly* 25 (1973): 134, 137; John S. Haller and Robin M. Haller, *The Physician and Sexuality in Victorian America* (New York: 1974), 200–1, 102–13, 130; G.J. Barker-Benfield, "The Spermatic Economy: A Nineteenth-Century View of Sexuality," in *The American Family in Social-Historical Perspective*, 2nd ed., ed. Michael Gordon (New York: 1978), 377; Ronald G. Walters, *Primers for Prudery: Sexual Advice to Victorian America* (Englewood Cliffs, NJ: 1974), 2, 17, 32, 49; Linda Gordon, *Woman's Body, Woman's Right: A Social History of Birth Control in America* (New York: 1976), 102–6, 183; Carroll Smith-Rosenberg, "A Richer and a Gentler Sex," *Social Research* 53 (1986): 289.

On women's sexuality, see Walters, *Primers*, 67; Nancy F. Cott, "Passionlessness: An Interpretation of Victorian Sexual Ideology, 1790–1850," *Signs* 4 (1978): 226–8; Carl N. Degler, "What Ought To Be and What Was: Women's Sexuality in the Nineteenth Century," *American Historical Review* 79 (1974): 1469–77. Degler argues that the notion of women's sexual passivity was part of an ideology in the process of being established rather than an account of majority opinion on the question. The fear underlying the ideology was that women did possess sexual drives and might not maintain control. See also Peter Filene, *Him/Her/Self: Sex Roles in Modern America*, 2nd ed. (Baltimore: 1986), 91. Peter Gay, in *Education of the Senses* (New York: 1984), argues like Degler that much behavior violated norms of sexual restraint and that the power of Victorian sexual ideology was thus incomplete.

For the Victorian definition of male sexuality, see Rosenberg,

"Sexuality, Class and Role," 140–1; Barbara Welter, "The Cult of True Womanhood: 1820–1860," in *The American Family*, ed. Gordon, 313–16, 318.

5 David J. Pivar, *Purity Crusade: Sexual Morality and Social Control, 1868–1900* (Westport, CT: 1973); John Paull Harper, "Be Fruitful and Multiply: Origins of Legal Restrictions on Planned Parenthood in Nineteenth-Century America," in *Women of America: A History*, ed. Carol Berkin and Mary Beth Norton (Boston: 1979), 260–2; Gertrude Marvin, "Anthony and the Devil," *The Masses* (February 1914), reprinted in *Echoes of Revolt: The Masses, 1911–1917*, ed. William L. O'Neill (Chicago: 1966), 39.

6 By 1914 Anglo-Saxon stock was no longer in the majority. Irish, Italian, and Jewish immigrants concentrated in the cities, built political machines that afforded them some control over urban life, and created cultural forms different from both European patterns and those of the native Yankees. Gilman M. Ostrander, *American Civilization in the First Machine Age, 1890–1940* (New York: 1970), 43–5, 277; Epstein, "Family, Sexual Morality," in *Powers of Desire*, ed. Snitow *et al.*, 123. For information on urban culture and leisure, see Lewis A. Erenberg, *Steppin' Out: New York Nightlife and the Transformation of American Culture, 1890–1930* (Westport, CT: 1981); Lary May, *Screening Out the Past: The Birth of Mass Culture and the Motion Picture Industry* (New York: 1980); Kathy Peiss, *Cheap Amusements: Working Women and Leisure in Turn-of-the-Century New York* (Philadelphia: 1986); Elizabeth Ewen, "City Lights: Immigrant Women and the Rise of the Movies," *Signs* 5 (supp.) (1980): S45–65.

7 Filene, *Him/Her/Self*, 19–38; Joseph A. Hill, *Women in Gainful Occupations, 1870 to 1920*, Census Monographs IX (Washington, DC: 1929), 19, 76; William H. Chafe, *The American Woman: Her Changing Social, Economic, and Political Role, 1920–1970* (New York: 1972), 51, 54; Lorine Pruette, "The Flapper," in *The New Generation: The Intimate Problems of Modern Parents and Children*, ed. V. F. Calverton and S. D. Schmalhausen (New York: 1930), 586–8.

Many sexual commentators made the connection between women's new status and new sexuality. See Horace Coon, *Coquetry for Men* (New York: 1932), 110–11; S. D. Schmalhausen, "The War of the Sexes," in *Woman's Coming of Age: A Symposium*, ed. V. F. Calverton and S. D. Schmalhausen (New York: 1931), 285–6; Dora Russell, "Sex Love," in *The Sex Problem in Modern Society*, ed. John F. McDermott (New York: 1931), 135; Ira S. Wile and Mary Winn, *Marriage in the Modern Manner* (New York: 1929), 28–9, 34; Phyllis Blanchard and Carlyn Manasses, *New Girls for Old* (New York: 1930), 235, 245–6.

The feminist quoted is Suzanne LaFollette, in *Concerning Women* (New York: 1926), 147. See also Gordon, *Woman's Body*, 192; Mari Jo Buhle, *Women and American Socialism, 1870–1920* (Urbana, IL: 1981), 260.

8 On men see Gordon, *Woman's Body*, 191–2; Filene, *Him/Her/Self*, 72–8; Joseph F. Kett, *Rites of Passage: Adolescence in America, 1790 to*

the Present (New York: 1977), 233–4, 240; Irvin G. Wyllie, *The Self-Made Man in America: The Myth of Rags to Riches* (New York: 1954), 144; Ostrander, *American Civilization*, 256; Erenberg, *Steppin' Out*, 66–7; Lawrence K. Frank, "Social Change and the Family," *Annals of the American Academy of Political and Social Science* 160 (March 1932): 100–1. Quotation from "Confessions of a Feminist Man," *The Masses* (March 1914): 8.

9 Alfred C. Kinsey et al., *Sexual Behavior in the Human Female* (1953; reprint, New York: 1965), 298–300, 380, 362–3, 358–9; Rachelle Yarros, *Modern Woman and Sex: A Feminist Physician Speaks* (New York: 1933), 65; Lewis M. Terman, *Psychological Factors in Marital Happiness* (New York: 1938), 318; Ben B. Lindsey, "The Promise and Peril of the New Freedom," in *Woman's Coming of Age*, ed. Calverton and Schmalhausen, 454–5. Kinsey found similar changes occurring between later generations. Comparing men in their youth between 1910 and 1925 with those growing up between 1930 and 1948, he found the later generation had intercourse with prostitutes only two-thirds to one-half as often as the older group though total sexual contact was of similar frequency. Hence, partners must have been changing from prostitutes to friends. Alfred C. Kinsey, *Sexual Behavior in the Human Male* (Philadelphia: 1948), 396, 411.

The sexual behavior of non–middle-class groups, on the other hand, had begun to diverge from Victorian standards by about 1880. Daniel Scott Smith, "The Dating of the American Sexual Revolution: Evidence and Interpretation," in *The American Family*, ed. Gordon, 431–3, 435.

10 Foucault, *History of Sexuality*, 1, 30, 41–6. On Freud's influence, see Nathan Hale, *Freud and the Americans: The Beginnings of Psychoanalysis in the United States, 1887–1917* (New York: 1971), 262, 271, 361, 416, 430; and Fred Matthews, "In Defense of Common Sense: Mental Hygiene as Ideology and Mentality in Twentieth-Century America," *Prospects* 4 (1979): 459–516.

For biographies, see *New York Times*, 27 March 1943, 13; 10 October 1943, 16; Christopher Lasch, *Haven in a Heartless World: The Family Besieged* (New York: 1977), 16, 23; "Ernest Groves," *Current Biography* 4 (1943): 21–3; Elaine Showalter, "Lorine Pruette," in *These Modern Women: Autobiographical Essays from the Twenties*, ed. Showalter (Old Westbury, NY: 1978), 68; Floyd Dell, *Homecoming: An Autobiography* (New York: 1933), 255, 350, 288, and *Intellectual Vagabondage: An Apology for the Intelligentsia* (New York: 1926), 174, 187–9; Gordon, *Woman's Body*, chs. 9, 10; Lewis, *Ann Vickers*; Fannie Hurst, *Back Street* (New York: 1930); Haim Gnizi, "V. F. Calverton: Independent Radical" (Ph.D. dissertation, City University of New York, 1968), 25, 31, 52–3, 90–8, 162–3.

11 Samuel D. Schmalhausen, "The Freudian Emphasis on Sex," in *The Sex Problem in Modern Society*, ed. McDermott, 61–2; Floyd Dell, *Love in the Machine Age: A Psychological Study of The Transition from Patriarchal Society* (New York: 1930), 6; Ben B. Lindsey and Wainwright Evans, *Companionate Marriage* (New York: 1927), 227–8.

12 Margaret Sanger, *Happiness in Marriage* (New York: 1926), 21, 48; Wile and Winn, *Modern Manner*, 213–14; LeMon Clark, *Emotional Adjustment in Marriage* (St. Louis, MO: 1937), 13.

13 Edwin W. Hirsch, *The Power to Love: A Psychic and Physiologic Study of Regeneration* (New York: 1935), 88, 119–20, 126; also Dell, *Machine Age*, 62; Sherwood Eddy, *Sex and Youth* (Garden City, NJ: 1929), 125, 21; Ernest R. Groves, *The Marriage Crisis* (New York: 1928), 214.

14 Schmalhausen, "Freudian Emphasis," in *The Sex Problem*, ed. McDermott, 69; Lindsey and Evans, *Companionate*, v–vi.

15 Smith-Rosenberg, "Richer and a Gentler Sex," 293–8; Gordon, *Woman's Body*, 103–6.

16 Sanger, *Happiness*, 89; Groves, *Marriage Crisis*, 100; Ernest R. Groves, Gladys Hoagland Groves, and Catherine Groves, *Sex Fulfillment in Marriage* (New York: 1942), 135, 144, 146, 150; Wile and Winn, *Modern Manner*, 54; Ernest R. Groves, *The American Family* (Chicago: 1934), 225. The brute image appeared sometimes, too, in discussion of the relation of Victorian fathers to their modern daughters, describing restrictive, punitive fathers. See Ben B. Lindsey and Wainwright Evans, *The Revolt of Modern Youth* (Garden City, NJ: 1925), 294.

17 Havelock Ellis, "Woman's Sexual Nature," in *Woman's Coming of Age*, ed. Calverton and Schmalhausen, 238. A few pessimistic female authors despaired of overcoming male aggression and used the same image to argue for a revival of chivalry. See Edith Stern, *Men Are Clumsy Lovers* (New York: 1934), 21.

18 Wile and Winn, *Modern Manner*, xiv, 147; Sanger, *Happiness*, 6.

19 Coon, *Coquetry*, 207, 49–50; Hirsch, *Power to Love*, 182; Lewis, *Ann Vickers*, 277; William J. Robinson, "Sexual Continence and Its Influence on the Physical and Mental Health of Men and Woman," and Victor G. Vecki, "The Dogma of Sexual Abstinence," in *Sexual Continence and Its Influence on the Physical and Mental Health of Men and Women*, ed. Robinson (New York: 1930), 39, 235–6. Several of the authors in this collection were influenced by Freud's 1908 essay " 'Civilized' Sexual Morality and Modern Nervousness," first translated into English by Robinson in 1915 (reprinted in *Sexuality and the Psychology of Love*, ed. Philip Rieff [New York: 1963], 20–40). Freud did criticize excessive repression but did not oppose all repression. See also Estelle Freedman, " 'Uncontrolled Desires': The Response to the Sexual Psychopath, 1920 to 1960," in *Passion and Power: Sexuality in History*, ed. Kathy Peiss and Christina Simmons (Philadelphia: 1989).

20 Hirsch, *Power to Love*, 203–4; Eddy, *Sex and Youth*, 134, 316; Wile and Winn, *Modern Manner*, 160; Lindsey and Evans, *Revolt*, 94, 325; Sanger, *Happiness*, 217–18.

21 Harry Elmer Barnes, "Sex Education," in *Sex in Civilization*, ed. V. F. Calverton and S. D. Schmalhausen (New York: 1929), 303; Groves *et al.*, *Sex Fulfillment*, 183–9; Dell, *Machine Age*, 311.

22 Floyd Dell, *Love Without Money* (New York: 1931), 6, 12, 18, 152–6, 273; Barnes, "Sex in Education," in *Sex in Civilization*, ed. Calverton

and Schmalhausen, 302. Barnes emphasizes women's religiosity and role in perpetuating wrong sexual ideas. Lindsey and Evans, *Companionate*, 117–23; Olga Knopf, *Women On Their Own* (Boston: 1935), 245–6; Clark, *Emotional Adjustment*, 97, 109; Lewis, *Ann Vickers*, 476.

23 Wile and Winn, *Modern Manner*, 162–70; Elizabeth M. Gilmer, *Dorothy Dix – Her Book: Every-day Help for Every-day People* (New York: 1926), 63, 157, 283–4; Pruette, "The Flapper," in *The New Generation*, ed. Calverton and Schmalhausen, 589; Hurst, *Back Street*, 54, 92–102; Winifred Rauschenbush, "The Idiot God Fashion," and Alice Beal Parson, "Man-Made Illusions About Woman," in *Woman's Coming of Age*, ed. Calverton and Schmalhausen, 442–3, 23; LaFollette, *Concerning Women*, 14, 83–4, 113; Dell, *Machine Age*, 65–6.

24 LaFollette, *Concerning Women*, 113; Lorine Pruette, "Why Women Fail," in *Woman's Coming of Age*, ed. Calverton and Schmalhausen, 246–7; see also Wile and Winn, *Modern Manner*, 132–3, and Calverton and Schmalhausen, Preface to *New Generation*, 8–10.

These female sexual revisionists were not to my knowledge lesbians, unlike the New Women whom Carroll Smith-Rosenberg describes in "The New Woman as Androgyne: Social Disorder and Gender Crisis, 1870–1936," in her collected essays, *Disorderly Conduct: Visions of Gender in Victorian America* (New York: 1985), 245–96. The situation of the revisionists as heterosexual women participating in the re-creation of heterosexual ideology is complex and needs further examination. For one example, see Mary Trigg, " 'The Characterization of Herself': Lorine Pruette on Women, Men, and Marriage in the 1920s," paper presented at the Seventh Berkshire Conference on the History of Women, Wellesley College, 1987.

25 Meredith Nicholson, *Broken Barriers* (New York: 1922), 79, 241, 320, 313, 315; Gertrude Atherton, *Black Oxen* (New York: 1923), 263; Marjorie Hillis, *Live Alone and Like It: A Guide for the Extra Woman* (Indianapolis: 1936), 90–1; Lindsey and Evans, *Companionate*, 311; Gilmer, *Dorothy Dix*, 56.

26 Knopf, *Women*, 110, 112, 125, 76; Phyllis Blanchard, *The Adolescent Girl* (New York: 1920), 113–14; C. Gasquoine Hartley, *Women's Wild Oats: Essays on the Re-fixing of Moral Standards* (New York: 1920), 21; Groves, *Marriage Crisis*, 3; Lindsey and Evans, *Revolt*, 294, 246; Frances R. Donovan, *The Schoolma'am* (New York: 1938), 39.

27 Gilbert V. Hamilton, "The Emotional Life of Modern Woman," in *Woman's Coming of Age*, ed. Calverton and Schmalhausen, 228–9; Ralph Hay, "Mannish Women or Old Maids?" *Know Yourself* 1 (July 1938): 78; Lindsey and Evans, *Companionate*, 187; David H. Keller, "Abnormal Love Between Women," *Your Body* 3 (March 1938): 426; Knopf, *Women*, 120; Clark, *Emotional Adjustment*, 70. Carroll Smith-Rosenberg discusses the charge of lesbianism extensively in "Androgyne," in her *Disorderly Conduct*.

28 Hurst, *Back Street*, 169, 175, 191, 377, 400–1; Lewis, *Ann Vickers*, 91–2, 189, 207, 320, 420, 460–1; Robinson, "Continence," in *Sexual Continence*, ed. Robinson, 40.

29 Rupert Hughes, *No One Man* (New York: 1930), 58; Gilmer, *Dorothy Dix*, 79, 216–20; Pruette, "The Flapper," in *The New Generation*, ed. Calverton and Schmalhausen, 589.
30 Pruette, "The Flapper," *The New Generation*, ed. Calverton and Schmalhausen, 589; Gilmer, *Dorothy Dix*, 17; Nicholson, *Broken Barriers*, 76; Dell, *Machine Age*, 139, 353, 358; Blanchard and Manasses, *New Girls*, 237; Robin Wise, *How To Make Love, in Six Easy Lessons* (New York: 1925), 36.
31 Nicholson, *Broken Barriers*, 273; Atherton, *Black Oxen*, 126; Blanchard and Manasses, *New Girls*, 218; Lindsey and Evans, *Companionate*, 124–31.
32 Sanger, *Happiness*, 127; Max J. Exner, *The Sexual Side of Marriage* (1932; reprint, New York: 1937), 20; Hannah M. Stone and Abraham Stone, *A Marriage Manual: A Practical Guide-Book to Sex and Marriage* (New York: 1937), 217–18. In " 'A New Generation of Women': Progressive Psychiatrists and the Hypersexual Female," *Feminist Studies* 13 (Fall 1987): 513–43, Elizabeth Lunbeck shows the resistance there was to accepting young women's sexual activity as normal.
33 Lindsey and Evans, *Revolt*, 88; Eddy, *Sex and Youth*, 137; Wile and Winn, *Modern Manner*, 176.
34 John D'Emilio, "Capitalism and Gay Identity," in *Powers of Desire*, ed. Snitow *et al.*, 105.
35 Elaine May, *Great Expectations: Marriage and Divorce in Post-Victorian America* (Chicago: 1980), 137–55, 104–9.
36 Filene, *Him/Her/Self*, 144–5; Raoul de Guchteneere, *Judgment on Birth Control* (New York: 1931), 177, 191–2; Lindsey and Evans, *Companionate*, 153; Schmalhausen, "War of the Sexes," in *Woman's Coming of Age*, ed. Calverton and Schmalhausen, 173.
37 Rosalind Pollack Petchesky, *Abortion and Woman's Choice: The State, Sexuality, and Reproductive Freedom* (1984; reprint, Boston: 1985), ch. 6, "Abortion and Heterosexual Culture: The Teenage Question."
38 Other writers making similar interpretations of this sexual ideology include Epstein in "Family, Sexual Morality," in *Powers of Desire*, ed. Snitow *et al.*; Smith-Rosenberg in "Androgyne," in her *Disorderly Conduct*; and Margaret Jackson in "Sexual Liberation or Social Control? Some aspects of the relationship between feminism and the social construction of sexual knowledge in the early twentieth century," *Women's Studies International Forum* 6 (1983): 1–17, in which she discusses the ideas of Havelock Ellis.

3

SEXUAL GEOGRAPHY AND GENDER ECONOMY

The furnished room districts of Chicago, 1890–1930

Joanne Meyerowitz

The physical space and cultural geography of the city provide a focus for Joanne Meyerowitz's innovative contribution to the discussion about the sexual revolution. Urban life opened up new possibilities for young women removed from the surveillance and supervision of families and small towns or rural communities. Meyerowitz acknowledges that such arrangements also rendered working-class women vulnerable to sexual exploitation, and she points to the low wages that motivated the exchange of sexual favors, whether in dating or in outright prostitution. But she cautions us not to take middle-class reformers' depictions of working-class women at face value: these women were not merely victims of city life and predatory men, but also active historical subjects who made their own choices about sexuality. At the same time, she questions a more positive representation of wage-earning women as it emerges in Hollywood movies and the work of urban sociologists: the image of the emancipated urban woman downplayed the constraints of poverty and the sexual vulnerability that women experienced. Finally, Meyerowitz challenges a view of the sexual revolution as a middle-class creation. Even as sexologists were articulating new theory about sexuality, working-class women were living out their own versions of a revised sexual code.

* * *

The broad outlines of the early twentieth-century sexual revolution in the United States are now well known.[1] From roughly 1890 to 1930, public discussions and displays of sexuality multiplied

43

in popular magazines, newspapers, and entertainments. At the same time, women began to adopt more sexual, or at least less modest, styles; shorter skirts, cosmetics, bobbed hair, and cigarettes, once the styles of prostitutes, all seemed evidence of a larger change in mores when adopted by "respectable" working- and middle-class women. Men and women mingled freely in new commercialized recreation industries and in workplaces. And surveys of the middle class revealed increases in premarital intercourse.

Historians have now written at least three versions of this sexual revolution. In the oldest and now standard account, young middle-class "flappers" rebelled against the repressive standards of their parents by engaging in shocking behavior, such as petting in automobiles, dancing to jazz music, and using bawdy language.[2] A second version of the sexual revolution developed with the growth of the field of US women's history. In this rendition, young feminist bohemians, or independent "new women," influenced by the writings of Freud and other sexologists, experimented sexually and rejected the homosocial* sisterhood of earlier women's rights activists.[3] A third variation points to a working-class component. Urban working-class "rowdy girls" appear as early as the 1830s, but seem to enter historical center stage in precisely the same years that the middle-class "new women" and "flappers" self-consciously rejected Victorian mores. In the workplace and in dance halls, theaters, and amusement parks, young working-class women adopted an overtly sexual style that dismayed both their parents and middle-class reformers.[4]

This article is a case study of working-class women's sexuality in the furnished room districts of turn-of-the-century Chicago. In a particular setting, how did women participate in the sexual revolution, and how was their behavior interpreted and publicized? This approach modifies the various versions of the sexual revolution. For one, it locates neglected geographical centers of urban sexual activity – the furnished room districts – and early active participants in the sexual revolution – the women lodgers. Second, it highlights economic imperatives that motivated and shaped at least part of the sexual revolution. And, finally, it shows how middle-class observers reshaped the experiences of sexually active working-class women and broadcast them to a larger national audience.

* The term "homosocial" pertains to activities and associations among members of the same sex; it connotes an affirmation of same-sex networks.

Recently US feminists have engaged in heated debates over the meaning of twentieth-century sexual expression. The debates are polarized between those who emphasize the sexual dangers, such as rape, that oppress women and those who focus on the sensual pleasures that await women.[5] While this article does not enter these debates directly, it suggests the importance of studying sexuality in context. Sexual behavior, of course, is neither inherently dangerous for women nor inherently pleasurable. Like other socially constructed behaviors, its meanings derive from the specific contexts in which it is enacted. This study examines how and why a particular group of women adopted the freer modes of sexual expression that characterized the early twentieth-century sexual revolution. It finds that neither sexual danger nor sensual pleasure provides adequate explanation.

Most major American cities today have a distinct geography of sexuality. That is, one can locate districts and neighborhoods known as the institutional and social centers of various sexual subcultures. Take San Francisco, for example, a city known for its celebration of sexual variety. Upscale heterosexual singles live in apartments and frequent bars in the Marina district. Downscale heterosexual men go to porn shops and massage parlors in the Tenderloin. Female prostitutes sell their services at the corner of 18th and Mission streets; male prostitutes sell their services on Polk Street. Gay men congregate in the Castro district, and lesbians meet in the bars and coffeehouses in the vicinity of Valencia Street.

A lesser-known geography of sexuality also existed in early twentieth-century American cities. In 1916, sociologist Robert Park identified what he called "moral regions" of the city, "detached milieus in which vagrant and suppressed impulses, passions, and ideals emancipate themselves from the dominant moral order."[6] Park was not the first to define neighborhoods by sexual behavior. At the end of the nineteenth century, a few urban investigators identified the furnished room districts, or areas where rooming houses abounded, as "moral regions" of sorts, distinct neighborhoods where unconventional sexual behavior flourished.[7] By the early twentieth century, reformers defined a "furnished room problem" more precisely. In 1906, for example, in a study of Boston's furnished room district, Albert Benedict Wolfe lamented the "contamination of young men, the deterioration in the modesty and morality of young women, the existence of actual houses of prostitution in the guise of lodging-houses, the laxity of landladies, the large number of informal unions, the general loosening of moral texture."[8] By the late 1910s and 1920s, more dispassionate sociologists explored "a new code of sex relationships" in the furnished room districts of Chicago.[9] Evidence from newspapers, autobiographies, vice reports, and social surveys also suggests that the furnished room districts were indeed the centers of sexually unconventional subcultures.[10]

By the end of the nineteenth century, most major American cities had furnished room districts. These often first appeared in the city center, and, later, as business displaced downtown housing, moved out farther along major transportation lines. The large proportion of adult residents and the small proportion of children distinguished these districts demographically from other neighborhoods of the city. A residential street in a furnished room district usually resembled others in the city: a typical block would consist of single-family homes, buildings of flats, large tenements, or older mansions. The owners of the buildings, however, converted the interiors into one- or two-room dwellings. They might divide a flat into two or three smaller units or divide a large tenement into an "apartment hotel" with as many as 100 furnished rooms.

In Chicago, three such districts emerged in the late nineteenth century. On the South Side, the furnished room district included major portions of the Chicago black community and also what was, before the 1912 raids, the segregated vice district of the city. On the West Side, the district housed a population of predominantly white service and factory workers. A transient male hobo population congregated on the inner boundaries. On the North Side, where rents were slightly higher, clerical and sales workers lived in rooming houses alongside white service and manufacturing workers, artists, bohemians, and radicals of all stripes. In the early twentieth century, the North Side district included substantial numbers of Irish and Swedish roomers.[11]

These districts burgeoned in the early 1890s when migrants and visitors streamed to Chicago for the World's Columbian Exposition. They continued to grow in the first decades of the twentieth century. By 1923, the Illinois Lodging House Register reported over 85,000 lodgers in about 5,000 rooming houses in the three major furnished room districts. By 1930, residents of the new small-unit apartments (with private bathrooms and kitchenettes) joined lodgers in these neighborhoods.[12]

Several distinctive features of the furnished room districts fostered the development of extramarital sexual relationships. Most obviously, women and men lived together in houses where most people did not live in families. In these neighborhoods, lodgers found numerous opportunities to create social and sexual ties with their peers. Further, the high geographic mobility in the furnished room districts made informal, transient relationships the norm. One writer went so far as to claim that the entire population of Chicago's North Side furnished room district changed every four months.[13] This high turnover rate created an atmosphere of anonymity in which lodgers rarely knew their neighbors well. Community pressures to conform to conventional familial roles were weaker than in more settled neighborhoods. And parental authorities were absent. Many rooming house keepers, eager to keep their tenants, refrained from criticizing or interfering with roomers' sexual behaviour.[14] In addition, the predominance of men in the North and West Side districts may have encouraged women to participate in extramarital heterosexual relationships: it would have been easy to meet men and difficult to avoid them.[15]

In any case, the prevalence of prostitution in the furnished room districts created a climate where open expressions of sexuality were common. In the first decade of the twentieth century, the most prominent vice district of Chicago lay in the South Side furnished room district. Brothels were tolerated in sections of the West and North Side districts as well.[16] In addition, on the South, West, and North Sides, some keepers of rooming houses and hotels rented rooms by the hour or night to prostitutes and their customers.[17] After the municipal government closed the brothels in the 1910s, social investigators repeatedly found rooming houses and hotels used for prostitution.[18]

In addition to hotels and rooming houses, the "bright light" centers of the furnished room districts provided settings in which men and women could socialize. Investors who hoped to profit from the demand by lodgers opened cafeterias, cheap restaurants, tea rooms, soft-drink parlors, saloons, dance halls, cabarets, and movie theaters. Residents of the districts turned these institutions into social centers. As one observer noted: "Considerable companionship grows up around these resorts. One is struck by the fact that the same people visit and re-visit the same cabaret time and again."[19]

On the North Side, Clark Street and, on the West Side, Halsted Street were well known for their nightlife. In 1918, Clark Street alone housed 57 saloons, 36 restaurants, and 20 cabarets.[20] On the South Side, the State Street "Stroll" and 35th Street emerged as the "bright light" centers of the black community. Dance halls, restaurants, movies, and saloons for black customers coexisted with "black and tan" cabarets which offered racially integrated recreation.[21] When young men and women who lived with their parents went out for a night on the town and when wealthier people went "slumming," they often went to the furnished room districts of the city.

These areas, it seems, were geographic settings where behavior considered unacceptable elsewhere was accepted matter-of-factly and even encouraged. In residential communities of Chicago, neighbors often stigmatized sexually active unmarried women. For example, Mamie, a young woman who lived with her parents in a working-class neighbourhood of Chicago, first encountered problems in 1918 when a policewoman reported her for "unbecoming conduct with sailors." Later, rumor had it that her neighbors talked of signing a petition to expel her from the neighborhood.[22] Contrast Mamie's brief case history with the comment of a student of Chicago's South Side furnished room district: "It is said that an attractive woman who does not 'cash in' is likely to be considered a fool by her neighbors, instead of any stigma being attached to a woman who 'hustles' in this neighborhood."[23]

By the early twentieth century, the furnished room districts of Chicago and other large cities were known as havens for women and men who chose to defy convention.[24] In addition to migrants and transients, they attracted women and men seeking adventures and a chance to break taboos in a community without parental supervision.[25] Here interested lodgers could enter peer-oriented subcultures that sanctioned extramarital sexual behavior. A 1918 account of Chicago's North Side shows the complex and casual nature of social and sexual relationships:

[I. and V.] went to the North Clark Street section where they posed as man and wife. They took a couple of furnished rooms. . ., and remained there for two years. Both of them worked, often bringing in as much as $30.00 a week together. They took their meals out and got along very well.

Then two of the girl's sisters came to Chicago to find work and rented rooms next to them. These girls had good intentions but not securing very lucrative positions, they soon learned how to supplement their wages by allowing young men to stay with them.

These girls struck up an acquaintanceship with another girl who used to remain overnight with them now and again when they had been out to a dance or cabaret. J. liked this new girl and as he put it could not "help monkeying with her" and when V. found it out she became extremely jealous and shortly afterwards left him. Her sisters and the other girl followed her.[26]

Other accounts provide additional glimpses of how women formed social networks in the furnished room districts. In 1911, two women, 17 and 20 years old, met at a South Side dance hall. The older woman persuaded the younger to room with her on Chicago's North Side. After they moved in together, they made "pick up acquaintances" with men at dance halls and on the street.[27] Around 1913, Myrtle S., who roomed on the North Side, made friends with a woman at the restaurant where she ate her meals. This woman introduced her to a man, Lew W., with whom she spent several evenings drinking beer. Myrtle testified that she lost her virginity when Lew took advantage of her: "one night she lost consciousness after her drink of beer and awoke next morning in the Superior Hotel." Despite this betrayal, she returned to the hotel with Lew on two other occasions. Later, Myrtle met another man at a "chop suey" restaurant.[28]

Some of the social circles that developed in the furnished room districts were distinguished by unconventional lifestyles, sexual preferences, or political leanings. In the North Side district, for example, a subculture of hoboes congregated in and around Washington, or Bughouse, Square. In her autobiography, hobo "Box Car Bertha" wrote, "Girls and women. . .

seemed to keep Chicago as their hobo center. . . . They all centered about the Near North Side, in Bughouse Square, in the cheap roominghouses and light housekeeping establishments, or begged or accepted sleeping space from men or other women there before them." The women hoboes whom Bertha described engaged casually in sexual relationships. One woman, she wrote, had "a group of sweethearts," others lived and traveled with men "to whom by chance or feeling they had attached themselves," and still others engaged in "careless sex relations."[29]

By the 1920s, lesbian communities were also visible.[30] According to blues singer Ma Rainey, a black bisexual, lesbians frequented State Street, in the South Side rooming house area. A song she recorded in 1924 included the following among other more sexually suggestive verses:

> Goin' down to spread the news
> State Street women wearing brogan shoes
> Hey, hey, daddy let me shave 'em dry. . .
> There's one thing I don't understand
> Some women walkin' State Street like a man,
> Eeh, hey, hey, daddy let me shave 'em dry.[31]

According to Box Car Bertha, "several tea shops and bootleg joints on the near-north side. . .catered to lesbians," including many among the Chicago hobo population.[32] Another observer found lesbians in the somewhat less transient population of the North Side furnished room district's bohemian circles. He, too, noted that homosexual women and men frequented the tea rooms of the area and held parties in their rented rooms.[33]

The best-known subcultures of the furnished room districts were undoubtedly the bohemian circles of artists, intellectuals, and political radicals. In Chicago, black bohemians congregated in the South Side furnished room district, and some white socialists and anarchists lived in the West Side district.[34] But the heart of Chicago's bohemia was on the North Side where one study found that "most of the experimenters are young women."[35] In most respects, Chicago's bohemians resembled those of New York's Greenwich Village. Chicago, though, had its own distinctive institutions. The informal Dill Pickle Club provided a setting for lectures, plays, and jazz performances.[36]

And the anarchist tradition of soap-box oratory in Washington Square provided a public forum for unconventional speakers.[37] As in the other subcultures of the furnished room districts, women who joined bohemian circles expected and often wanted to participate in extramarital sexual activities. For example, Natalie Feinberg, the daughter of working-class Jewish immigrants from Russia, expressed an interest in "free love" before she moved away from her family in Chicago, changed her name to Jean Farway, and "frequented the various gathering places" of the bohemians. According to the sociologist who described her, "She won the reputation of wishing to become a great courtesan."[38]

Historians remember the furnished room districts primarily for the articulate, "emancipated" middle- and upper-class members of bohemian communities. Such people are often seen as vanguards of modern sexuality, women and men who experimented freely with new sexual possibilities learned from Sigmund Freud, Havelock Ellis, and other sexologists.[39] The geography of sexuality helps place the bohemians in context, as only one subculture among several. The furnished room districts housed working-class women and men as well as middle- and upper-class bohemians. There is no evidence that the "revolution" of a bohemian and middle-class vanguard trickled down to the working class. In fact, it seems more likely that bohemians learned of new sexual possibilities not only from the "highbrow" writings of the sexologists but also from the "lowbrow" behavior of their less intellectual neighbors.[40]

The furnished room districts not only provide a setting for observing various participants in the sexual revolution; they also reveal the social and economic context that shaped changing sexual mores. Heterosexual relationships in the furnished room districts included "dating," "pick ups," "occasional prostitution," and "temporary alliances." Like professional prostitution and marriage, these were economic as well as sexual and social relationships. Because employers paid self-supporting women wages intended for dependent daughters and wives, many women lodgers worked in low-paying jobs that barely covered subsistence.[41] In an era of rapidly expanding urban consumerism, these women were forced into scrimping and self-denial. By entering sexual relationships, however, they could

51

supplement their wages with free evenings on the town, free meals in restaurants, and sometimes gifts and money. In many cases, the new sexual expression allowed women to participate in the urban consumer economy.

Even in the most innocent dating, men customarily paid for the evening's entertainment. Women, in return, gave limited sexual favors, ranging from charming companionship to sexual intercourse. A 1910 federal report on self-supporting working women stressed the economic value of dating:

> Even if most of the girls do not spend money for amuse-ments, it is no proof that they go without them. Many of the girls have "gentlemen friends" who take them out. "Sure I go out all the time, but it doesn't cost me anything; my gentleman friend takes me," was the type of remark again and again. . . . [G]irls who have "steadies" are regarded as fortunate indeed.[42]

A woman need not have a "steady," however, to benefit from dating. In "pick ups," women met male strangers casually on street corners or in dance halls, restaurants, and saloons. They then spent the evening and sometimes the night with them. In Chicago women attempted to pick men up in dance halls and on the streets. In 1911, for example, a vice investigator in a North Side dance hall encountered several women who asked him "to take them to shows or dances."[43] Ten years later, in the heart of the South Side furnished room district, Gladys B., an 18-year-old black woman, "went cabareting" with James P. after she picked him up at the corner of 35th and State streets. They ended the evening in a hotel room.[44] Presumably James paid for the cabarets, the room, and perhaps for Gladys's sexual ser-vices. (In this case, he paid more than he bargained for: this mundane pick up became newsworthy only when Gladys escaped in the night with James's wad of money.)

In the early twentieth century, young working-class women who lived in their parents' homes also participated avidly in the new urban dating patterns promoted by commercialized recrea-tion facilities.[45] For many women lodgers in the furnished room districts, though, the necessity of supporting themselves on low wages added a special imperative. Lodgers themselves were highly aware of the economic benefits of dating. A waitress said bluntly, "If I did not have a man, I could not get along on my wages."[46] And a taxi dancer stated, "It's a shame a girl can't go straight and have a good time but I've got to get what I get by Sex Appeal."[47] One male resident of the North Side furnished room district concluded: "[Women] draw on their sex as I would on my bank account to pay for the kind of clothes they want to wear, the kind of shows they want to see."[48]

"Occasional prostitution" resembled dates and pick ups, but here the economic benefits were even clearer. Women asked men explicitly to pay for the sexual services provided them. These women worked in stores, offices, factories, and restaurants by day and sold their sexual services on occasional nights for extra money. While many women who dated probably exchanged only companionship, flirtation, and petting for evenings on the town, the smaller group of occasional prostitutes stepped up the barter, exchanging sexual intercourse for gifts or money. These women did not necessarily see themselves as prostitutes; they simply played the "sex game" for somewhat higher stakes.[49]

Without watchful relatives nearby, women lodgers could engage in occasional prostitution more easily than working women who lived in their parents' homes. Accordingly, vice investigators in search of occasional prostitutes went to the furnished room districts to find them. In a North Clark Street saloon, for example, a vice investigator met two women who lived in the North Side district. They worked in a department store for $5.50 per week. "They can't live on this," he reported, "so they 'hustle' on the side." In another case, the investigator reported on a 19-year-old migrant from Indiana, who worked in a South Side restaurant: "Is not a regular prostitute, goes with men for presents or money. Is poorly paid at restaurant."[50]

With pick ups and occasional prostitution, the relationships usually lasted for one night only. In a "temporary alliance," a woman maintained a sexual relationship with one or more "steady" boyfriends or lived with a man as if she were married. Amy, a 20-year-old woman who lived on the South Side, worked as a cashier in a downtown restaurant until she met a streetcar conductor who agreed to "keep" her. He had given her a new fall hat and promised to buy her a new winter coat. Amy occasionally went out with other men "to get a little more spending money."[51] Another account of temporary alliances in furnished rooms stated tersely, "For ten months, Marion lived a hand-to-mouth existence, dependent upon the bounty of several men with whom she became intimate."[52] Such alliances were motivated in some cases by "genuine and lasting regard," but in others, "the motive of the girl is simply to find support, and that of the man gratification."[53]

From the limited evidence available, it seems that economic concerns also shaped sexual relationships in the lesbian subculture. Some lesbians depended on men, earning money as prostitutes. Others found higher-paid or wealthier women to support them. For example, in the North Side district in the late 1920s, one lesbian, Beatrice, was supported by her lover Peggy who earned money as a prostitute. Peggy had "had a dozen sweethearts, all lesbian" and had "always supported them." On at least one occasion, some lesbians also adopted a form of gold-digging or, more precisely, veiled blackmail. After a North Side party, some lesbians persuaded the wealthier women attending to pay for their companionship: "The lesbians would get their names and addresses and borrow money by saying, 'I met you at. . .[the] party.' " Some lesbians also prostituted themselves to other women.[54]

This emphasis on the economics of sexual relationships should not obscure the sexual dangers or the sensual pleasures that many women experienced. On the one hand, some women lodgers encountered undeniable sexual violence, including rape, and others found themselves betrayed by false promises of marriage.[55] On the other hand, many women clearly enjoyed sexual relationships in which they found physical pleasure, excitement, and companionship. As one woman stated bluntly, "Frankly, I like intercourse!"[56] Further, the economic dependency in these relationships was not necessarily more exploitative or more oppressive than wives' traditional dependence on husbands or daughters' traditional dependence on fathers.

The financial imperatives are important, though, for they point to a neglected economics of the early-twentieth-century sexual revolution. The exchange of sexual services for monetary support moved beyond the marital bedroom and the brothel and into a variety of intermediate forms including dating, pick ups, temporary alliances, and occasional prostitution. The sexual revolution was not simply, as one historian has written, "prosperity's child."[57] In the furnished room districts, economic need shaped sexual experimentation. "What I get is mine. And what they have is mine, too, if I am smart enough to get it," said one self-avowed gold-digger, ". . .I'll show you how to take their socks away."[58] "Modern" sexual expression, then, not only threatened women with danger and promised women pleasure; in a variety of forms, it also offered financial reward.

Contemporary feminists who debate the meanings of sexual expression are not the first to define sexuality in terms of danger and pleasure. In the past century and a half, middle-class American commentators, including feminists, have often invested sexual expression with one of two opposing meanings. On the one side, many observers, especially in the nineteenth century, have described nonmarital sexual expression with various stories of danger, disease, decay, and disorder. On the other side, some observers, primarily in the twentieth century, have represented nonmarital sexuality with stories of pleasure, vitality, adventure, and freedom.[59] In both constructions, sexuality is stripped of its everyday contexts and inflated with symbolic meaning.

In the early twentieth century, the bourgeois attack on Victorian "sexual repression" marked a self-conscious shift in the dominant discourse from sex as danger to sex as pleasure.[60] As this conception of sexuality changed, the woman lodger played a central symbolic role. Through local and national media, a variety of commentators constructed conflicting interpretations of her unconventional sexual behavior. Reformers, manufacturers of popular culture, and sociologists dominated these debates.[61]

At the turn of the century, reformers presented the woman lodger as a symbol of endangered womanhood. In the organized boarding home movement, the antiprostitution crusade, and the campaign to improve women's wages, reformers wrote with genuine concern for poorly paid self-supporting women. With a sense of female solidarity, they deplored the economic hardships faced by the wage-earning women, but they reserved their greatest distress for her sexual vulnerability.[62] Like most middle-class Americans of their day, they lamented female sexual expression outside marriage, but, unlike many, they rarely blamed the women involved.[63] Following earlier female moral reformers, they read sexual expression as a symbol of female victimization in an increasingly ruthless urban world.[64] These writers portrayed sexually active women lodgers as passive, pure, and impoverished orphans duped, forced, or unduly tempted by scheming men. While they occasionally criticized women lodgers for their "tendency. . .to drift away from sweet and tender home influences," most often they condemned the "vampires" who trapped "poor, innocent little girls."[65] The reformers acknowledged that a woman lodger might enjoy the companionship she found in the furnished room districts, but "the glare of cheap entertainments and the dangers of the street," they feared, would overpower her.[66] In short, they adopted a stereotype of female weakness and innocence that absolved the woman lodger of responsibility for her own sexual behavior.

The reformers appointed themselves as maternal protectors. In Chicago and other cities, they opened subsidized boarding homes – "veritable virtue-saving stations" – to lure women from commercial rooming houses.[67] By the 1920s, Chicago had more than sixty organized homes managed by Protestant, Catholic, Jewish, African-American, German, Swedish, Polish, and Norwegian-Danish middle-class women for working women of their own religious, racial, and ethnic background.[68] They established room registries that placed women lodgers with private families in residential neighborhoods. They campaigned for minimum-wage laws because they saw the low pay of women lodgers as a major cause of "immorality." To "outwit evil agents, who would deceive the innocent," they placed charity workers in train stations and police matrons in public dance halls.[69] While they helped women in need of support, they obscured the actions that women lodgers took on their own behalf and elaborated instead an image of weak-willed women in sexual danger. In fact, well after most reformers had acknowledged the competence of working women living with parents, the "woman adrift," who lodged on her own, bereft of protectors, remained a symbol of endangered womanhood.

A variant of the reformers' discourse reached into popular culture. In the late nineteenth and early twentieth centuries, popular "working girl" romance novels, printed as cheap books or story-paper serials, adopted the image of orphaned, innocent, and imperiled "women adrift."[70] In these melodramatic stories, young, virtuous, native-born, white women endured countless agonies when alone in the city and eventually married wealthy men. Here the language of female victimization reached its most sensational. Listen to Charlotte M. Stanley, the author of "Violet, the Beautiful Street Singer; or, an Ill-Starred Betrothal": "Oh, what cruel fate was it that had so suddenly altered the safe, smooth current of her young existence and cast her adrift in this frightful seething whirlpool of vice and crime?"[71] In romance novels, the gravest dangers a woman faced were threats to her sexual purity, generally seduction, abduction, procurement, and forced marriage. The queen of romance was probably Laura Jean Libbey, the author of more than sixty novels in the late nineteenth century. Libbey created especially naive heroines who endured unusually frequent and frightening perils. In the opening chapters of one Libbey novel, beautiful Junie, an "artless little country lass" alone in the city, spurns the advances of a cad, follows a seemingly kind male stranger "without the least thought of her danger," and falls in the clutches of the cruel Squire Granger who abducts her.[72] Like the reformers, Libbey publicized the perils of life in the city and sympathized with the lone woman whom she portrayed as passive, innocent, and endangered.

The reformers and romance novelists, though, were fighting a losing battle, in part because the women they hoped to help belied the image of helpless victim. In fact, some women lodgers themselves directly attacked the reformers who treated them as pathetic orphans. In 1890, several "self-respecting and self-supporting" residents of the Chicago YWCA home wrote a blistering letter to a local newspaper:

> The idea seems to be in circulation that we who are unfortunate enough to be independent, are a collection of ignorant, weak-minded young persons, who have never had any advantages, educational or otherwise, and that we are brought here where we will be philanthropically cared for, and the cold winds tempered for us. A matron is provided, and a committee of women who happen to be blessed with a few thousand dollars worth of aristocracy, has charge of the matron.

The women also complained of the furniture and food, and referred to themselves as the "victims of the home."[73]

By the early twentieth century, some reformers began to reassess their outlook. Managers of organized homes and other astute observers could not help but note that many women lodgers were competent, assertive, and sexual by choice. Using the fact-gathering methods of the new social science, social investigators met face to face with women who pursued sexual companionship actively.[74] While reformers' concern for the woman lodger continued, they dropped their earlier emphasis on her passivity. Some also began to recognize that wage-earning women had sexual feelings. In 1910, one Chicago anti-vice crusader, who described self-supporting women as innocent, naive, and unprotected, admitted that "every normal girl or woman has primal instincts just as strong as her brother's."[75] Jane Addams, Louise DeKoven Bowen, and other Chicago reformers rejected earlier images of female passionlessness and instead blamed overwork, commercialized recreation, and alcohol for bringing out natural yearnings and instincts that they preferred to see repressed.

As reformers observed women lodgers, their fears about sexual danger diminished. They saw that women in the furnished room districts lived in a world that attached less stigma to female sexual activity. Reformers interviewed women who had given up their chastity without an inkling that they had chosen "a fate worse than death," and they saw that a wage-earning woman might choose to sell or exchange sexual services without ruining her life. "The fact that she has earned money in this way does not stamp her as 'lost'. . .," a 1911 federal report stated. "And the ease with which, in a large city, a woman may conceal a fall of this kind, if she desires to do so, also helps make a return to virtuous ways easy. . . . [O]ccasional prostitution holds its place in their minds as a possible resource, extreme, to be sure, but not in the least unthinkable."[76]

By the mid-1910s the observations of reformers coincided with broader changes in middle-class thought and behavior. In the years before the First World War, increasing numbers of middle-class urban women adopted the more open sexual behavior of women in the furnished room districts. This change in middle-class morals further undermined the older image of female innocence and passionlessness and challenged reformers' fear that female sexual behavior denoted female victimization. After the First World War, in a conservative political climate, reformers suffered further from declining public interest and from government repression and indifference.[77]

Ultimately reformers' views on sexuality could not compete with a newer discourse emerging in popular culture. In the early twentieth century, cabaret reviews and movies attracted audiences by using the woman lodger as an appealing symbol of urban vitality, allure, and adventure. In these newer texts, the woman lodger, headstrong and openly sexual, lived freely in a fast-paced urban environment. In the earlier romance novels, unfortunate circumstance – poverty or death in the family – forced timid young women, soon to be victims, from happy parental homes, or foolish young women left home and soon regretted it. In the newer scenarios, opportunistic women, like Theodore Dreiser's Sister Carrie, chafed at the restriction of domesticity and the dullness of the small town. As one writer concluded, "[The city] is her frontier and in it she is the pioneer."[78] In the earlier discourse, the woman victim's suffering signified the high cost of urban living; in the newer, the woman pioneer's pleasure pointed to its rewards.[79]

By the first decade of the twentieth century, the new image reached national audiences in stories of chorus girls who achieved stardom and married wealth.[80] These women strutted boldly across the stage, displaying their bodies and commanding attention through their sexual appeal. They won wide publicity in 1908 when the trial of Henry Thaw made sensational headlines and reached larger audiences still in a movie, *The Great Trial*. Thaw had murdered architect Stanford White in a jealous rage over White's affair with Thaw's wife, Evelyn Nesbit. During the trial, Nesbit, a former chorus girl, told how wealthy men entertained, courted, and, in her case, married the sexually attractive dancers in cabarets and theaters. As she recounted her rise from the life of a hard-working chorus girl to a life of luxury and extravagance, she announced the material and romantic pleasures available to the sexual, independent, wage-earning woman.[81]

In the following years, as the number of movie theaters expanded rapidly and the size of audiences grew, the woman lodger emerged as a central character in the new feature films. At first, in early "white slavery" films, the heroines faced threats to their virtue and sometimes eventual victimization. At the same time, though, in early serials – *The Perils of Pauline* and *The Hazards of Helen* – the heroines, independent from family, were "healthy, robust, and self-reliant." They met available and often moneyed men whom they attracted with their native allure. While they encountered dangers and difficulties, they also enjoyed a daring nightlife in cabarets and dance halls as well as the high life in opulent villas.[82] By 1915, Mary Pickford, the first major movie queen, was portraying women lodgers who flirted, danced, wore revealing clothing, and enjoyed energetic activities. Always chaste, she combined the purity of the Victorian orphan with the healthy sexuality of the chorus girl. Her exuberance and spunk attracted male suitors, leading to upwardly mobile marriages.[83]

By the 1920s, the movies drew clear connections between independence from family, on the one side, and female sexuality and material gain, on the other. In some movies, the woman lodger was the stock heroine in rags-to-riches stories. *At the Stage Door* typifies the formula: "Mary leaves home to become a chorus girl in New York, and soon she achieves stardom. Philip Pierce, a young millionaire, is attracted to her."[84] As the heterosexual activities and assertive behavior of the independent working woman became more explicit in movies, so did the threat she posed to men.[85] The woman lodger as gold-digger appeared at least as early as 1915. In *The Model; Or, Women and Wine*, wealthy young Dick Seymour pursues an independent working woman, Marcelle Rigadont, an artist's model. Marcelle, as one character advises her, wants to "play him for a sucker . . .and bleed him for every cent he's got." She finally confesses, "I never loved you – It was only your money I was after."[86] In the 1920s, at least thirty-four films included the gold-digger with her "aggressive use of sexual attraction."[87]

Although unrecorded forms of entertainment are harder to document, it seems that similar themes appeared in chorus revues at cabarets and theaters. In the opening number of the Midnight Frolic's "Just Girls," staged in 1915, "girls from 24 cities and one small home town came to New York for adventure, men, and a new life." "Sally," a Ziegfeld revue staged in 1920, told the story of a working-class orphan who climbed from "the chorus to theatrical fame, wealthy admirers, and riches."[88] By the 1920s, variations on these plot lines appeared repeatedly in new monthly pulp romance magazines such as *True Story* and *True Romances*.

In the late 1910s and 1920s, the new image of women lodgers achieved academic legitimacy in writings by urban sociologists at the University of Chicago. Inaugurated in the 1890s, the academic discipline of sociology moved quickly from an anti-urban moralism to more rarefied theoretical questions. In Chicago, sociologists, predominantly male, undertook intensive investigations of urban life, using census data, interviews, and observation. They showed little interest in women or in sexuality *per se*; rather, they used sexual behavior in the furnished room districts to bolster their theories of "urban evolution." Sociologist Robert Park wrote, "Everywhere the old order is passing, but the new has not arrived. . . . This is particularly true of the so-called rooming-house area."[89] In this view, the furnished room districts became the vanguard of urban change, characterized by "disorganization" and "individuation." As these terms suggest, some sociologists saw the furnished room districts as disturbed, soulless, and lonely.[90] For the most part, though, sociologists had a stronger faith in progress. As the vanguard of urban evolution, the furnished room districts were, in a sense, the most advanced development of urban life. With a marked ambivalence, sociologists described the residents of furnished room districts as "emancipated" as frequently as they called them "disorganized."[91]

For sociologists, the woman of the furnished room districts represented the freedom of urban life. As in movies, the urban woman was seen as released from the "monotony of settled family life" in the small town.[92] From a barren, restricted existence, she moved to "a section of the old frontier transplanted to the heart of the modern city" where, competent and self-seeking, she could pursue her individual desires and ambitions.[93] One particularly blunt sociology student stated, "The homeless woman of modern cities is the emancipated woman."[94] In areas where earlier reformers had discovered sexual exploitation of unprotected women, sociologists now found willing participation. Of dating for money, Frances Donovan wrote, "She is not. . .exploited nor driven into it, but goes with her eyes wide open."[95] Another sociologist asserted, more dubiously, that prostitutes were no longer exploited by procurers or pimps.[96] And, as in the movies, some sociologists depicted the sexually "emancipated" woman as a potential threat to men: "In the quest after the material equipment of life. . .the girl becomes not only an individualist but also – frankly – an opportunist."[97] In earlier reformers' portrayals, men exploited naive women; in sociologists' constructions, women lodgers, like Hollywood gold-diggers, took advantage of men.

No less than earlier images of the innocent victim, new images of the urban pioneer reduced women in furnished room districts to stereotypes, exaggerating certain features of their lives and neglecting others. Sociologists used self-supporting women as examples of uniquely urban personalities, emphasizing those traits that supported their theories of urban evolution: individualism, unconventional sexual behavior, transient personal relationships, and freedom from social control. Their commitment to the idea of evolutionary progress encouraged them to view these urban features as at least somewhat positive and liberating. At the same time, sociologists undermined reform efforts to alleviate female poverty. They downplayed the negative constraints of low wages, sexual harassment, and economic dependence, and thus suggested that reformers were superfluous, even meddling.

Reformers and romance novelists portrayed women lodgers as passive, passionless, and imperiled, while sociologists, moviemakers, and pulp magazine writers depicted them as active, pleasure seeking, and opportunistic. The changing discourse marks the waning influence of moral reformers and the rise to cultural power of manufacturers of mass entertainment and academic social scientists. It also highlights a larger change in the portrayal of women in America, from the Victorian angel to the sexy starlet. In the late nineteenth century, women lodgers, alone in the city, epitomized the purity of endangered womanhood; in the early twentieth century, the same women were among the first "respectable" women broadcast as happy sexual objects.

The sexual behavior of women in turn-of-the-century furnished room districts is not an isolated episode in women's history. Other US historians also describe sexual expression among women lodgers. From at least the 1830s to at least the 1960s, women who supported themselves in the cities sometimes explored the boundaries of sexual convention.[98] In other societies as well, "modern" sexual behavior has reflected in part the changing social and economic relations wrought by wage work and urbanization. The migration of labor to cities has removed some women workers from traditional forms of community or family control and protection, thus opening possibilities for both sexual experimentation and sexual coercion. At the same time, the worldwide gender gap in wages has sustained women's dependence on others, especially on men. In new urban, industrial settings, the traditional exchange of services for support has taken on extrafamilial, sexual forms, including temporary alliances and occasional prostitution.[99]

In turn-of-the-century Chicago, the volume of migrants led entrepreneurs to invest in restaurants, furnished rooming houses, theaters, cabarets, and dance halls. Women and men flocked to and shaped these institutions, creating new peer-oriented subcultures in specific urban districts. In these districts, most women could not afford to view sex solely in terms of sexual danger or sensual pleasure, for sexual expression was also tied inextricably to various forms of economic reward. In this context, the sexual revolution was, most likely, sometimes oppressive, sometimes exciting, and often an exchange.

The history of women lodgers in the furnished room districts is important, for these women helped shape the modern sexual expression that other women later adopted. In the furnished room districts themselves, middle and upper-class bohemian "new women" observed the unconventional behavior of working-class women who were their neighbors. Middle-class pleasure seekers and "flappers" may have copied the blueprints of "sexy" behaviour they observed while slumming in the districts' cabarets and dance halls. And moviegoers and magazine readers learned from the portrayals of women lodgers, as films, cabarets, and romance magazines used the sexuality of independent wage-earning women to attract and titillate viewers and readers. In these ways, turn-of-the-century women lodgers helped chart the modern American sexual terrain.

NOTES

First published in *Gender & History* 2, 3 (Autumn 1990): 274–96. Used by permission.

1 This article is reprinted in slightly revised form from Nancy Hewitt, ed., *Women, Families, and Communities: Readings in American History* (New York: 1990). It draws on material in Joanne Meyerowitz,

Women Adrift: Independent Wage-Earners in Chicago, 1880–1930 (Chicago: 1988). Thanks to Estelle Freedman, Zane Miller, Leila Rupp, Christina Simmons, and Bruce Tucker for their helpful comments. And special thanks to Nancy Hewitt who helped sustain this article through its strange publication history.

2 Frederick Lewis Allen, *Only Yesterday* (New York: 1931); William Leuchtenburg, *The Perils of Prosperity, 1914–1932* (Chicago: 1958); James McGovern, "The American Woman's Pre-World War I Freedom in Manners and Morals," *Journal of American History* 55 (1968): 315–33; Gerald E. Critoph, "The Flapper and Her Critics," in Carol V. R. George, ed., *"Remember the Ladies": New Perspectives on Women in American History* (Syracuse: 1975). See also Paula S. Fass, *The Damned and the Beautiful: American Youth in the 1920s* (New York: 1977); John Modell, "Dating Becomes the Way of American Youth," in Leslie Page Moch and Gary Stark, ed., *Essays on the Family and Historical Change* (College Station, TX: 1983).

3 June Sochen, *The New Woman: Feminism in Greenwich Village, 1910–1920* (New York: 1972); Elaine Showalter, ed., *These Modern Women: Autobiographical Essays from the Twenties* (Old Westbury, NY: 1978); Carroll Smith-Rosenberg, "The New Woman as Androgyne: Social Disorder and Gender Crisis, 1870–1936," in Smith-Rosenberg, ed., *Disorderly Conduct: Visions of Gender in Victorian America* (New York: 1985); Esther Newton, "The Mythic Mannish Lesbian: Radclyffe Hall and the New Woman," *Signs* 9 (Summer 1984): 557–75; Ellen Carol DuBois and Linda Gordon, "Seeking Ecstasy on the Battlefield: Danger and Pleasure in Nineteenth-Century Feminist Sexual Thought," in Carole S. Vance, ed., *Pleasure and Danger: Exploring Female Sexuality* (Boston: 1984); Leila J. Rupp, "Feminism and the Sexual Revolution in the Early Twentieth Century: The Case of Doris Stevens," *Feminist Studies* 15 (Summer 1989): 289–309. For an earlier account, see Henry F. May, *The End of American Innocence: A Study of the First Years of Our Own Time, 1912–1917* (New York: 1986).

4 Kathy Peiss, *Cheap Amusements: Working Women and Leisure in Turn-of-the-Century New York* (Philadelphia: 1986); for the nineteenth century, see Christine Stansell, *City of Women: Sex and Class in New York, 1789–1860* (New York: 1986).

5 For a summary of these debates, see "Forum: The Feminist Sexuality Debates," *Signs* 10 (Autumn 1984): 102–35; Carole S. Vance, "Pleasure and Danger: Toward a Politics of Sexuality," in Vance, ed., *Pleasure and Danger.*

6 Robert Park, "The City: Suggestions for the Investigation of Human Behavior in the Urban Environment," in Richard Sennett, ed., *Classic Essays on the Culture of Cities* (New York: 1969), 128–9.

7 Robert Woods, ed., *The City Wilderness: A Settlement Study* (Boston: 1898); see especially William I. Cole's article, "Criminal Tendencies," 166–9.

8 Albert Benedict Wolfe, *The Lodging House Problem in Boston* (Boston: 1906), 171. See also Franklin Kline Fretz, *The Furnished Room Problem in Philadelphia* (Ph.D. dissertation, University of Pennsylvania,

1912); S. P. Breckinridge and Edith Abbott, "Chicago's Housing Problems: Families in Furnished Rooms," *American Journal of Sociology* (November 1910): 289–308.

9 Harvey Warren Zorbaugh, *Gold Coast and Slum: A Sociological Study of Chicago's Near North Side* (Chicago: 1929), 153.

10 To avoid being unduly influenced by the sociologists' discourse, I have accepted the sociologists' conclusions only when I could corroborate them with evidence from other sources, such as newspaper accounts, reports of reformers, and memoirs.

11 In the 1910s, the South Side district ran from 16th to 33rd streets and from Clark Street to Prairie Avenue; the West Side district ran from Washington to Harrison streets and from Ashland Boulevard to Halsted Street; the North Side district went from Division Street to the Chicago River and from Wells to Rush streets. Edith Abbott, *The Tenements of Chicago, 1908–1935* (Chicago: 1936).

Information on the population of the furnished room districts was derived from sociological studies and from the Federal Manuscript Census, (Meyerowitz's) samples of Chicago "women adrift," 1880 and 1910, and the tract-by-tract census data found in Ernest W. Burgess and Charles Newcomb, eds, *Census Data of the City of Chicago, 1920* (Chicago: 1931), and Ernest W. Burgess and Charles Newcomb, eds, *Census Data of the City of Chicago, 1930* (Chicago: 1933).

12 On growth of districts, see Abbott, *Tenements of Chicago*, ch. 10; also Kimball Young, "Sociological Study of a Disintegrated Neighborhood" (M.A. dissertation, University of Chicago, 1918). On the number of lodgers, see T. W. Allison, "Population Movement in Chicago," *Journal of Social Forces* (May 1924): 529–33. The lodging houses included in the 1923 register were only those with more than ten roomers.

13 Zorbaugh, *Gold Coast and Slum*, 72.

14 See Wolfe, *The Lodging House Problem in Boston*; for examples of permissive landladies in Chicago, see Louise DeKoven Bowen, *The Straight Girl on the Crooked Path: A True Story* (Chicago: 1916).

15 In 1920, the ratio of women to men in the North Side district was 1:4, and in the West Side district, 1:6. In 1930, the ratio in the North Side district was 1:3 and in the West Side district 2:0. In both years, the South Side district, which was more dispersed over a larger area, had a ratio of 1:0. These ratios were derived from tract-by-tract census data found in Burgess and Newcomb, eds, *Census Data of the City of Chicago, 1920* and *Census Data of the City of Chicago, 1930*.

16 Vice Commission of Chicago, *The Social Evil in Chicago: A Study of Existing Conditions with Recommendations by the Vice Commission of Chicago* (Chicago: 1911), 87–91.

17 Ibid., 73, 74, 92–4.

18 "Investigation of Commercialized Prostitution," December 1922, Juvenile Protective Association of Chicago Papers 5.92, University of Illinois at Chicago Manuscript Collections, Chicago.

19 Young, "Sociological Study of a Disintegrated Neighborhood," 52.

20 Young, "Sociological Study of a Disintegrated Neighborhood," 42; Abbott, *Tenements of Chicago*, 322.
21 James R. Grossman, *Land of Hope: Chicago, Black Southerners, and the Great Migration* (Chicago: 1989), 117; E. Franklin Frazier, *The Negro Family in Chicago* (Chicago: 1932), 103. See also Carroll Binder, "Negro Active in Business World," Chicago *Daily News*, 5 August 1927; Junius B. Wood, *The Negro in Chicago*, reprint of articles in Chicago *Daily News*, 11–27 December 1916, p. 25.
22 Walter Reckless, "The Natural History of Vice Areas in Chicago" (Ph.D. dissertation, University of Chicago, 1925), 381.
23 E. H. Wilson, "Chicago Families in Furnished Rooms" (M.A. dissertation, University of Chicago, 1929), 100.
24 See Young, "Sociological Study of a Disintegrated Neighborhood," 54; also Zorbaugh, *Gold Coast and Slum*. As early as 1898, Frederick Bushee suggested that "The lodging houses themselves [in Boston's South End district] are the homes of the queer and questionable of every shade," in Woods, ed., *The City Wilderness*, 50.
25 See, for example, Walter C. Reckless, *Vice in Chicago* (Chicago: 1933), 53–4. I use Claude Fischer's definition of subcultures: "social worlds. . .inhabited by persons who share relatively distinctive traits (like ethnicity or occupation), who tend to interact especially with one another, and who manifest a relatively distinct set of beliefs and behaviors." Claude S. Fischer, *The Urban Experience* (New York: 1976), 36.
26 Young, "Sociological Study of a Disintegrated Neighborhood," 79.
27 Case record from Chicago Vice Study File, cited in Reckless, *Vice in Chicago*, 53, 54.
28 *Chicago Examiner*, 12 April 1913.
29 Box Car Bertha as told to Dr. Ben L. Reitman, *Sister of the Road: The Autobiography of Box-Car Bertha* (New York: 1937), 68, 70, 62, 29.
30 There is some evidence of a lesbian community among prostitutes in Paris as early as the 1880s, and also evidence suggesting that some lesbians in New York participated in the male homosexual subculture there by the 1890s. In general, though, American lesbian communities were not visible until the 1920s, perhaps because the majority of women had fewer opportunities than men to leave family life. Moreover, romantic attachments between women were not usually labeled deviant in America until the early twentieth century. Middle- and upper-class women who lived together as couples in "Boston marriages," for example, were not segregated as outcasts from heterosexual family and friends. On early male homosexual subcultures in American cities, see Jonathan Katz, ed., *Gay American History: Lesbians and Gay Men in the U.S.A.* (New York: 1976), 61–81; John D'Emilio, "Capitalism and Gay Identity," in Ann Snitow, Christine Stansell, and Sharon Thompson, *Powers of Desire: The Politics of Sexuality* (New York: 1983), 100–16; eds, and George Chauncey, Jr., "Christian Brotherhood or Sexual Perversion? Homosexual Identities and the Construction of Sexual Boundaries in the World War I Era," this volume, 72. On lesbian prostitutes in

Paris and on turn-of-the-century tolerance for lesbianism, see Lillian Faderman, *Surpassing the Love of Men: Romantic Friendship and Love Between Women from the Renaissance to the Present* (New York: 1981), 282, 298.

31 Paul Oliver, *Screening the Blues: Aspects of the Blues Tradition* (London: 1968), 225, 226.

32 Box Car Bertha, *Sister of the Road*, 65.

33 "A nurse told me of being called on night duty in an apartment in the 'village' and of being entertained every night by the girls in the apartment across the well, some of whom would put on men's evening clothes, make love to the others, and eventually carry them off in their arms into the bedrooms." Zorbaugh, *Gold Coast and Slum*, 100.

34 Frazier, *The Negro Family in Chicago*, 103; interview with Eulalia B., conducted by author, 16 October 1980.

35 Zorbaugh, *Gold Coast and Slum*, 91.

36 "Dill Pickle Club," in Vivien Palmer, "Documents of History of the Lower North Side," vol. 3, part 2, document 52, Chicago Historical Society, Chicago.

37 Zorbaugh, *Gold Coast and Slum*, 114–15.

38 Reckless, "The Natural History of Vice Areas," 374, 375. For a similar rejection of social background, see the story of Christina Stranski (a.k.a. DeLoris Glenn) in Paul G. Cressey, *The Taxi-Dance Hall: A Sociological Study in Commercialized Recreation and City Life* (Chicago: 1932), 56.

39 On bohemians as a vanguard of sex radicalism, see May, *The End of American Innocence*, 307–10, 341.

40 A few other historians have suggested that working-class women were pioneers in changing sexual mores. See, for example, Nathan G. Hale, Jr., *Freud and the Americans: The Beginnings of Psychoanalysis in the United States, 1876–1917* (New York: 1971), 477; Lewis A. Erenberg, *Steppin' Out: New York Nightlife and the Transformation of American Culture, 1890–1930* (Westport, CT: 1981); Daniel Scott Smith, "The Dating of the American Sexual Revolution: Evidence and Interpretation," in Michael Gordon, ed., *The American Family in Social-Historical Perspective* (New York: 1973).

41 On women's wages, see Leslie Woodcock Tentler, *Wage-Earning Women: Industrial Work and Family Life in the United States, 1900–1930* (New York: 1979).

42 Charles P. Neill, *Wage-Earning Women in Stores and Factories*, vol. 5, *Report on Condition of Woman and Child Wage-Earners in the United States* (Washington, DC: 1910), 75.

43 *The Social Evil in Chicago*, 186.

44 *Chicago Defender*, 20 August 1921.

45 See Kathy Peiss, " 'Charity Girls' and City Pleasures: Historical Notes on Working-Class Sexuality, 1880–1920," in Snitow, *et al.*, eds, *Power of Desire*.

46 Louise DeKoven Bowen, *The Girl Employed in Hotels and Restaurants* (Chicago: 1912).

47 "Alma N. Z——r," Paul Cressey notes [c. 1926], p. 5, Ernest Burgess Papers 129:6, University of Chicago Manuscript Collections, Chicago.
48 Zorbaugh, *Gold Coast and Slum*, 86.
49 Frances Donovan, *The Woman Who Waits* (1920; reprint, New York: 1974), 211–20.
50 *The Social Evil in Chicago*, 133, 95.
51 Ibid., 188.
52 Ruth Shonle Cavan, *Suicide* (Chicago: 1928), 206.
53 Wolfe, *The Lodging House Problem in Boston*, 142. In these accounts of heterosexual relationships, most of the women lodgers seem to be under 30 years of age. Older women lodgers were probably somewhat less attractive to the predominantly young male suitors. They also seemed to tire of the nightlife, preferring the more stable support and companionship sometimes provided in marriage. In fact, most women lodgers in Chicago did eventually marry. For a revealing interview with an older woman, see Anderson, "Life History of a Rooming House Keeper," c. 1925, Ernest Burgess Papers 127:2, University of Chicago Manuscript Collections, Chicago.
54 Box Car Bertha, *Sister of the Road*, 223, 66, 69, 288. This limited evidence of dependent relationships is corroborated by other evidence that early-twentieth-century working-class lesbians often adopted somewhat traditional gender roles, with one partner assuming a masculine role. See Katz, *Gay American History*, 383–90. See also Joan Nestle, "The Fem Question," in Vance, ed., *Pleasure and Danger*; and Elizabeth Lapovsky Kennedy and Madeline Davis, "The Reproduction of Butch-Fem Roles: A Social Constructionist Approach," in Kathy Peiss and Christina Simmons, eds, *Passion and Power: Sexuality in History* (Philadelphia: 1989).
55 See, for example, Louise DeKoven Bowen, *A Study of Bastardy Cases* (Chicago: 1914).
56 "Lillian S. W——n," Paul Cressey notes, p. 18, Ernest Burgess Papers 129:6, University of Chicago Manuscript Collections, Chicago.
57 Kenneth Yellis, "Prosperity's Child: Some Thoughts on the Flapper," *American Quarterly XXI* (Spring 1969): 44–64.
58 *Chicago Daily Times*, 31 January 1930.
59 I'm not suggesting that the contemporary feminist sexuality debates replicate the earlier discourse, only that contemporary debates are a new, different, and interesting variant of older associations. On sex as danger, see Carroll Smith-Rosenberg, "Sex as Symbol in Victorian Purity: An Ethnohistorical Analysis of Jacksonian America," in John Demos and Sarane Spence Boocock, eds, *Turning Points: Historical and Sociological Essays on the Family* (Chicago: 1978); Paul Boyer, *Urban Masses and Moral Order in America, 1820–1920* (Cambridge, MA: 1978); on sex as pleasure, see Paul Robinson, *The Modernization of Sex: Havelock Ellis, Alfred Kinsey, William Masters and Virginia Johnson* (New York: 1976). For a general history of the changing dominant discourses on sexuality, see John D'Emilio and Estelle

Freedman, *Intimate Matters: A History of Sexuality in America* (New York: 1988). On late nineteenth- and early twentieth-century feminist variants of the shift from sex as danger to sex as pleasure, see DuBois and Gordon, "Seeking Ecstasy on the Battlefield," in Vance, ed., *Pleasure and Danger*. For formulations in Britain, see Judith Walkowitz, *Prostitution and Victorian Society: Women, Class and the State* (Cambridge: 1980); Susan Kingsley Kent, *Sex and Suffrage in Britain, 1860–1914* (Princeton, NJ: 1987); Frank Mort, *Dangerous Sexualities: Medico-Moral Politics in England Since 1830* (London: 1987). In general, representations of sex as vitality, pleasure, adventure, and freedom have not been studied as closely by historians as representations of sex as danger, disease, decay, and disorder.

60 On the attack on Victorian "sexual repression," see Christina Simmons, "Modern Sexuality and the Myth of Victorian Repression," in this volume, 17. See also Michel Foucault, *The History of Sexuality*, vol. 1 (New York: 1980).

61 For psychiatrists' contribution to these public discussions, see Elizabeth Lunbeck, "A New Generation of Women: Progressive Psychiatrists and the Hypersexual Woman," *Feminist Studies* 13 (Fall 1987): 513–43.

62 On late-nineteenth-century reformers' interest in working women, see Mari Jo Buhle, "The Nineteenth Century Woman's Movement: Perspectives on Women's Labor in Industrializing America," unpublished paper, Bunting Institute of Radcliffe College (Cambridge, MA: 1979).

63 For a more detailed discussion of the reformers' position, see Meyerowitz, *Women Adrift*, ch. 3. For a similar combination of feminist sympathy and middle-class moralism in the early to mid-nineteenth century, see Stansell, *City of Women*, 70–4.

64 On earlier reformers, see especially Mary P. Ryan, "The Power of Women's Networks: A Case Study of Female Moral Reform in Antebellum America," *Feminist Studies* 5 (Spring: 1979) 66–85; Carroll Smith-Rosenberg, "Beauty, the Beast, and the Militant Woman: A Case Study of Sex Roles and Social Stress in Jacksonian America," in Nancy F. Cott and Elizabeth H. Pleck, eds, *A Heritage of Her Own: Toward a New Social History of American Women* (New York: 1979).

65 Young Women's Christian Association of Chicago, *Fifth Annual Report* (1881), 12; Charles Bryon Chrysler, *White Slavery* (Chicago: 1909), 13.

66 Annie Marion MacLean, "Homes for Working Women in Large Cities," *Charities Review* (July 1899): 228.

67 Ibid., 228.

68 Josephine J. Taylor, "Study of YWCA Room Registry," unpublished paper [1928] Ernest Burgess Papers 138:9, University of Chicago Manuscript Collections, Chicago. Essie Mae Davidson, "Organized Boarding Homes for Self-Supporting Women in the City of Chicago" (M.A. dissertation, University of Chicago, 1914); Ann Elizabeth Trotter, *Housing of Non-Family Women in Chicago: A Survey*

(Chicago: c. 1921).

69 YWCA of Chicago, *18th Annual Report* (1894), 33. On the national Travelers' Aid movement, see Lynn Y. Weiner, *From Working Girl to Working Mother: The Female Labor Force in the United States, 1820–1980* (Chapel Hill, NC: 1985), 49–52, 78–9. On reforming the dance halls, see Elisabeth I. Perry, " 'The General Motherhood of the Commonwealth': Dance Hall Reform in the Progressive Era," *American Quarterly* 37 (Winter 1985): 719–33.

70 For a brief description of the "working girl" novel, see Cathy N. Davidson and Arnold E. Davidson, "Carrie's Sisters: The Popular Prototypes for Dreiser's Heroine," *Modern Fiction Studies* 23 (Autumn 1977): 395–407.

71 Charlotte M. Stanley, "Violet, the Beautiful Street Singer; or an Ill-Starred Betrothal," *The New York Family Story Paper*, 5 September 1908. See also T. W. Hanshew, "Alone in New York: A Thrilling Portrayal of the Dangers and Pitfalls of the Metropolis," *The New York Family Story Paper*, 30 April 1887.

72 Laura Jean Libbey, *Junie's Love Test* (New York: 1883), 66.

73 *Sunday Inter Ocean*, 16 November 1890. The women who lived in this YWCA home tended to be white, native-born women who held middle-class jobs in offices and stores. Black women and immigrant women also expressed displeasure with forms of housing that invaded their privacy and reduced their initiative. See Meyerowitz, *Women Adrift*, ch. 4.

74 See, for example, Louise DeKoven Bowen, *Safeguards of City Youth at Work and at Play* (New York: 1914), 23; Clara E. Laughlin, *The Work-A-Day Girl* (1913; reprint, New York: 1974), 51.

75 Leona Prall Groetzinger, *The City's Perils* (n.p., c. 1910), 110.

76 Mary Conyngton, *Relation Between Occupation and Criminality of Women*, vol. 15, *Report on Condition of Woman and Child Wage-Earners in the United States* (Washington, DC: 1911), 102–3.

77 Other factors undermining the reformers' image of passive, endangered women lodgers included the First World War venereal disease campaign, the decline in the number of women immigrants arriving from Europe, and a slight rise in women's real wages in the 1920s. As these changes occurred, most reformers lost interest in women lodgers; those who maintained their interest lost the power to shape cultural images.

78 Donovan, *The Woman Who Waits*, 9.

79 For a more detailed discussion of this newer image, see Meyerowitz, *Women Adrift*, ch. 6.

80 Lois Banner, *American Beauty* (Chicago: 1983), 180–4.

81 On the Thaw trial, see Erenberg, *Steppin' Out*, 53; Lary May, *Screening Out the Past: The Birth of Mass Culture and the Motion Picture Industry* (New York: 1980), 34, 43.

82 May, *Screening Out the Past*, 108.

83 Ibid., 119, 142, 143. For a discussion of "heterosocial culture" in earlier films, see Peiss, *Cheap Amusements*, 153–8.

84 Kenneth Munden, ed., *The American Film Institute Catalog, Feature*

Films, 1921–1929 (New York: 1971), 29.

85 The 1920s stories which represented sexual expression as pleasurable and adventurous often had a subtext of potential danger (especially to men), as the "gold-digger" movies attest.

86 *"The Model; Or, Women and Wine," Picture-Play Weekly*, 12 June 1915, pp. 12–16.

87 Mary P. Ryan "The Projection of a New Womanhood: The Movie Moderns in the 1920s," in Jean E. Friedman and William G. Shade, eds, *Our American Sisters: Women in American Life and Thought*, 2nd ed. (Boston: 1976), 376.

88 Erenberg, *Steppin' Out*, 210, 223.

89 Robert E. Park, "Introduction," in Zorbaugh, *Gold Coast and Slum*, viii.

90 Cavan, *Suicide*, 81; Robert E. L. Faris, *Chicago Sociology, 1920–1932* (1967; reprint, Chicago: 1979), 35.

91 See, for example, Ernest Mowrer, *Family Disorganization: An Introduction to Sociological Analysis* (Chicago: 1927), 111; Faris, *Chicago Sociology*, 79.

92 Reckless, "The Natural History of Vice Areas," 211.

93 Zorbaugh, *Gold Coast and Slum*, 199.

94 Reckless, "The Natural History of Vice Areas," 209.

95 Donovan, *The Woman Who Waits*, 220.

96 W. I. Thomas, *The Unadjusted Girl, With Cases and Standpoint for Behavioral Analysis* (Boston: 1923), 150.

97 Cressey, *The Taxi-Dance Hall*, 47.

98 Stansell, *City of Women*, 83–101, 171–92; Linda Gordon, *Woman's Body, Woman's Right: A Social History of Birth Control in America* (New York: 1977), 203–4; Babara Ehrenreich, Elizabeth Hess, and Gloria Jacobs, *Re-Making Love: The Feminization of Sex* (Garden City, NY: 1986), 39–42, 54–62.

99 There is a recent and growing literature on contemporary women migrants in third world nations. For a good introduction, see the special issue of *International Migration Review* (Winter 1984); and Annette Fuentes and Barbara Ehrenreich, *Women in the Global Factory* (Boston: 1983). For additional references to sexuality, see also Ilsa Schuster, "Marginal Lives: Conflict and Contradiction in the Position of Female Traders in Lusaka, Zambia," in Edna G. Bay, ed., *Women and Work in Africa* (Boulder, CO: 1982); and Sharon Stichter, *Migrant Laborers* (Cambridge: 1985). On capitalism, urbanization, migration, and sexuality in Europe, see the now classic accounts of the eighteenth century in Edward Shorter, "Illegitimacy, Sexual Revolution and Social Change in Modern Europe," *Journal of Interdisciplinary History* (Autumn 1971); and Louise A. Tilly, Joan W. Scott, and Miriam Cohen, "Women's Work and Fertility Patterns," *Journal of Interdisciplinary History* (Winter 1976). Shorter emphasizes the sexual pleasure pursued by women, while Tilly, Scott, and Cohen underscore women's sexual vulnerability. For a more recent account, see Nicholas Rogers, "Carnal Knowledge: Illegitimacy in Eighteenth-Century Westminster," *Journal of Social History* (Winter 1989).

4

CHRISTIAN BROTHERHOOD OR SEXUAL PERVERSION?

Homosexual identities and the construction of sexual boundaries in the World War I era[1]

George Chauncey, Jr.

"Homosexuality" (as we currently use it) refers to behavior between same-sex partners, male or female. But, as George Chauncey demonstrates, that view of homosexuality is itself a social construction, not a straightforward or inevitable definition.

Historians of sexuality confront special problems of evidence, for sexual experience is private and seldom documented in the kinds of records that historians use. George Chauncey seizes the opportunity provided by a widely publicized 1919 investigation into homosexuality in the US Navy. In the hands of this imaginative historian, reams of testimony become the instrument for gaining a rare glimpse into homosexual subcultures, revealing the prevailing constructions of masculinity that defined both the "queer" and his sexual partner. He finds that his subjects saw homosexuality as a matter of gender roles rather than of sexual partners: men who appeared effeminate or took the "woman's part" in sex were considered homosexual, but their male partners were not. Chauncey also explores homosexual identities as they are supported and constrained by a distinctive homosexual subculture.

Public controversies often involve disputes over the boundaries of discourse, and in the controversy that followed the investigation, Chauncey traces ministers' self-image of a masculinity of "Christian brotherhood," which led them to challenge the investigators' methods and their definition of homosexuality. Like Meyerowitz, Chauncey raises questions about the reach of medical discourses: the many voices in his records show little awareness of the sexologists' views of homosexuality.

* * *

In the spring of 1919, officers at the Newport (Rhode Island) Naval Training Station dispatched a squad of young enlisted men into the community to investigate the "immoral conditions" obtaining there. The decoys sought out and associated with suspected "sexual perverts," had sex with them and learned all they could about homosexual activity in Newport. On the basis of the evidence they gathered, naval and municipal authorities arrested more than twenty sailors in April and sixteen civilians in July and the decoys testified against them at a naval court of inquiry and several civilian trials. The entire investigation received little attention before the navy accused a prominent Episcopal clergyman who worked at the YMCA of soliciting homosexual contacts there. But when civilian and then naval officials took the minister to trial on charges of being a "lewd and wanton person," a major controversy developed. Protests by the Newport Ministerial Union and the Episcopal Bishop of Rhode Island and a vigorous editorial campaign by the *Providence Journal* forced the navy to conduct a second inquiry in 1920 into the methods used in the first investigation. When that inquiry criticized the methods but essentially exonerated the senior naval officials who had instituted them, the ministers asked the Republican-controlled Senate Naval Affairs Committee to conduct its own investigation. The Committee agreed and issued a report in 1921 that vindicated the ministers' original charges and condemned the conduct of the highest naval officials involved, including Franklin D. Roosevelt, President Wilson's Assistant Secretary of the Navy and the 1920 Democratic vice-presidential candidate.[2]

The legacy of this controversy is a rich collection of evidence about the organization and phenomenology of homosexual relations among white working-class and middle-class men and about the changing nature of sexual discourse in the World War I era.[3] On the basis of the 3,500 pages of testimony produced by the investigations it is possible to reconstruct the organization of a homosexual subculture during this period, how its participants understood their behavior, and how they were viewed by the larger community, thus providing a benchmark for generalizations about the historical development of homosexual identities and communities. The evidence also enables us to reassess current hypotheses concerning the relative significance of medical discourse, religious doctrine, and folk tradition in the shaping of popular understandings of sexual behavior and character. Most importantly, analysis of the testimony of the government's witnesses and the accused churchmen and sailors offers new insights into the relationship between homosexual behavior and identity in the cultural construction of sexuality. Even when witnesses agreed that two men had engaged in homosexual relations with each other they disagreed about whether both men or only the one playing the "woman's part" should be labeled as "queer." More profoundly, they disagreed about how to distinguish between a "sexual" and a "nonsexual" relationship: the navy defined certain relationships as homosexual and perverted which the ministers claimed were merely brotherly and Christian. Because disagreement over the boundary between homosexuality and homosociality[*] lay at the heart of the Newport controversy, its records allow us to explore the cultural construction of sexual categories in unusual depth.

THE SOCIAL ORGANIZATION OF HOMOSEXUAL RELATIONS

The investigation found evidence of a highly developed and varied gay subculture in this small seaport community and a strong sense of collective identity on the part of many of its participants. Cruising areas, where gay men and "straight" sailors[4] alike knew that sexual encounters were to be had, included the beach during the summer and the fashionable Bellevue Avenue close to it, the area along Cliff Walk, a cemetery and a bridge. Many men's homosexual experiences consisted entirely (and irregularly) of visits to such areas for anonymous sexual encounters, but some men organized a group life with others who shared their inclinations. The navy's witnesses mentioned groups of servants who worked in the exclusive "cottages" on Bellevue Avenue and of civilians who met at places such as Jim's Restaurant on Long Wharf.[5] But they focused on a tightly knit group of sailors who referred to themselves as "the gang,"[6]

---

[*] The term "homosociality" pertains to same-sex networks and associations; it is used here in contrast to same-sex associations that include overtly erotic and sexual behavior.

and it is this group whose social organization the first section of this paper will analyze.

The best-known rendezvous of gang members and of other gay sailors was neither dark nor secret: "The Army and Navy YMCA was the headquarters of all cocksuckers [in] the early part of the evening," commented one investigator, and, added another, "everybody who sat around there in the evening. . . knew it."[7] The YMCA was one of the central institutions of gay male life; some gay sailors lived there, others occasionally rented its rooms for the evening so that they would have a place to entertain men, and the black elevator operators were said to direct interested sailors to the gay men's rooms.[8] Moreover, the YMCA was a social center, where gay men often had dinner together before moving to the lobby to continue conversation and meet the sailors visiting the YMCA in the evening.[9] The ties which they maintained through such daily interactions were reinforced by a dizzying array of parties; within the space of three weeks, investigators were invited to four "faggot part[ies]" and heard of others.[10]

Moreover, the men who had developed a collective life in Newport recognized themselves as part of a subculture extending beyond a single town: they knew of places in New York and other cities "where the 'queens' hung out," made frequent visits to New York, Providence, and Fall River, and were visited by gay men from those cities. An apprentice machinist working in Providence, for instance, spent "week-ends in Newport for the purpose of associating with his 'dear friends,' the 'girls,' " and a third of the civilians arrested during the raids conducted in the summer were New York City residents working as servants in the grand houses of Newport. Only two of the arrested civilians were local residents.[11]

Within and sustained by this community, a complex system of personal identities and structured relationships took shape, in which homosexual behavior per se did not play a determining part. Relatively few of the men who engaged in homosexual activity, whether as casual participants in anonymous encounters or as partners in ongoing relationships, identified themselves or were labeled by others as sexually different from other men on that basis alone. The determining criterion in labeling a man as "straight" (their term) or "queer" was not the extent of his homosexual activity, but the gender role he assumed. The

75

only men who sharply differentiated themselves from other men, labeling themselves as "queer," were those who assumed the sexual and other cultural roles ascribed to women; they might have been termed "inverts" in the early twentieth-century medical literature because they not only expressed homosexual desire but "inverted" (or reversed) their gender role.[12]

The most prominent queers in Newport were effeminate men who sometimes donned women's clothes – when not in uniform – including some who became locally famous female impersonators. Sometimes referred to as "queens," these men dominated the social activities of the gang and frequently organized parties at their off-base apartments to which gay and "straight" sailors alike were invited. At these "drags" gang members could relax, be openly gay, and entertain straight sailors from the base with their theatrics and their sexual favors.

Female impersonation was an unexceptional part of Navy culture during the World War I years, sufficiently legitimate – if curious – for the *Providence Journal* and the Navy's own magazine, *Newport Recruit*, to run lengthy stories and photo essays about the many theatrical productions at the navy base in which men took the female roles.[13] The ubiquity of such drag shows and the fact that numerous "straight" identified men took part in them sometimes served to protect gay female impersonators from suspicion. The landlord of one of the gay men arrested by the navy cited the sailor's stage roles in order to explain why he hadn't regarded the man's wearing women's clothes as "peculiar," and presumably the wife of the training station's commandant, who loaned the man "corsets, stockings, shirt waists, [and] women's pumps" for his use in *H. M. S. Pinafore*, did not realize that he also wore them at private parties.[14]

But if in some circles the men's stage roles served to legitimate their wearing drag, for most sailors such roles only confirmed the impersonators' identities as queer. Many sailors, after all, had seen or heard of the queens' appearing in drag at parties where its homosexual significance was inescapable. According to the navy's investigators, for instance, numerous sailors in uniform and "three prize fighters in civilian clothes" attended one "faggot party" given in honor of a female impersonator visiting Newport to perform at the Opera House. Not only were some of the men at the party – and presumably the guest of honor – in drag, but two men made out on a bed in full view of the others, who "remarked about their affection for each other."[15] Moreover, while sailors commonly gave each other nicknames indicating ethnic origin (e.g., "Wop" Bianchia and "Frenchman" La Favor) or other personal characteristics (e.g., "Lucky" and "Pick-axe"), many of them knew the most prominent queers *only* by their "ladies' names," camp nicknames they had adopted from the opera and cinema such as "Salome," "Theda Bara," and "Galli Curci."[16]

Several of the navy's witnesses described other signs of effeminacy one might look for in a queer. A straight investigator explained that "it was common knowledge that if a man was walking along the street in an effeminate manner, with his lips rouged, his face powdered, and his eye-brows pencilled, that in the majority of cases you could form a pretty good opinion of what kind of a man he was. . .'fairy.' "[17] One gay man, when pressed by the court to explain how he identified someone as "queer," pointed to more subtle indicators: "He acted sort of peculiar; walking around with his hands on his hips. . . . [H]is manner was not masculine. . . . The expression with the eyes and the gestures. . . . If a man was walking around and did not act real masculine, I would think he was a cocksucker."[18] A sailor, who later agreed to be a decoy, recalled that upon noticing "a number of fellows. . .of effeminate character" shortly after his arrival at Newport, he decided to look "into the crowd to see what kind of fellows they were and found they were perverts."[19] Effeminacy had been the first sign of a deeper perversion.

The inverts grouped themselves together as "queers" on the basis of their effeminate gender behavior,[20] and they all played roles culturally defined as feminine in sexual contacts. But they distinguished among themselves on the basis of the "feminine" sexual behavior they preferred, categorizing themselves as "fairies" (also called "cocksuckers"), "pogues" (men who liked to be "browned," or anally penetrated), and "two-way artists" (who enjoyed both). The ubiquity of these distinctions and their importance to personal self-identification cannot be overemphasized. Witnesses at the naval inquiries explicitly drew the distinctions as a matter of course and incorporated them into their descriptions of the gay subculture. One "pogue" who cooperated with the investigation, for instance, used such categories to label his friends in the gang with no prompting from the court: "Hughes said he was a pogue; Richard said he was a cocksucker; Fred Hoage said he was a two-way artist. . . ." While there were some men about whom he "had to draw my own conclusions: they never said directly what they was or wasn't," his remarks made it clear he was sure they fit into one category or another.[21]

A second group of sailors who engaged in homosexual relations and participated in the group life of the gang occupied a more ambiguous sexual category because they, unlike the queers, conformed to masculine gender norms. Some of them were heterosexually married. None of them behaved effeminately or took the "woman's part" in sexual relations, they took no feminine nicknames, and they did not label themselves – nor were they labeled by others – as queer. Instead, gang members, who reproduced the highly gendered sexual relations of their culture, described the second group of men as playing the "husbands" to the "ladies" of the "inverted set." Some husbands entered into steady, loving relationships with individual men known as queer; witnesses spoke of couples who took trips together and maintained monogamous relationships.[22] The husbands' sexual – and sometimes explicitly romantic – interest in men distinguished them from other men: one gay man explained to the court that he believed the rumor about one man being the husband of another must have "some truth in it because [the first man] seems to be very fond of him, more so than the average man would be for a boy."[23] But the ambiguity of the sexual category such men occupied was reflected in the difficulty observers found in labeling them. The navy, which sometimes grouped such men with the queers as "perverts," found it could only satisfactorily identify them by describing what they *did*, rather than naming what they *were*. One investigator, for instance, provided the navy with a list of suspects in which he carefully labeled some men as "pogues" and others as "fairies," but he could only identify one man by noting that he "went out with all the above named men at various times and had himself sucked off or screwed them through the rectum."[24] Even the queers' terms for such men – "friends," and "husbands" – identified the men only *in relation to* the queers, rather than according them an autonomous sexual identity. Despite the uncertain definition of their sexual identity, however, most observers recognized these men as regular – if relatively mar- ginal – members of the gang.

The social organization of the gang was deeply embedded in that of the larger culture; as we have seen, its members repro- duced many of the social forms of gendered heterosexuality, with some men playing "the woman's part" in relationships with conventionally masculine "husbands." But the gang also helped men depart from the social roles ascribed to them as biological males by that larger culture. Many of the "queers" interrogated by the navy recalled having felt effeminate or otherwise "different" most of their lives. But it was the existence of sexual subcultures – of which the gang was one – that provided them a means of structuring their vague feelings of sexual and gender difference into distinctive personal identities. Such groups facilitated people's exploration and organization of their homosexuality by offering them support in the face of social opprobrium and providing them with guidelines for how to organize their feelings of difference into a particular social form of homosexuality, a coherent identity and way of life. The gang offered men a means of assuming social roles which they perceived to be more congruent with their inner natures than those prescribed by the dominant culture, and sometimes gave them remarkable strength to publicly defy social convention.

At the same time, the weight of social disapprobation led people within the gang to insist on a form of solidarity which required conformity to its own standards. To be accepted by the gang, for instance, one had to assume the role of pogue, fairy, two-way artist, or husband, and present oneself publicly in a manner consistent with that labeling. But some men appear to have maintained a critical perspective on the significance of the role for their personal identities. Even while assuming one role for the purpose of interaction in the gang, at least some con- tinued to explore their sexual interests when the full range of those interests was not expressed in the norms for that role. Frederick Hoage, for instance, was known as a "brilliant woman" and a "French artist" (or "fairy"), but he was also reported surreptitiously to have tried to "brown" another mem- ber of the gang – behavior inappropriate to a "queer" as defined by the gang.[25]

Gang members, who believed they could identify men as pogues or fairies even if the men themselves had not yet recognized their true natures, sometimes intervened to accelerate the process of self-discovery. The gang scrutinized newly arrived recruits at the YMCA for likely sexual partners and "queers," and at least one case is recorded of their approaching an effeminate but "straight" identified man named Rogers in order to bring him out as a pogue. While he recalled always having been somewhat effeminate, after he joined the gang Rogers began using makeup "because the others did," assumed the name "Kitty Gordon," and developed a steady relationship with another man (his "husband").[26] What is striking to the contemporary reader is not only that gang members were so confident of their ability to detect Rogers's homosexual interests that they were willing to intervene in the normal pattern of his life, but that they believed they could identify him so precisely as a "latent" (not their word) pogue.

Many gay witnesses indicated that they had at least heard of "fairies" before joining the service, but military mobilization, by removing men like Rogers from family and neighborhood supervision and placing them in a single-sex environment, increased the chances that they would encounter gay-identified men and be able to explore new sexual possibilities. Straight witnesses at the naval inquiry also demonstrated remarkable familiarity with homosexual activity in Newport; like gay men, they believed that "queers" constituted a distinct group of people, "a certain class of people called 'fairies.' "[27] Most of them believed that one could identify certain men as queer by their mannerisms and carriage. Most also realized that such men had organized a collective life, even if they were unfamiliar with its details. As we have seen, many sailors at the naval training station knew that the YMCA was a "headquarters" for such people, and Newport's mayor recalled that "it was information that was common. . .in times gone by, summer after summer," that men called "floaters" who appeared in town "had followed the fleet up from Norfolk."[28] In a comment that reveals more about straight perceptions than gay realities, a navy officer described gay men to the Newport Chief of Police as "a gang who were stronger than the Masons. . .[and who] had signals and a lot of other stuff. . . . [T]hey were perverts and well organized."[29]

"Straight" people's familiarity with the homosexual subculture resulted from the openness with which some gay men rejected the cultural norms of heterosexuality. Several service-men, for instance, mentioned having encountered openly homosexual men at the naval hospital, where they saw patients and staff wear makeup and publicly discuss their romances and homosexual experiences.[30] The story of two gang members assigned to the Melville coaling station near Newport indicates the extent to which individual "queers," with the support of the gang, were willing to make their presence known by defying social convention, even at the cost of hostile reactions. "From the time that they arrived at the station they were both the topic of conversation because of their effeminate habits," testified several sailors stationed at Melville. They suffered constant harassment; many sailors refused to associate with them or abused them physically and verbally, while their officers assigned them especially heavy work loads and ordered their subordinates to "try to get [one of them] with the goods."[31] Straight sailors reacted with such vigor because the gay men flaunted their difference rather than trying to conceal it, addressing each other with "feminine names," witnesses com-plained, and "publish[ing] the fact that they were prostitutes and such stuff as that."[32] At times they were deliberately provo-cative; one astounded sailor reported that he had "seen Richard lying in his bunk take one leg and, putting it up in the air, ask everyone within range of his voice and within range of this place how they would like to take it in this position."[33]

Even before the naval inquiry began, Newport's servicemen and civilians alike were well aware of the queers in their midst. They tolerated them in many settings and brutalized them in others, but they thought they knew what they were dealing with: perverts were men who behaved like women. But as the inquiry progressed, it inadvertently brought the neat bound-aries separating queers from the rest of men into question.

DISPUTING THE BOUNDARIES OF THE "SEXUAL"

The testimony generated by the navy investigation provided unusually detailed information about the social organization of men who identified themselves as "queer." But it also revealed that many more men than the queers were regularly engaging in some form of homosexual activity. Initially the navy expressed little concern about such men's behavior, for it did not believe that straight sailors' occasional liaisons with queers raised any questions about their sexual character. But the authorities decision to prosecute men not normally labeled as queer ignited a controversy which ultimately forced the navy and its opponents to define more precisely what they believed constituted a homosexual act and to defend the basis upon which they categorized people participating in such acts. Because the controversy brought so many groups of people – working- and middle-class gay- and straight-identified enlisted men, middle-class naval officers, ministers, and town officials – into conflict, it revealed how differently those groups interpreted sexuality. A multiplicity of sexual discourses coexisted at a single moment in the civilian and naval seaport communities.

The gang itself loosely described the male population beyond its borders as "straight" but its members further divided the straight population into two different groups: those who would reject their sexual advances, and those who would accept them. A man was "trade," according to one fairy, if he "would stand to have 'queer' persons fool around [with] him in any way, shape or manner."[34] The boundary separating trade from the rest of men was easy to cross. There were locations in Newport where straight men knew they could present themselves in order to be solicited. Even among "trade," gay men realized that some men would participate more actively than others in sexual encounters. Most gay men were said to prefer men who were strictly "straight and [would] not reciprocate in any way," but at least one fairy, as a decoy recorded, "wanted to kiss me and love me [and]. . . insisted and begged for it."[35] Whatever its origins, the term "trade" accurately described a common pattern of interaction between gay men and their straight sexual partners. In Newport, a gay man might take a sailor to a show or to dinner, offer him small gifts, or provide him with a place to stay when he was on overnight leave; in exchange, the sailor allowed his host to have sex with him that night, within whatever limits the sailor cared to set. The exchange was not always so elaborate: The navy's detectives reported several instances of gay men meeting and sexually servicing numerous sailors at the YMCA in a single evening. Men who were "trade" normally did not expect or demand direct payment for their services, although gay men did sometimes lend their partners small amounts of money without expecting it to be returned, and they used the term "trade" to refer to some civilians who, in contrast to the sailors, paid *them* for sexual services. "Trade" normally referred to straight-identified men who played the "masculine" role in sexual encounters solicited by "queers."[36]

Almost all straight sailors agreed that the effeminate members of the gang should be labeled "queer," but they disagreed about the sexual character of a straight man who accepted the sexual advances of a queer. Many straight men assumed that young recruits would accept the sexual solicitations of the perverts. "It was a shame to let these kids come in and run in to that kind of stuff," remarked one decoy; but his remarks indicate he did not think a boy was "queer" just because he let a queer have sex with him.[37] Most pogues defined themselves as "men who like to be browned," but straight men casually defined pogues as "[people] *that you can 'brown'* " and as men who "offered themselves in the same manner which women do."[38] Both remarks imply that "normal" men could take advantage of the pogues' availability without questioning their own identities as "straight"; the fact that the sailors made such potentially incriminating statements before the naval court indicates that this was an assumption they fully expected the court to share (as in fact it did). That lonesome men could unreservedly take advantage of a fairy's availability is perhaps also the implication, no matter how veiled in humor, of the remark made by a sailor stationed at the Melville coaling station: "It was common talk around that the Navy Department was getting good. They were sending a couple of 'fairies' up there for the 'sailors in Siberia.' As we used to call ourselves. . .meaning that we were all alone."[39] The strongest evidence of the social acceptability of trade was that the enlisted men who served as decoys volunteered to take on the role of trade for the purpose of infiltrating the gang, but were never even asked to consider assuming the role of queer. Becoming trade, unlike becoming a queer, posed no threat to the decoys' self-image or social status.

While many straight men took the sexual advances of gay men in stride, most engaged in certain ritual behavior designed to reinforce the distinction between themselves and the "queers." Most importantly, they played only the "masculine" sex role in their encounters with gay men – or at least claimed that they did – and observed the norms of masculinity in their own demeanor. They also ridiculed gay men and sometimes beat them up after sexual encounters. Other men, who feared it brought their manhood into question simply to be approached by a "pervert," were even more likely to attack gay men. Gang members recognized that they had to be careful about whom they approached. They all knew friends who had received severe beatings upon approaching the wrong man.[40] The more militant of the queers even played on straight men's fears. One of the queers at the Melville coaling station "made a remark that 'half the world is queer and the other half trade,' " recalled a straight sailor, who then described the harassment the queer suffered in retribution.[41]

It is now impossible to determine how many straight sailors had such sexual experiences with the queers, although Alfred Kinsey's research suggests the number might have been large. Kinsey found that 37 per cent of the men he interviewed in the 1930s and 1940s had engaged in some homosexual activity, and that a quarter of them had had "more than incidental homosexual experience or reactions" for at least three years between the ages of 16 and 55, even though only 4 per cent were exclusively homosexual throughout their lives.[42] Whatever the precise figures at Newport, naval officials and queers alike believed that very many men were involved. Indeed, as the investigation progressed, even the court of inquiry became concerned about the extent of homosexual activity uncovered. The chief investigator later claimed that the chairman of the first court had ordered him to curtail the investigation because " 'If your men [the decoys] do not knock off, they will hang the whole state of Rhode Island.' "[43]

Naval officials never considered prosecuting the many sailors who they fully realized were being serviced by the fairies each year, because they did not believe that the sailors' willingness to allow such acts "to be performed upon them" in any way implicated their sexual character as homosexual. Instead, they chose to prosecute only those men who were intimately involved in the gang, or otherwise demonstrated (as the navy tried to prove in court) that homosexual desire was a persistent, constituent element of their personalities, whether or not it manifested itself in effeminate behavior. The fact that naval and civilian authorities could prosecute men only for the commission of specific acts of sodomy should not be construed to mean that they viewed homosexuality simply as an act rather than as a condition characteristic of certain individuals; the whole organization of their investigation suggests otherwise. At the January 1920 trial of Reverend Samuel Kent the prosecution contended that

> we may offer evidence of other occurrences similar to the ones the indictment is based on for the purpose of proving the disposition on the part of this man. I submit that it is a well known principle of evidence that in a crime of this nature where disposition, inclination, is an element, that we are not confined to the specific conduct which we have complained of in the indictment, that the other incidents are gone into for their corroborative value as to intent, as to disposition, inclination.[44]

As the investigation and trials proceeded, however, the men prosecuted by the navy made it increasingly difficult for the navy to maintain standards which categorized certain men as "straight" even though they had engaged in homosexual acts with the defendants. This was doubtless particularly troubling to the navy because, while its opponents focused their questions on the character of the decoys in particular, by doing so they implicitly questioned the character of *any* man who had sex with a "pervert". The decoys testified that they had submitted to the queers' sexual advances only in order to rid the navy of their presence, and the navy, initially at least, guaranteed their legal immunity. But the defendants readily charged that the decoys themselves were tainted by homosexual interest and had taken abnormal pleasure in their work. Reverend Kent's lawyers were particularly forceful in questioning the character of any man who would volunteer to work as a decoy. As one decoy after another helplessly answered each question with a quiescent "Yes, sir," the lawyers pressed them:

Q. You volunteered for this work?
A. Yes, sir.
Q. You knew what kind of work it was before you volunteered, didn't you?
A. Yes, sir.
Q. You knew it involved sucking and that sort of thing, didn't you?
A. I knew that we had to deal with that, yes, sir.

Q. You knew it included sodomy and that sort of thing, didn't you?

A. Yes, sir.

Q. And you were quite willing to get into that sort of work?

A. I was willing to do it, yes, sir.

Q. And so willing that you volunteered for it, is that right?

A. Yes, sir. I volunteered for it, yes, sir.

Q. You knew it included buggering fellows, didn't you?[45]

Such questions about the decoys' character were reinforced when members of the gang claimed that the decoys had sometimes taken the initiative in sexual encounters.

The defendants thus raised questions about the character of any man capable of responding to the advances of a pervert, forcing the navy to reexamine its standards for distinguishing "straight" from "perverted" sexuality. At the second naval court of inquiry, even the navy's judge advocate asked the men about how much sexual pleasure they had experienced during their contacts with the suspects. As the boundaries distinguishing acceptable from perverted sexual response began to crumble, the decoys recognized their vulnerability and tried to protect themselves. Some simply refused to answer any further questions about the sexual encounters they had described in graphic detail to the first court. One decoy protested that he had never responded to a pervert's advances: "I am a man. . . . The thing was so horrible in my sight that naturally I could not become passionate and there was no erection," but was immediately asked, "Weren't [the other decoys] men, too?" Another, less fortunate decoy had to plead:

Of course, a great deal of that was involuntary inasmuch as a man placing his hand on my penis would cause an erection and subsequent emission. That was uncontrollable on my part. . . . Probably I would have had it [the emission] when I got back in bed anyway. . . . It is a physiological fact.[46]

But if a decoy could be suspected of perversion simply because he had a certain physiological response to a pervert's sexual advances, then the character of countless other sailors came under question. Many more men than the inner circle of queers and husbands would have to be investigated. In 1920, the navy was unprepared to take that step. The decision of the

Dunn Inquiry to condemn the original investigation and the navy's decision to offer clemency to some of the men imprisoned as a result of it may be interpreted, in part, as a quiet retreat from that prospect.

CHRISTIAN BROTHERHOOD UNDER SUSPICION

The navy investigation raised fundamental questions concerning the definition of a "sexual relationship" itself when it reached beyond the largely working-class milieu of the military to label a prominent local Episcopal clergyman, Samuel Kent, and a YMCA volunteer and churchman, Arthur Leslie Green, as homosexual. When Kent fled the city, the navy tracked him down and brought him to trial on sodomy charges. Two courts acquitted him despite the fact that five decoys claimed to have had sex with him, because the denials of the respected minister and of the numerous clergymen and educators who defended him seemed more credible. Soon after Kent's second acquittal in early 1920, the Bishop of Rhode Island and the Newport Ministerial Union went on the offensive against the navy. The clergymen charged that the navy had used immoral methods in its investigation by instructing young enlisted men "in details of a nameless vice" and sending them into the community to entrap innocent citizens. They wrote letters of protest to the Secretary of the Navy and the President, condemned the investigation in the press, and forced the navy to convene a second court of inquiry into the methods used in the first inquiry. When it exculpated senior naval officials and failed to endorse all of the ministers' criticisms, the ministers persuaded the Republican-controlled Senate Naval Affairs Committee to undertake its own investigation, which eventually endorsed all of the ministers' charges.[47]

The simple fact that one of their own had been attacked did not provoke the fervor of the ministers' response to the navy investigation, nor did they oppose the investigation simply because of its "immoral" methods. Close examination of the navy's allegations and of the ministers' countercharges suggests that the ministers feared that the navy's charges against the two churchmen threatened to implicate them all. Both Green and Kent were highly regarded local churchmen; Kent had been asked to preach weekly during Lent, had received praise for his work at the Naval Hospital during the influenza epidemic, and at the time of the investigation was expected to be named superintendent of a planned Seaman's Church Institute.[48] Their behavior had not differed markedly from that of the many other men who ministered to the needs of the thousands of boys brought to Newport by the war. When the navy charged that Kent's and Green's behavior and motives were perverted, many ministers feared that they could also be accused of perversion, and, more broadly, that the inquiry had questioned the ideology of nonsexual Christian brotherhood that had heretofore explained their devotion to other men. The confrontation between the two groups fundamentally represented a dispute over the norms for masculine gender behavior and over the boundaries between homosociality and homosexuality in the relations of men.

The investigation threatened Newport's ministers precisely because it repudiated those conventions that had justified and institutionalized a mode of behavior for men of the cloth or of the upper class that would have been perceived as effeminate in other men. The ministers' perception of this threat is reflected in their repeated criticism of the navy operatives' claim that they could detect perverts by their "looks and actions."[49] Almost all sailors and townspeople, as we have seen, endorsed this claim, but it put the ministers as a group in an extremely awkward position, for the major sign of a man's perversion according to most sailors was his being effeminate. As the ministers' consternation indicated, there was no single norm for masculine behavior at Newport; many forms of behavior considered effeminate on the part of working-class men were regarded as appropriate to the status of upper-class men or to the ministerial duties of the clergy. Perhaps if the navy had accused only working-class sailors, among whom "effeminacy" was more clearly deviant from group norms, of perversion, the ministers might have been content to let this claim stand. But when the naval inquiry also identified as perverted churchmen associated with such an upper-class institution as the Episcopal Church of Newport because of their perceived effeminacy, it challenged the norms which had heretofore shielded men of their background from such suspicions.

One witness tried to defend Kent's "peculiar" behavior on the basis of the conventional norms when he contended that "I don't know whether you would call it abnormal. He was a minister."[50] But the navy refused to accept this as a defense, and witnesses repeatedly described Kent and Green to the court as "peculiar," "sissyfied," and "effeminate." During his daily visits to patients at the hospital, according to a witness named Brunelle, Green held the patients' hands and "didn't talk like a man – he talk[ed] like a woman to me."[51] Since there is no evidence that Green had a high-pitched or otherwise "effeminate" *voice*, Brunelle probably meant Green addressed men with greater affection than he expected of a man. But all ministers visited with patients and spoke quiet, healing words to them; their position as ministers had permitted them to engage in such conventionally "feminine" behavior. When the navy and ordinary sailors labeled this behavior "effeminate" in the case of Green and Kent, and further claimed that such effeminacy was a sign of sexual perversion, they challenged the legitimacy of many Christian social workers' behavior.

During the war, Newport's clergymen had done all they could to minister to the needs of the thousands of boys brought to the Naval Training Station. They believed they had acted in the spirit of Christian brotherhood, but the naval inquiry seemed to suggest that less lofty motives were at work. Ministers had loaned sailors money, but during the inquiry they heard Green accused of buying sex. They had visited boys in the hospital and now heard witnesses insinuate that this was abnormal: "I don't know what [Kent's] duties were, but he was always talking to some boys. It seems though he would have special boys to talk to. He would go to certain fellows [patients] and probably spend the afternoon with them."[52] They had given boys drives and taken them out to dinner and to the theater, and now heard Kent accused of lavishing such favors on young men in order to further his salacious purposes. They had opened their homes to the young enlisted men, but now heard Kent accused of inviting boys home in order to seduce them.[53] When one witness at the first court of inquiry tried to argue that Green's work at the YMCA was inspired by purely "charitable" motives, the court repudiated his interpretation and questioned the motives of *any* man who engaged in such work:

Do you think a normal active man would peddle stamps and paper around a Hospital and the YMCA?. . .

Do you think that a man who had no interest in young boys would voluntarily offer his services and work in the YMCA where he is constantly associated with young boys?[54]

The ministers sought to defend Kent – and themselves – from the navy's insinuations by reaffirming the cultural interpretation of ministerial behavior as Christian and praiseworthy. While they denied the navy's charge that Kent had had genital contact with sailors, they did not deny his devotion to young men, for to have done so would have implicitly conceded the navy's interpretation of such behavior as salacious – and thus have left all ministers who had demonstrated similar devotion open to suspicion. Reverend John H. Deming of the Ministerial Union reported that numerous ministers shared the fear of one man who was "frantic after all he had done for the Navy":

When this thing [the investigation] occurred, it threw some of my personal friends into a panic. For they knew that in the course of their work they had had relations with boys in various ways; they had been alone with them in some cases. As one boy [a friend] said, frequently boys had slept in the room with him. But he had never thought of the impropriety of sleeping alone with a navy boy. He thought probably he would be accused.[55]

Rather than deny the government's claim that Kent had sought intimate relationships with sailors and devoted unusual attention to them, therefore, Kent and his supporters depicted such behavior as an honorable part of the man's ministry. Indeed, demonstrating just how much attention Kent had lavished on boys became as central to the strategy of the ministers as it was to that of the government, but the ministers offered a radically different interpretation of it. Their preoccupation with validating ministerial behavior turned Kent's trial and the second naval inquiry into an implicit public debate over the cultural definition of the boundaries between homosociality and homosexuality in the relations of men. The navy had defined Kent's behavior as sexual and perverted; the ministers sought to reaffirm that it was brotherly and Christian.

Kent himself interpreted his relations with sailors as "[t]rying to be friends with them, urging them to come to my quarters and see me if they wanted to, telling them – I think, perhaps, I can best express it by saying 'Big Brotherhood.' " He quoted a letter from another minister commending his "brotherly assistance" during the influenza epidemic, and he pointed out that the Episcopal War Commission provided him with funds with which to take servicemen to the theater "at least once a week" and to maintain his automobile in order to give boys drives "and get acquainted with them."[56] He described in detail his efforts to minister to the men who had testified against him, explaining that he had offered them counsel, a place to sleep, and other services just as he had to hundreds of other enlisted men. But he denied that any genital contact had taken place, and in some cases claimed he had broken off the relationships when he realized that the *decoys* wanted sexual contact.

Kent's lawyers produced a succession of defense witnesses – respected clergymen, educators, and businesspeople who had known Kent at every stage of his career – to testify to his obvious affection for boys, even though by emphasizing this aspect of his character they risked substantiating the navy's case. The main point of their testimony was that Kent was devoted to boys and young men and had demonstrated such talent in working with them that they had encouraged him to focus his ministry on them. The Bishop of Pennsylvania recalled that, as Kent's teacher at the Episcopal Theological School in Cambridge in 1908, he had asked Kent to help him develop a ministry to Harvard men, "because [Kent] seemed peculiarly fitted for it in temperament and in experience, and in general knowledge of how to approach young men and influence them for good." The sentiments of Kent's character witnesses were perhaps best summarized by a judge who sat on the Episcopal War Commission which employed Kent. The judge assured the court that Kent's reputation was "excellent; I think he was looked upon as an earnest Christian man [who] was much interested in young men."[57]

The extent to which Kent's supporters were willing to interpret his intimacy with young men as brotherly rather than sexual is perhaps best illustrated by the effort of Kent's defense lawyer to show how Kent's inviting a decoy named Charles Zipf to sleep with him was only another aspect of his ministering to the boy's needs. Hadn't the decoy told Kent he was "lonesome" and had no place to sleep that night, the defense attorney pressed Zipf in cross-examination, before Kent invited him to spend the night in his parish house? And after Kent had set up a cot for Zipf in the living room, hadn't Zipf told Kent that he was "cold" before Kent pulled back the covers and invited him to join him in his bed?[58] The attorney counted on the presumption of Christian brotherhood to protect the minister's behavior from the suspicion of homosexual perversion, even though the same evidence would have seemed irrefutably incriminating in the case of another man.

Kent's defense strategy worked. Arguments based on assumptions about ministerial conduct persuaded the jury to acquit Kent of the government's charges. But Newport's ministers launched their campaign against the navy probe as soon as Kent was acquitted because they recognized that it had succeeded in putting their devotion to men under suspicion. It had raised questions about the cultural boundaries distinguishing homosexuality from homosociality that the ministers were determined to lay to rest.

But while it is evident that Newport's ministers feared the consequences of the investigation for their public reputations, two of their charges against the navy suggest that they may also have feared that its allegations contained some element of truth. The charges reflect the difference between the ministers' and the navy's understanding of sexuality and human sinfulness, but the very difference may have made the navy's accusations seem plausible in a way that the navy could not have foreseen. First, the ministers condemned the navy for having instructed young enlisted men – the decoys – "in the details of a nameless vice," and having ordered them to use that knowledge. The naval authorities had been willing to let their agents engage in sexual acts with the "queers" because they were primarily concerned about people manifesting a homosexual disposition rather than those engaging occasionally in homosexual acts. The navy asserted that the decoys' investigative purpose rendered them immune from criminal prosecution even though they had committed illegal sexual acts. But the ministers viewed the decoys' culpability as "a moral question. . .not a technical question at all"; when the decoys had sex with other men, they had "scars placed on their souls" because, inescapably, "having immoral relations with men is an immoral act."[59] The sin was in the act, not the motive or the disposition. In addition, the ministers charged that the navy had directed the decoys to entrap designated individuals and that no one, no matter how innocent, could avoid entrapment by a skillful decoy. According to Bishop Perry, the decoys operated by putting men "into compromising positions, where they might be suspected of guilt, [even though they were] guiltless persons." Anyone could be entrapped because an "innocent advance might be made by the person operated upon and he might be ensnared against his will."[60] Implicitly, any clergyman could have done what Kent was accused of doing. Anyone's defenses could fall.

The ministers' preoccupation with the moral significance of genital sexual activity and their fear that anyone could be entrapped may reflect the continued saliency for them of the Christian precept that *all* people, including the clergy, were sinners subject to a variety of sexual temptations, including those of homosexual desire.[61] According to this tradition, Christians had to resist homosexual temptations, as they resisted others, but simply to desire a homosexual liaison was neither a singular failing nor an indication of perverted character. The fact that the ministers never clearly elucidated this perspective and were forced increasingly to use the navy's own terms while contesting the navy's conclusions may reflect both the ministers' uncertainty and their recognition that such a perspective was no longer shared by the public.

In any case, making the commission of specified physical acts the distinguishing characteristic of a moral pervert made it definitionally impossible to interpret the ministers' relationships with sailors – no matter how intimate and emotionally moving – as having a "sexual" element, so long as they involved no such acts. Defining the sexual element in men's relationships in this narrow manner enabled the ministers to develop a bipartite defense of Kent which simultaneously denied he had had sexual relationships with other men and yet celebrated his profound emotional devotion to them. It legitimized (nonphysical) intimacy between men by precluding the possibility that such intimacy could be defined as sexual. Reaffirming the boundaries between Christian brotherhood and perverted sexuality was a central objective of the ministers' very public debate with the navy. But it may also have been of private significance to churchmen forced by the navy investigation to reflect on the nature of their brotherhood with other men.

CONCLUSION

The richly textured evidence provided by the Newport controversy makes it possible to re-examine certain tenets of recent work in the history of sexuality, especially the history of homosexuality. Much of that work, drawing on sociological models of symbolic interactionism and the labeling theory of deviance, has argued that the end of the nineteenth century witnessed a major reconceptualization of homosexuality. Before the last century, according to this thesis, North American and European cultures had no concept of the homosexual-as-person; they regarded homosexuality as simply another form of sinful behavior in which anyone might choose to engage. The turn of the century witnessed the "invention of the homosexual," that is, the new determination that homosexual desire was limited to certain identifiable individuals for whom it was an involuntary sexual orientation of some biological or psychological origin. The most prominent advocates of this thesis have argued that the medical discourse on homosexuality that emerged in the late nineteenth century played a determining role in this process, by creating and popularizing this new model of homosexual behavior (which they have termed the "medical model" of homosexuality). It was on the basis of the new medical models, they argue, that homosexually active individuals came to be labeled in popular culture – and to assume an identity – as sexual deviants different in nature from other people, rather than as sinners whose sinful nature was the common lot of humanity.[62]

The Newport evidence suggests how we might begin to refine and correct our analysis of the relationship between medical discourse, homosexual behavior, and identity. First, and most clearly, the Newport evidence indicates that medical discourse still played little or no role in the shaping of working-class homosexual identities and categories by World War I, more than thirty years after the discourse had begun. There would be no logical reason to expect that discussions carried on in elite journals whose distribution was limited to members of the medical and legal professions would have had any immediate effect on the larger culture, particularly the working class. In the

Newport evidence, only one fairy even mentioned the favored medical term "invert," using it as a synonym for the already existing and widely recognized popular term "queer." Moreover, while "invert" was commonly used in the medical literature there is no reason to assume that it originated there, and the Newport witness specified that he had first heard it in theater circles and not through reading any "literature." The culture of the sexual underground, always in a complex relationship with the dominant culture, played a more important role in the shaping and sustaining of sexual identities.

More remarkably, medical discourse appears to have had as little influence on the military hierarchy as on the people of Newport.[63] Throughout the two years of navy investigations related to Newport, which involved the highest naval officials, not a single medical expert was invited to present the medical perspective on the issues at stake. The only member of the original board of inquiry who even alluded to the published literature (and this on only one occasion during the Foster hearings, and once more at the second inquiry) was Dr E. M. Hudson, the welfare officer at the naval hospital and one of the decoys' supervisors. Hudson played a prominent role in the original investigation not because of his medical expertise, but because it was the flagrantly displayed (and normally tolerated) effeminacy and homosexuality of hospital staff and patients that first made naval officials consider undertaking an investigation. As the decoys' supervisor, Hudson drew on his training in fingerprinting and detective work considerably more than his medical background. Only after he became concerned that the decoys might be held legally culpable for their homosexual activity did he "read several medical books on the subject and read everything that I could find out as to what legal decisions there were on these cases."[64] But he never became very familiar with the medical discourse on sexual nonconformity; after his reading he still thought that the term "invert," which had first appeared in US medical journals almost forty years earlier, was "practically a new term," less than two years old.[65]

Moreover, Hudson only accepted those aspects of the medical analysis of homosexuality that confirmed popular perceptions. Thus he accepted as authoritative the distinction that medical writers drew between "congenital perverts" (called "queers" in common parlance) and "normal people submitting to acts of perversion, as a great many normal people do, [who] do not become perverts themselves," such as men isolated from women at a military base. He accepted this "scientific" distinction because it only confirmed what he and other naval officials already believed: that many sailors had sex with the queers without being "queer" themselves. But when the medical literature differed from the assumptions he shared with most navy men, he ignored it. Rather than adopting the medical viewpoint that homosexuals were biological anomalies who should be treated medically rather than willful criminals who should be deterred from homosexuality by severe legal penalties, for instance, he agreed with his colleagues that "these conditions existed and should be eradicated and the men guilty of offenses should be rounded up and punished."[66] In the course of 109 days of hearings, Dr Hudson referred to medical authorities only twice, and then only when they confirmed the assumptions of popular culture.

It thus appears more plausible to describe the medical discourse as a "reverse discourse," to use Michel Foucault's term, rather than as the central force in the creation of new sexual categories around which individuals shaped their personal identities. Rather than creating such categories as "the invert" and "the homosexual," the turn-of-the-century medical investigators whom Hudson read were trying to describe, classify and explain a pre-existing sexual underground whose outlines they only vaguely perceived. Their scientific categories largely reproduced those of popular culture, with "queers" becoming "inverts" in medical parlance but retaining the characteristic cross-gender behavior already attributed to them in popular culture. Doctors developed generalizations about homosexuals based on their idiosyncratic observations of particular individuals and admitted from the beginning that they were responding to the existence of communities of such people whose mysterious behavior and social organization they wished to explore. As one of the first American medical commentators observed in 1889, in explaining the need to study sexual perversion, "[t]here is in every community of any size a colony of male sexual perverts; they are usually known to each other, and are likely to congregate together."[67] By the time of the Newport investigation, medical researchers had developed an elaborate system of sexual classification and numerous explanations for individual cases of homosexuality, but they still had little comprehension of the complex social and cultural structure of gay life.

The Newport evidence helps put the significance of the medical discourse in perspective; it also offers new insights into the relationship between homosexual behavior and identity. Recent studies which have established the need to distinguish between homosexual behavior (presumably a transhistorically evident phenomenon) and the historically specific concept of homosexual identity have tended to focus on the evolution of people whose *primary* personal and political "ethnic" identification is as gay, and who have organized a multidimensional way of life on the basis of their homosexuality. The high visibility of such people in contemporary Western societies and their growing political significance make analysis of the historical development of their community of particular scholarly interest and importance.[68] But the Newport evidence indicates that we need to begin paying more attention to *other* social forms of homosexuality – other ways in which homosexual relations have been organized and understood, differentiated, named, and left deliberately unnamed. We need to specify the *particularity* of various modes of homosexual behavior and the relationships between those modes and particular configurations of sexual identity.

For even when we find evidence that a culture has labeled people who were homosexually active as sexually deviant, we should not assume a priori that their homosexual activity was the determinative criterion in the labeling process. As in Newport, where many men engaged in certain kinds of homosexual behavior yet continued to be regarded as "normal," the assumption of particular sexual roles and deviance from gender norms may have been more important than the coincidence of male or female sexual partners in the classification of sexual character. "Fairies," "pogues," "husbands," and "trade" might all be labeled "homosexuals" in our own time, but they were labeled – and understood themselves – as fundamentally different kinds of people in World War I-era Newport. They all engaged in what we would define as homosexual behavior, but they and the people who observed them were more careful than we to draw distinctions between different modes of such behavior. To classify their behavior and character using the simple polarities of "homosexual" and "heterosexual" would be to misunderstand the complexity of their sexual system. Indeed, the very terms "homosexual behavior" and "identity," because of their tendency to conflate phenomena that other cultures may have regarded as quite distinct, appear to be insufficiently precise to denote the variety of social forms of sexuality we wish to analyze.[69]

The problems that arise when different forms of homosexual activity and identity are conflated are evidenced in the current debate over the consequences of the development of a medical model of homosexuality. Recent studies, especially in lesbian history, have argued that the creation and stigmatization of the public image of the homosexual at the turn of the century served to restrict the possibilities for intimacy between all women and all men by making it possible to associate such intimacy with the despised social category of the homosexual. This thesis rightly observes that the definition of deviance serves to establish behavioral norms for everyone, not just for the deviant. But it overlooks the corollary of this observation, that the definition of deviance serves to legitimize some social relations even as it stigmatizes others; and it assumes that the turn-of-the-century definition of "sexual inversion" codified the same configuration of sexual and gender phenomena which "homosexuality" does today. But many early twentieth-century romantic friendships between women, for instance, appear to have been unaffected by the development of a public lesbian persona, in part because that image characterized the lesbian primarily as a "mannish woman," which had the effect of excluding from its stigmatizing purview all conventionally feminine women, no matter how intimate their friendships.[70]

The stigmatized image of the queer also helped to legitimate the behavior of men in Newport. Most observers did not label as queer either the ministers who were intimate with their Christian brothers or the sailors who had sex with effeminate men, because neither group conformed to the dominant image of what a queer should be like. Significantly, though, in their own minds the two groups of men legitimized their behavior in radically different ways: The ministers' conception of the boundary between acceptable and unacceptable male behavior was almost precisely the opposite of that obtaining among the sailors. The ministers made it impossible to define their relationships with sailors as "sexual" by making the commission of specified physical acts the distinguishing characteristic of a moral pervert. But even as the ministers argued that their relatively feminine character and deep emotional intimacy with other men were acceptable so long as they engaged in no physical contact with them, the sailors believed that their physical sexual contact with the queers remained acceptable so long as they avoided effeminate behavior and developed no emotional ties with their sexual partners.

At the heart of the controversy provoked and revealed by the Newport investigation was a confrontation between several such definitional systems, a series of disputes over the boundaries between homosociality and homosexuality in the relations of men and over the standards by which their masculinity would be judged. The investigation became controversial when it verged on suggesting that the homosocial world of the navy and the relationships between sailors and their Christian brothers in the Newport ministry were permeated by homosexual desire. Newport's ministers and leading citizens, the Senate Naval Affairs Committee, and to some extent even the navy itself repudiated the Newport inquiry because they found such a suggestion intolerable. Although numerous cultural interpretations of sexuality were allowed to confront each other at the inquiry, ultimately certain cultural boundaries had to be reaffirmed in order to protect certain relations as "nonsexual," even as the sexual nature of others was declared and condemned. The Newport evidence reveals much about the social organization and self-understanding of men who identified themselves as "queer." But it also provides a remarkable illustration of the extent to which the boundaries established between "sexual" and "nonsexual" relations are culturally determined, and it reminds us that struggles over the demarcation of those boundaries are a central aspect of the history of sexuality.

NOTES

1 First published in *Journal of Social History* 19 (1985): 189–212. Used by permission. This is a revised version of a paper originally presented at the conference "Among Men, Among Women: Sociological and Historical Recognition of Homosocial Arrangements," held at the University of Amsterdam, 22–6 June 1983. I am grateful to Allan Bérubé, John Boswell, Nancy Cott, Steven Dubin, James Schultz, Anthony Stellato, James Taylor, and my colleagues at the

Amsterdam conference for their comments on earlier versions.

2 The Newport investigation was brought to the attention of historians by Frank Freidel, *Franklin D. Roosevelt: The Ordeal* (Boston: 1954), 41, 46–7, 96–7, and Jonathan Katz, *Gay American History: A Documentary* (New York: 1976), 579n. Katz reprinted the Senate report in *Government Versus Homosexuals* (New York: 1975), a volume in the Arno Press series on homosexuality he edited. A useful narrative account of the naval investigation is provided by Lawrence R. Murphy. "Cleaning Up Newport: The U.S. Navy's Prosecution of Homosexuals After World War I," *Journal of American Culture* 7 (Fall 1984): 57–64.

3 Murphy J. Foster presided over the first Court of Inquiry which began its work in Newport on 13 March 1919 and heard 406 pages of testimony in the course of 23 days (its records are hereafter cited as *Foster Testimony*). The second court of inquiry, convened in 1920 "to inquire into the methods employed. . .in the investigation of moral and other conditions existing in the Naval Service; [and] to ascertain and inquire into the scope of and authority for said investigation," was presided over by Rear Admiral Herbert O. Dunn and heard 2500 pages of testimony in the course of 86 days (hereafter cited as *Dunn Testimony*). The second trial of Reverend Kent, *U.S. v. Samuel Neal Kent*, heard in Rhode Island District Court in Providence beginning 20 January 1920, heard 532 pages of evidence (hereafter cited as *Kent Trial*). The records are held at the National Archives, Modern Military Field Branch, Suitland, Maryland, R. G. 125.

4 I have used "gay" in this essay to refer to men who identified themselves as sexually different from other men – and who labeled themselves and were labeled by others as "queer" – because of their assumption of "feminine" sexual and other social roles. As I explain below, not all men who were homosexually active labeled themselves in this manner, including men, known as "husbands," who were involved in long-term homosexual relationships but nonetheless maintained a "masculine" identity.

5 *Foster Testimony*, Ervin Arnold, 5; F. T. Brittain, 12; Thomas Brunelle, 21; *Dunn Testimony*, Albert Viehl, 307; Dudley Marriott, 1737.

6 Frederick Hoage, using a somewhat different construction than most, referred to them as "the inverted gang" (*Foster Testimony*, Hoage, 255).

7 *Foster Testimony*, Arnold, 5: *Dunn Testimony*, Clyde Rudy, 1783. For a few of the many other comments by "straight" sailors on the presence of gay men at the YMCA, see *Dunn Testimony*, Claude McQuillin, 1759; and Preston Paul, 1836.

8 A man named Temple, for instance, had a room at the Y where he frequently took pickups (*Foster Testimony*, Brunelle, 207–8); on the role of the elevator operators, see William McCoy, 20; and Samuel Rogers, 61.

9 *Foster Testimony*, Arnold, 27; Hoage, 271; Harrison Rideout. 292.

10 Ibid., Hoage, 267; Rogers, 50; Brunelle, 185.

11 Ibid., Gregory A. Cunningham, 30; Arnold, 6; *Dunn Testimony*, John S. Tobin, 720–1.

12 For an elaboration of the conceptual distinction between "inversion" and "homosexuality" in the contemporary medical literature, see my article, "From Sexual Inversion to Homosexuality: Medicine and the Changing Conceptualization of Female Deviance," *Salmagundi* 58/59 (Fall 1982/Winter 1983): 114–46.

13 E.g., an article which included the following caption beneath a photograph of Hughes dressed in women's clothes: "This is Billy Hughes, Yeo. 2c. It's a shame to break the news like that, but enough of the men who saw 'Pinafore' fell in love with Bill, without adding to their number. 'Little Highesy,' as he is affectionately known, dances like a Ziegfeld chorus girl. . . ." (" 'We Sail the Ocean Blue': 'H.M.S. Pinafore' as Produced by the Navy," *Newport Recruit* 6 [August 1918]: 9). See also, e.g., "Mayor Will Greet Navy Show Troupe: Official Welcome Arranged for 'Jack and Beanstalk' Boys," which quoted an admiral saying, " 'It is a corker. I have never in my life seen a prettier 'girl' [a man] than 'Princess Mary.' She is the daintiest little thing I ever laid eyes on' " (*Providence Journal* [26 May 1919]: 9). I am grateful to Lawrence Murphy for supplying me with copies of these articles.

14 *Dunn Testimony*, Tobin, 716; *Foster Testimony*, Charles Zipf, 377; confirmed by Hoage, 289, and Arnold (*Dunn Testimony*, 1405). The man who received the women's clothes was the Billy Hughes mentioned in the newspaper article cited in the previous note. I am grateful to Allan Bérubé for informing me of the regularity with which female impersonators appeared in navy shows during and immediately following World War I.

15 *Foster Testimony*. Hoage called it a "faggot party" and "a general congregation of inverts" (*Foster Testimony*, 267); Brunelle, who claimed to have attended the party for only fifteen minutes, noted the presence of the sailors and fighters; he also said only one person was in drag, but mentioned at least two (*Foster Testimony*, 194, 206); John E McCormick observed the lovers (*Foster Testimony*, 332).

16 For the straight sailors' nicknames, see *Foster Testimony*, William Nelson Gorham, 349. On the ubiquity of nicknames and the origins of some of them, see *Foster Testimony*, Hoage, 253, 271: Whitney Delmore Rosenszweig, 397.

17 *Dunn Testimony*, E. M. Hudson, 1663.

18 *Foster Testimony*, Rideout, 76–7.

19 Ibid., Cunningham, 29. For other examples, see Wade Stuart Harvey, 366; and *Dunn Testimony*, Tobin, 715.

20 *Foster Testimony*, George Richard, 143; Hoage, 298.

21 Ibid., Rideout, 69; see also, for example, Rogers, 63; Viehl, 175; Arnold, 3.

22 An investigator told the Navy that one gay man had declined to make a date with him because "he did not like to 'play with fire'. . .[and] was afraid Chief Brugs would beat him up" (*Foster Testimony*, Arnold, 36); the same gay man told the court he had

traveled to Providence with Brugs two weekends in a row and gone to shows with him (Rogers, 53–4). Speaking of another couple, Hoage admitted he had heard "that Hughes has traveled with Brunelle separately for two months or so" and that "they were lovers." He added that "of course that does not indicate anything but friendship," but that "naturally I would suspect that something else was taking place" (Hoage, 268).

23 Ibid., Hoage, 313.
24 Ibid., Arnold, 5.
25 Ibid., Viehl, 175; Brunelle, 235; Rideout, 93. Hoage, when cross-examined by Rosenszweig, denied another witness's charge that he, Hoage, had *boasted* of browning Rosenszweig, but he did not deny the act itself – nor did Rosenszweig ask him to do so (396).
26 Ibid., Hoage, 271; Rogers, 131–6.
27 Ibid., Rideout, 78.
28 *Dunn Testimony*, Jeremiah Mahoney, 698.
29 Ibid., Tobin, 717.
30 Witnesses who encountered gay men at the hospital or commented on the presence of homosexuals there included Cunningham, *Foster Testimony*, 29; Brunelle, 210; *Dunn Testimony*, McCormick, 1780; and Paul, 1841. Paul also described some of the open homosexual joking engaged in by patients, *Foster Testimony*, 393–4.
31 *Foster Testimony*, Hervey, 366; Johnson, 153, 155, 165, 167; Walter F. Smith, 221.
32 Ibid., Johnson, 153; Smith, 169.
33 Ibid., Smith, 171.
34 Ibid., Hoage, 272. Hoage added that "[t]rade is a word that is only used among people temperamental [i.e., gay]," although this does not appear to have been entirely the case.
35 Ibid., Hoage, 269, 314; Rudy, 14. The decoy further noted that, despite the fairy's pleas, "I insisted that he do his work below my chest."
36 Hoage provided an example of this pattern when he described how a gay civilian had taken him to a show and dinner, let him stay in his room, and then "attempted to do what they call 'browning.' " But he devoted much of his testimony to *denying* that *his* "tak[ing] boys to dinner and to a show," offering to share his bed with sailors who had nowhere else to stay, and giving them small gifts and loans had the sexual implications that the court obviously suspected (*Foster Testimony*, Hoage, 261, 256, 262, 281–2). For other examples of solicitation patterns, see *Foster Testimony*, Maurice Kreisberg, 12; Arnold, 26; *Dunn Testimony*, Paul, 1843. Edward Stevenson described the "trade" involved in military prostitution in *The Intersexes: A History of Semisexualism* (privately printed, 1908), 214. For an early sociological description of "trade," see Albert Reiss, Jr., "The Social Integration of Queers and Peers," *Social Problems* 9 (1961): 102–20.
37 *Dunn Testimony*, Paul, 1836; see also, e.g., Mayor Mahoney's comments, 703.
38 *Foster Testimony*, James Daniel Chase, 119 (my emphasis); Zipf, 375.

39 Ibid., Smith, 169.
40 See, e.g., the accounts of Hoage, *Foster Testimony*, 271–2, and Rideout, 87.
41 *Foster Testimony*, Smith, 169.
42 Alfred Kinsey, Wardell Pomeroy, and Clyde Martin, *Sexual Behavior in the Human Male* (Philadelphia: 1948), 650–1.
43 *Foster Testimony*, Arnold, 6; *Dunn Testimony*, Arnold, 1495.
44 *Kent Trial*, 21.
45 Ibid., defense attorney's interrogation of Charles McKinney, 66–7. See also, e.g., the examination of Zipf in *Kent Trial*, esp. 27–8.
46 Ibid., Zipf, 2113, 2131 (the court repeatedly turned to the subject). The "manly" decoy was Clyde Rudy, 1793.
47 The ministers' efforts are reviewed and their charges affirmed in the Senate report, 67th Congress, 1st session, Committee on Naval Affairs, *Alleged Immoral Conditions of Newport (R.I.) Naval Training Station* (Washington, DC: 1921), and in the testimony of Bishop Perry and Reverend Hughes before the Dunn Inquiry.
48 *Dunn Testimony*, Reverend Deming, 30; Reverend Forster, 303.
49 Hudson quoted in the Senate report, *Alleged Immoral Conditions*, 8: see also *Dunn Testimony*, Tobin, 723; cf. Arnold, 1712. For the ministers' criticism, see, e.g., Bishop Perry, 529, 607.
50 *Foster Testimony*, Hoage, 319.
51 Ibid., Brunelle, 216. He says the same of Kent on p. 217.
52 *Kent Trial*, cross-examination of Howard Rider, 296.
53 Ibid., Malcolm C. Crawford, 220–3; Dostalik, 57–71.
54 *Foster Testimony*, interrogation of Hoage, 315, 318.
55 *Dunn Testimony*, Reverend Deming, 43.
56 *Kent Trial*, Kent, 396, 419, 403.
57 Ibid., Bishop Philip Rhinelander, 261–2: Judge Darius Baker, 277; see also Reverend Henry Motett, 145–9, 151.
58 Ibid., interrogation of Zipf, 37–8.
59 *Dunn Testimony*, Reverend Deming, 42; Bishop Perry, 507.
60 Ibid., Bishop Perry, 678.
61 Jonathan Katz argues that such a perspective was central to Puritan concepts of homosexuality. "The Age of Sodomitical Sin, 1607–1740," in his *Gay/Lesbian Almanac: A New Documentary* (New York: 1983), 23–65. But see also John Boswell, "Revolutions, Universals and Sexual Categories," *Salmagundi* 58/59 (Fall 1982 Winter 1983): 89–113.
62 This argument was first introduced by Mary McIntosh, "The Homosexual Role," *Social Problems* 16 (1968): 182–92, and has been developed and modified by Jeffrey Weeks, *Coming Out: Homosexual Politics in Britain from the Nineteenth Century to the Present* (London: 1977); Michel Foucault, *The History of Sexuality: An Introduction*, trans. Robert Hurley (New York: 1978); Lillian Faderman, *Surpassing the Love of Men: Romantic Friendships and Love Between Women from the Renaissance to the Present* (New York: 1981); Kenneth Plummer, ed., *The Making of the Modern Homosexual* (London: 1981); and Katz, *Gay/Lesbian Almanac*. Although these historians and sociologists

subscribe to the same general model, they disagree over the timing and details of the emergence of a homosexual role, and McIntosh's original essay did not attribute a key role in that process to medical discourse.

63 The situation had changed considerably by the Second World War when psychiatrists occupied a more influential position in the military, which used them to help select and manage the more than fifteen million men and women it mobilized for the war. See, for instance, the role of psychiatrists in the records of courts-martial conducted in 1941–3 held at the National Archives (Army A. G. 250.1) and the 1944 investigation of lesbianism at the Third WAC Training Center, Fort Oglethorpe, Georgia (National Archives, Modern Military Field Branch, Suitland, Maryland, R. G. 159, Entry 26F). Allan Bérubé's important study, *Coming Out Under Fire: The History of Gay Men and Women in World War Two* (New York: 1990), discusses at length the role of psychiatrists in the development and implementation of Second World War-era military policies.

64 *Dunn Testimony*, Hudson, 1630.

65 *Foster Testimony*, 300. The transcript does not identify the speaker, but the context strongly suggests it was Hudson.

66 *Dunn Testimony*, 1628, 1514.

67 George Frank Lydston, "Sexual Perversion, Satyriasis, and Nymphomania," *Medical and Surgical Reporter* 61 (1889): 254. See also Chauncey, "From Sexual Inversion to Homosexuality," 142–3.

68 John D'Emilio has provided the most sophisticated analysis of this process in *Sexual Politics, Sexual Communities: The Making of a Homosexual Minority in the United States, 1940–1970* (Chicago: 1983). See also Toby Moratta, *The Politics of Homosexuality* (Boston: 1981), and the pioneering studies by Jeffrey Weeks and Lillian Faderman cited in note 62.

69 One would also hesitate to assert that a single definition of homosexuality obtains in our own culture. Jonathan Katz has made a similar argument about the need to specify the meaning of homosexual behavior and identity in his *Gay/Lesbian Almanac*, although our analyses differ in a number of respects (see my review in *The Body Politic* 97 (1983): 33–4).

70 Lillian Faderman, in "The Mordification of Love Between Women by 19th-Century Sexologists," *Journal of Homosexuality* 4 (1978): 73–90, and *Surpassing the Love of Men*, is the major proponent of the argument that the medical discourse stigmatized romantic friendships. Alternative analyses of the role of the medical literature and of the timing and nature of the process of stigmatization have been proposed by Martha Vicinus, "Distance and Desire: English Boarding-School Friendships," *Signs* 9 (1984): 600–22; Carroll Smith-Rosenberg, "The New Woman as Androgyne: Social Disorder and Gender Crisis, 1870–1936," in Smith-Rosenberg, *Disorderly Conduct: Visions of Gender in Victorian America* (New York: 1985), 245–96; and Chauncey, "From Sexual Inversion to Homosexuality." On the apparent ubiquity of the early twentieth-century public image

of the lesbian as a "mannish woman," see Esther Newton, "The Mythic Mannish Lesbian: Radclyffe Hall and the New Woman," *Signs* 9 (1984): 557–75. Nineteenth-century medical articles and newspaper accounts of lesbian couples stigmatized only the partner who played "the man's part" by dressing like a man and seeking male employment, but found the "womanly" partner unremarkable, as if it did not matter that her "husband" was another female so long as she played the conventionally wifely role (see Chauncey, "From Sexual Inversion to Homosexuality," 125ff). The medical reconceptualization of female deviance as homosexual object choice rather than gender role inversion was underway by the 1920s, but it is difficult to date any such transition in popular images, in part because they remained so inconsistent.

5

THE MEANINGS OF LESBIANISM IN POSTWAR AMERICA

Donna Penn

"Homosexual" describes both gay men and lesbians, but that usage may be deceptive for historians seeking to understand the emergence of homosexual identities. By the mid-twentieth century, most historians have argued that homosexuality becomes defined by the choice of sexual partner, replacing an older definition of homosexuality as gender disorder – the condition of the man, often effeminate in demeanor, who wanted to take the "woman's part" in sex. In this essay Donna Penn suggests that lesbianism, more than male homosexuality, has been persistently defined in reference to gender. In "expert" opinion, popular culture, and lesbian subcultures alike, the "masculine" woman or the "butch" has been a crucial signifier of lesbianism.

Penn begins with a brief commentary on two historical models of homosexuality. Women's historians have rejected sexual activity as the defining characteristic of lesbianism, instead emphasizing the significance of women's emotional relationships and life choices (for example, not marrying, living with other women). Historians of homosexuality, by contrast, have relied more heavily on sexual behavior, especially choice of sexual partner, in defining homosexual practice and the emergence of homosexual identities.

Penn argues that we must consider both sexuality and gender as they shape the social construction of lesbianism. In medical and popular discourses, the representation of lesbianism focused on the lesbian's refusal of heterosexual marriage and motherhood, her defiant social and sexual autonomy – that is, experts described the "pathology" of lesbianism not as a problem of abnormal sexuality, but of disordered gender. Lesbians themselves disagreed about proper gender roles and practiced butch/femme roles to varying degrees, but the "mannish" woman, or the butch, declared a difference that others could observe; the butch was thus crucial to the formation of lesbian subcultures and to the emergence of lesbian identities.

* * *

I had been a closet gay before I got married, about 1948, which means I had a relationship with a woman, and I'd been in love with her but I thought I was the only person in the world. There was no others in the world. I had never read a gay book. I didn't even know the word "gay". . .I didn't know the word "lesbian". . . . And I really believe that women used to dress mannish simply to get you to know who they were. . . . In those days it was very important.[1]

In recounting her experience as a young lesbian in the 1950s, Joan reminds us of the very different cultural landscape that existed for gays and lesbians in the days before the emergence of the gay liberation movement. With the relative absence of strictly defined gay political institutions and social organizations, women who "used to dress mannish" played a vital role in introducing others to gay life and its social centers. They were the vehicle by which those who thought they were the "only ones" found others. Further, by dressing mannish during a period when strict gender boundaries were being revitalized and reinforced, these women announced lesbianism to the general public as well. Now publicly identifiable, the masculine woman became the object of study among experts on sexual deviance, while popular disseminators of expert opinion embarked on something resembling a crusade to make meaning of the masculine woman. This essay explores the various meanings assigned to the masculine woman by social scientists and their popularizers and by lesbians themselves, in an effort to unravel the competing and conflicting discourses over lesbianism during the postwar years.

Scholarship in the history of lesbianism is at a curious crossroads. On the one hand, we have a slim body of scholarship written by women's historians, born in part out of the second wave of feminism, which has sought to reclaim a lost history of women-loving-women. In an effort to remedy what Blanche Cook called the "historical denial of lesbianism," these scholars rejected the use of sexual activity as the primary criterion for determining who was and who wasn't a lesbian and instead assigned the identity to those who derived emotional and at times economic and political sustenance from a homosocial world of women or in a couple relationship with another woman. This approach to determining who was a lesbian historically led scholars to attach the label to women who, given their social and cultural context, certainly would not have defined themselves as such. This weakness is a consequence, in part, of the failure to account for the role of deviance in the cultural construction of lesbianism.[2]

On the other hand, historians of homosexuality, who have in large part taken their cue from Michel Foucault, have offered historically specific accounts of the emergence of homosexuality as a species of being, an identity distinct from mere behavior which is in deviant relationship to dominant cultural notions pertaining to sex and sexuality.[3] Although this work has been useful in its adoption of social construction theory to explain the changing character of sexual meanings, identities, and discourses over time, it has for the most part failed to consider gender as a significant variable. This tendency has been reinforced by our current efforts to discredit the explanatory power of essentialism,[*] thereby allowing gender, as a social category that may shape a history specific to lesbians, to slip away. Thus, we have a gendered history that is desexualized, and a sexual history that is degendered.

Two papers that appeared in 1982 may have, unwittingly, helped bring us to this crossroads. Gayle Rubin delivered a talk on sexual stratification at the Barnard Conference in which she urged us to differentiate between gender and sexuality and, thereby, to develop a theory of sexual oppression distinct from that of gender. She argued:

> Feminism is the theory of gender oppression. To automatically assume that this makes it the theory of sexual oppression is to fail to distinguish between gender, on the one hand, and erotic desire, on the other. . . .Feminist conceptual tools were developed to detect and analyze gender-based hierarchies. . . .But as issues become less those of gender and more those of sexuality, feminist analysis becomes irrelevant and often misleading.[4]

---

* "Essentialism" is the position that differences between men and women are "natural" – that is, determined and explained by biological differences. See also *Introduction*, this volume.

Then George Chauncey, in a 1982 *Salmagundi* essay, charted medical doctors' understanding of homosexuality between 1880 and 1930 as they shifted from theories of complete *gender* inversion to those of same-sex *sexual* object choice as the defining characteristic of homosexuality. Chauncey claimed that although one set of theories never fully and completely replaced previous ones, "by the turn of the century. . .researchers increasingly distinguished passive or aggressive sexual behavior from sexual object, and the latter became the more important element in the medical classification of sexuality."[5]

Both these scholars contributed to a way of thinking about the history of homosexuality that focused on sexuality itself, or sexual object choice. They encouraged us to reconsider and in part at least to reject the previously dominant paradigms – the medical discourse that viewed gender inversion as the defining characteristic assigned to homosexuality, and the feminist discourse of the 1970s that claimed theories of gender as the key to understanding the particular oppression of lesbians.

Greatly influenced by these works, I thought that what would make me a historian of sexuality, or female sexuality, or lesbianism, would be a concern for differentiating notions of sexuality from those of gender – for viewing sex and gender as distinct categories of analysis. I expected to find in my own research notions of gender playing a less dominant role. Then I began examining the period from about 1945 through the 1960s. In both the expert discourse and in the memories of members of the lesbian subculture itself, I found that concerns about proper gender roles for women played a very prominent role in the construction of meaning of and about lesbian lives. Although Chauncey argues for a switch in conceptualization from gender inversion to sexual object choice as the defining characteristic of homosexuality, a review of the literature suggests this may be more true for men than for women.

Here, by re-examining some of the expert and popular discourse pertaining to lesbianism in the postwar period, I propose a reconsideration of the approach presented by Rubin and Chauncey. The significant preoccupation with and anxiety over the way lesbians transcended prescribed gender roles and expectations revealed in this literature demands another reading of the relations between sex and gender. Apparently the paradigm of gender inversion carried more meaning for a longer period of time with respect to lesbians than it did for male homosexuals. Certainly well into the postwar years, this way of thinking about the "problem" of female homosexuality still held enormous sway. The near obsession with the "masculine" woman or the "butch" as the "true homosexual" was asserted repeatedly by the so-called experts as well as by members of the subculture itself. Finally, in her defiance of prescribed gender appearance, the butch lesbian made an otherwise private sexuality public and visible and, in so doing, open to public scrutiny. While she reaffirmed the dominant culture's perception of what a lesbian was, she also made possible the creation and maintenance of a lesbian subculture and sense of community that existed beyond the boundaries of home.

EXPERT AND POPULAR OPINION IN THE POSTWAR ERA

By the 1950s, some consensus had been reached concerning the causes of homosexuality. Theories of glandular and hormonal imbalance as well as those of congenital or hereditary defect gave way to the opinion that homosexuality was psychological in origin. Although experts and popularizers offered different views on the psychological development of lesbians, most agreed that at its heart, lesbianism was a flight from adult responsibility. They argued that it was a flight, as well, from heterosexuality, but sexual object choice was not the key here. Rather, heterosexuality was taken to mean all the social responsibilities associated with a heterosexual way of life, most importantly marriage and family. Frank Caprio stated this position clearly in his 1954 study of what he called the psychodynamics of lesbianism. He asserted: "The lesbian who deliberately renounces marriage and motherhood is blind to the realization that her attitude represents a defensive rationalization for her inadequacy and flight from life's responsibilities."[6] W. Beran Wolfe, former Director of the Community Church Mental Hygiene Clinic of New York, concurred, claiming that "lesbian love. . .represents an evasion of the responsibilities of marriage and motherhood. . . ."[7]

According to the experts, this failure to assume life's responsibilities relegated the lesbian to a life of frustration and loneliness unless she could find a substitute outlet for her unconscious maternal desires. In some cases, this might be accomplished, in

Caprio's view, by "lavish[ing] their affections on a pet cat, dog, or bird, or they become attached to some childlike male invert and practically 'mother him.' "[8] For others, the adjustment to maternal desires was thought to be satisfied by a woman developing a mother/child relationship with her sexual partner. In both cases, she sublimated her "natural" instincts in socially, culturally, and psychologically deficient ways.

The blame for what was perceived to be the rising rate of lesbianism was placed at the doorsteps of so-called emancipated women and of parents who did not offer culturally appropriate gender role models for their children. In the wake of wartime changes, cultural anxiety concerning the future of the American family led experts and popularizers to view "psychic masculinity," or the so-called defeminization of American women, as both the cause and symptom of lesbianism.

This sentiment was echoed time and again by purveyors of the dominant discourse. The degree to which sexual maladjustment was a consequence of an improper balance between masculine and feminine attributes in both the parent(s) and the lesbian herself was most explicitly argued by George Henry who went so far as to describe homosexuals as "those who suffer from masculine-feminine conflicts."[9] While director of the Committee on Sex Variants, he conducted studies of hundreds of sexually deviant types. His cases and findings are reported in his more than 1,000-page tome entitled *Sex Variants*, which was then rewritten for a lay audience under the title *All the Sexes* in 1955.

In this volume, notably subtitled "A Study of Masculinity and Femininity," Henry was explicit about his belief that meddling in the balance between prescribed gender roles was both the source of and description for homosexuality. Domineering or masculine mothers and weak or feminine fathers produced children who failed to identify with and learn their appropriate sex role. The consequence was sexually deviant children who themselves suffered from false gender identification. Nonetheless, he was hopeful that if girls and women were encouraged to pursue feminine ideals they would be capable of attaining the "preferred goal in life; [that is] establishing and maintaining a home which involves the rearing of children."[10]

Similarly, in his 1964 journalistic investigation of the lesbian world, Jess Stearn provided the public with one of the first and most accessible accounts of lesbian life as he claimed to have witnessed it. In so doing, he covered a lot of old ground in new form for a lay audience. Among the views he helped to further was, again, that the root of lesbianism rested in the so-called emancipation of women. He noted that homosexuality, including lesbianism, had been spreading since the Second World War and that "the so-called emancipation of women, with the fairer sex taking a more active role in outside affairs, had a lot to do with the rise of homosexuality. . . . With the woman frequently absent from the home, there was no longer the emotional security and assurance that sensitive children required; no longer a strong parent image."[11]

Thus, inversion of traditional gender roles for women, resulting in the so-called masculine woman, was once again presented as the source of and description for lesbians. Increasingly, lesbianism came to be viewed less as a condition in which women choose other women as sexual objects than as an inversion of gender identity among women.

Caprio credits noted German sexologist Magnus Hirschfeld for providing him with a picture of a typical lesbian's childhood which included a preference for boys' games and a distaste for "feminine occupations."[12] Henry's study concurred. Masculinizing influences and tendencies were reported in more than 40 per cent of the "female variants" in his sample "who wished they had been boys. . .which agrees with the general impression that female sex variants are inclined to be masculine."[13] His evidence, like Hirschfeld's, harkened back to the subjects' childhoods during which a dislike of dolls was offered as an indication of masculine tendencies. Other masculine propensities included an interest in sports, fighting, and male clothing.

As late as 1967 the Research Committee on Female Homosexuality established by the Society of Medical Psychoanalysts included among its published findings items from the developmental history of their subjects which indicated a potential predisposition to homosexual adaptation. These items overwhelmingly consisted of examples of the failure of these women, when girls, to fulfil gender expectations, including a tendency toward fighting and the rejection of dolls in favor of guns and other boys' games. Thus, the Committee concluded, ". . .we see a significant avoidance of feminine activities, or of the female role itself. . . . We feel that the observation of this configuration in a preadult female. . .should alert the parents or the family physician to the possibility of developing homosexual orientation."[14]

The obsession with the so-called masculine lesbian reached a feverish pitch in Henry's book. With meticulous detail, he measured every inch of the variant's body in an effort to describe with exact precision the adaptation to gender characteristics of the opposite sex. Despite widespread belief in the psychosexual origins of homosexuality and lesbianism, and despite the contentions of historians who have argued that by this era homosexuality was understood as same-sex sexual object choice, Henry's tabulations suggested that lesbianism still had everything to do with gender inversion and a "flight from femininity." What Henry called "Sex Variant Characteristics" were reduced to a two-page table including the following images of lesbians:

> athletic with broad shoulders and narrow hips. . .; hair kept short, coarse, straight, brushed straight back with an excess on face, body and extremities; eyes are subtle with a scrutinizing appraisal of women; mouth is small with thin lips and demonstrates a limited, conservative movement of lips and tongue; voice is deep,. . .sharp,. . .and petulant with cold, harsh, cautious, and biting speech though sometimes soft, seductive, appealing or babyish with own sex. . . .[15]

The table continues, in the same vein, to chart clothing, presence or absence of jewelry and cosmetics, build and body type, carriage and gait – all decidedly unfeminine.

The near hysteria reflected in such writings was the culmination of at least a half century of anxiety with regard to the transformation of prescribed gender roles particularly as they pertained to women. Although experts have offered examples of lesbian activity in all ages and cultures, there was an apocalyptic quality to its appearance at this particular juncture in human history. By reading properly the disturbance in the masculine–feminine balance, those who focused on female sexual deviance believed one could foretell the destruction of the human race, albeit a white, middle-class race.

This disturbance in gender identity was, according to the prevailing wisdom, due in no small part to the so-called emancipation of women which had been accelerated by war and women's labor force participation. Failure to restore equilibrium between the sexes would result in future generations of sexual variants whose failure to reproduce would bring an end to civilization. Henry asserted:

> The rebellion of women. . .in the form of feminism. . .has resulted in equal suffrage and virtual elimination of the double standard of morals. Women now own more property than do men, they outlive men, and if they united they could control the government. . . . The present Occidental trend is in the direction of a matriarchal system, with increasing masculinity on the part of women. The ascendency of women has been fostered by political and industrial competition between the sexes, the increasing tendency on the part of both sexes to avoid parental and homemaking responsibilities, and the destruction of masculine males and preservation of feminine males by modern warfare. This gradual change may foreshadow for Western civilization a decline and fall such as that of the Roman Empire.[16]

Note that these are not the voices of a lunatic fringe, but in fact represent the opinion of respected mainstream "experts."

This conflation of gender and sexuality was presented again by Richard Robertiello in *Voyage from Lesbos*, a tedious 1959 account of his psychoanalytic sessions with a woman named Connie. The author cites as an indication of the success of treatment Connie's awakening interest in things "feminine." He notes,

> during the next session she told me that she was getting very interested in sewing and that she was busy fixing up her apartment. She said she was thinking how nice it would be to get into a domestic life again. She spoke of getting a rotisserie. The role of the housewife was beginning to look a little more appealing to Connie.[17]

He further encouraged her to believe that the level of responsibility she brought to her analytic work indicated that she was certainly responsible enough to handle the role of wife and mother.[18] The assumption operating here was that if Connie's interests could be made consistent with her gender, a reassignment in her choice of sexual object would necessarily follow.

Ward and Kasselbaum's 1965 sociological study of female prison life in Frontera, California, further illustrates that what was at issue was the degree to which lesbians came to be viewed as masculine women, and that it was on this basis that they were considered deviant and lesbian. The study noted that so-called masculine women were instructed to grow their hair longer, even report to the cosmetology department to wave or curl it, thereby reducing the overt manifestations of homosexuality. Evidence of deviance reported by the staff included more than merely sexual encounters between inmates. A woman "whose hair is crewcut and whose dress and mannerisms are strongly masculine" was thereby considered deviant.[19] Here, in an effort to differentiate between the so-called "true homosexuals" and the jailhouse turnouts – those merely engaging in homosexual behavior during their term in prison – the researchers focused intensely on masculine appearance as a feature of lesbianism. Particular attention was paid to body structure, feminine attractiveness, gait, carriage, posture, smoking technique, hairstyle and use or absence of makeup as evidence of particular women's assault on feminine virtues.[20]

This preoccupation with the masculine lesbian, the butch, was in no small part a consequence of her obvious violation of prescribed gender roles as reflected in her appearance. The concern with feminine lesbians, or femmes, on the part of the experts, centered around these women being unfortunate victims of the aggressive masculine type. The femme was a suitable candidate for successful psychotherapy since it was believed she could readjust her sexual desires toward men and thereby achieve heterosexuality and its attendant virtues of home and family. She was not a "true homosexual" in that she did not suffer from gender inversion; thus what barred her from achieving normal sexuality could be eliminated by some hours on the couch. For the butch, however, her choice of an inappropriate sexual object was desperately compounded by a gender misidentification. According to Ward and Kasselbaum, "the butch changes the love object *and* her own appearance and behavior, thereby substituting a role; the femme changes only the love object" (emphasis mine).[21]

Frequently, experts on homosexuality like to make note of the perception that public sanctions against lesbianism are not as severe as those pertaining to male homosexuality. They argue that, unlike male homosexuality, lesbianism has gone largely unnoticed by the culture or by professionals, owing to a variety of factors. First, they suggest that lesbians are not considered responsible for the spread of syphilis, which was the venereal disease of primary concern during the period under consideration; therefore, they did not pose a public health threat. In addition, lesbians, these experts argue, practice discretion in their sexual activity which has kept them relatively free of the legal authorities. Reported instances of solicitation or sexual activity in public places – the two crimes, along with child molestation, that formed the basis of much public fear of homosexuality and that landed many a gay man in prison – are statistically insignificant with respect to lesbians. Finally, experts and popularizers repeatedly stress, almost with a taint of regret, that in this culture women are permitted significant latitude in their affectionate expressions which, at best, masks female homosexuality behind acceptable standards of interaction, and at worst, arouses no suspicion. Thus, according to these experts, female homosexuality is generally overlooked. Further, they admit with disdain that many identified lesbians have no wish to change and staunchly assert that they are happy with their lives.

If, then, these women do not break the taboos of sexual expression and are not often tormented by their condition, what's the fuss? What is the basis upon which they are labeled deviant? I would argue that lesbians were labeled deviant to the degree that they symbolized, represented and actualized lives that defied strict gender distinctions during a period of profound anxiety regarding gender roles and the postwar restoration and maintenance of "normal" family life. Thus, increasingly, masculine appearance became the yardstick against which lesbianism was measured. Stearn, for instance, identified appearance as a criterion for spotting lesbians and was surprised when they did not fit his image. He wrote of one encounter, ". . .I couldn't help but note how wholesomely middle class she appeared. She would have been the last person I would have taken for a lesbian."[22]

As late as 1965, Howard Becker noted with amusement the disparity between his preconceived notions of lesbian appearance and what he discovered as reality, interestingly enough at a meeting of the foremost lesbian organization of the 1950s and 1960s, the Daughters of Bilitis:

> I was surprised. . .at how much the group looked like a middle-class women's club having a meeting to decide how to run the next charity bazaar. Since they were conventionally dressed, not in the least "butch," I found myself amused by the disparity between my conception of them and the reality.[23]

During this same period, the Massachusetts Society for Social Hygiene investigated locations suspected of commercial vice and attendant immorality and reported its findings to the local authorities, whether police or licensing boards. A report issued in 1959 included a list of bars that were described by the investigators as places that "were found to be frequented by individuals who bore characteristics of homosexuals."[24] These "apparent homos," as they were called, which included women, were identified by what the investigators termed "characteristics indicative of homosexuals."[25] One would be hard pressed to argue that by "characteristics" they meant choice of sexual object. Instead, although they are not explicit in this regard, I would argue that "characteristics" implies that which was visible, meaning qualities of appearance that failed to measure up to proper, culturally sanctioned gender traits.

And yet, despite my emphasis on the trespassing of gender boundaries as the defining characteristic for lesbianism during this period, we must be careful as scholars not to separate gender and sex in rigid analytical categories. Perhaps butch style was as much about sex as it was about gender, for acting and dressing like a man – assuming male privilege – included having sexual access to other women. Clearly lesbians of the time, like Joan whose words open this essay, understood that butch women would lead them to other women who chose women for sex. The "others" were not merely other women who dressed like men but, rather, other lesbians – women whose sexual object choices were other women. Among social scientists, as well, the concern about gender identity may have been a code for sexual desire. Therefore, in our efforts to reintroduce gender as a variable, we must be careful not to lose sight of the role of sex. The work of Liz Kennedy and Madeline Davis, Joan

Nestle, and Esther Newton all point to the sexual meanings of butch attire and remind us that butch style signaled, at least in part, someone who sought female sexual partners.[26] Consequently, although this essay focuses on the ways in which lesbianism was signified by butch women who defied gender role characteristics, at the very least in their appearance, we must not understate the extent to which traits of gender inversion also marked the presence of an "inverted" or "deviant" sexual identity.

VOICES FROM THE SUBCULTURE

The concern with masculine women did not escape the attention of lesbians themselves. Some attempted to dispel the notion of lesbians as masculine women by defending what they perceived as the very real femininity they experienced in lesbian circles. One mid-1950s witness criticized Radclyffe Hall's portrayal of Stephen Gordon, the lesbian protagonist of *The Well of Loneliness* (1928):

> I think it was bad science to suggest that an interest in sports, the habit of wearing tailored clothes, a desire to have a career are symptoms of sexual inversion in women. These things are not signs of sexual inversion and anyone who has any real knowledge of the subject knows that they are not. Most [female] homosexuals are usually very feminine in appearance, behavior, mannerisms, [and] taste. . . .[27]

In this context, Daughters of Bilitis (DOB) represented quite an interesting position. To the extent that they, too, understood that deviation from prescribed gender roles was the root of social discomfort and worse against lesbians, they sought to remedy the situation, in part, by helping lesbians rediscover their femininity. DOB asserted that when lesbians adhered to the rules of the subculture, particularly with respect to butch/femme appearance, an alternative conformity emerged that directed women away from their true nature as women. A primary mission of DOB was to reaffirm and reassert womanly qualities among lesbians. They viewed bars, for instance as sites of false gender consciousness in which conformity to perverse notions of gender was encouraged. Whereas, according to DOB, the bars fostered a complete depreciation of femininity, DOB sought to help lesbians be proud of their womanliness and femininity and to refuse to transform themselves into a "mockery" of men or "perversion" of themselves.

This tension within the subculture between those who participated in the lesbian bar culture, with its attendant commitment to a butch/femme way of life, and those who held the DOB position was articulated in the pages of the DOB journal, *The Ladder*. A message from the president of the organization that appeared in the November 1956 issue speaks directly to the organization's interest in clarifying the gender identity of lesbians by reminding them that they are women first, regardless of the object of their sexual desires. She stated: "Our organization has already. . .converted a few to remembering that they are women first and a butch or fem secondly, so their attire should be that which society will accept."[28]

Such notable literary figures as Marion Zimmer Bradley and Lorraine Hansberry addressed this point directly in letters to the editor of *The Ladder*. They each reaffirmed and supported DOB's position that the lesbian should adopt a mode of dress and behavior acceptable to society.[29] Zimmer expressed her feelings in the following way:

> I think Lesbians themselves could lessen the public attitudes by confining their differences to their friends and not force themselves deliberately upon public notice by deliberate idiosyncracies of dress and speech. . . .I believe that homosexuals and Lesbians might well. . .realize that their private life is of little interest to the public and to keep it to themselves.[30]

The efforts of the DOB to encourage lesbians to reassert and recommit themselves to an appropriate gender identity was in part intended as a challenge to a flourishing and largely working-class bar culture that was rooted in a butch/femme sensibility.

Given this context, how do we make meaning of the stories lesbians tell about their lives? Although there is a great range of opinion on the butch/femme dichotomy in the subculture itself, there remains a singular acknowledgment of its importance in the lesbian world, particularly the postwar lesbian world. Even those who were appalled by it comment on it with vigor – their distaste frequently rooted in the often-expressed sentiment, "we didn't really like the idea that they [butches and femmes] were representing us" to the outside world.[31]

And yet, to the lesbian who sought access to a gay world beyond herself, who sought a remedy to her isolation, who sought to interrupt the often-held belief that she was the only one, the butch played an absolutely key role that cannot be overemphasized. "Masculine" women made lesbianism public; they made an otherwise privatized sexuality visible. For the very reasons the purveyors of the dominant discourse, as well as members of DOB, were disturbed by these women, women who sought access to others found them crucial. Through butch women, they found their way to a lesbian subculture in which they could be among others like themselves. As one woman describes her own introduction to the gay world:

When I was 22, I brought my car to the car wash. . .and I see these butches, these women all in men's clothes working in this car wash and they fascinated me. . . . So I had my car washed almost every day. . . . I feel that in the '50s the only way we brought the ones that came out into our community was by usually looking gay to let them know "here we are, come join us." And it was the butch that did that. . . . I look at it as, if I had never found them, what would my life have been like? If you stop and think of it, how [else] would I have met them?[32]

This woman went on to explain her own experience of serving as the so-called masculine woman through whom others found access to the lesbian world. She and her friend, dressing in full butch attire, entered a straight bar in downtown Worcester, Massachusetts, for a quick drink:

. . .there were two women in there. . .and through the waitress they sent us a note, they said, "we would like to meet you but not in here. Outside". . . . What happened was they were gay and they lived down in the other section of town and they didn't know anybody who was gay and they spotted us. We introduced them to the other people and they came to our house parties and before you knew it, they were part of the community. So you see where that worked? Being butch brought other people into the community. . . . That's what the butch role was as far as I was concerned because that's how we made friends,

that's how people came into our community, became our
family. . . . The butch role had a reason, a purpose of
identification. . . . A real important purpose.[33]

It is my contention that whereas recent scholarship has urged
us to be careful to sort out gender and sexuality as distinct
categories of analysis, the writings of experts and the testimo-
nies of lesbians suggest that the postwar construction of lesbianism had much to do with gender. I do not mean to suggest that
in our efforts to restore gender to the analysis sex be overlooked;
merely that there must be a place for both in our investigation of
lesbianism in America. Further, I do not mean to suggest that
butch appearance was merely a signifier of lesbianism or a
statement about gender. Certainly there were specific butch as
well as femme identities that spoke directly to sexuality.
Instead, I am arguing that cultural anxiety and concern over
lesbianism had less to do with women choosing other women as
sexual objects than with the degree to which lesbians, particularly butch women who in their very appearance defied strict
adherence to prescribed gender roles, challenged what it was to
be a woman in American society. We need to appreciate the
very deep ways dominant cultural notions concerning gender
formed the basis for the assault on lesbians and, conversely,
how notions concerning lesbians were used to attack women
who challenged prescribed gender roles. Further, the construction of a history of lesbianism distinct from that of male homosexuality must account for the ways in which gender informs
this experience.

FINAL THOUGHTS OR NOTES ON FUTURE
DIRECTIONS

In a field as new as lesbian history, there remain numerous
areas yet untouched as well as important conceptual issues still
unsolved. In my own work I have encountered a critical problem represented in this essay: the problem of whether the
"experts" constructed lesbianism or merely discovered and described it. Recent scholarship in this field has tended to focus on
the subculture and its institutions as the context from which
cultural meaning was derived, developed, and imparted to new
members.[34] Yet this community did not exist in a subcultural

vacuum. However alternative or oppositional the subculture was, it and its members did not exist completely detached or distanced from the messages of the dominant culture. How then do we evaluate the relationship between hegemonic and oppositional discourses? How do we explore the language of the experts without offering them complete cultural authority over defining the meaning of lesbianism? At the same time, when examining the words of lesbians themselves, how do we make meaning of their experiences without, similarly, presenting a world untouched by dominant cultural messages? If, as Joan states at the beginning of this essay, she never even knew the word "lesbian," in what ways and in what contexts did this word acquire meaning for her? Was her relationship to the meaning and experience of lesbianism completely shaped by her participation in the lesbian subculture or was it in part derived from popular and expert ideology concerning lesbianism?

Clearly at issue here is the question of who gains authority over the discourse and, following from that, who holds cultural authority over defining the meaning of the experience. I have tried in this essay to convey a sense of competing discourses over the meanings of lesbianism during the postwar period even though the essay presents "expert" ideology first and then asks how well lesbians themselves subverted, resisted, or absorbed the opinions of the authorities. In so doing, I have given these "experts" at least partial control of *my* discourse. Only when we find a remedy to this problem will we be able to paint a more reliable portrait of the cultural history of lesbianism in America.

NOTES

First published in *Gender & History* 3, 2 (Summer 1991): 190–203. Used by permission. The author would like to thank Mari Jo Buhle, John D'Emilio, and especially Estelle Freedman for their comments on an earlier draft of this essay.

1 Interview with "Joan," conducted 7 January 1990.
2 For some of the literature that equates nineteenth-century women's relationships with lesbianism, see Blanche Wiesen Cook, "Historical Denial of Lesbianism," *Radical History Review* 20 (1979): 60–5; Cook, "Women Alone Stir My Imagination," *Signs* 4 (1979): 718–39; Frances Doughty, "Lesbian Biography, Biography of Lesbians," *Frontiers* 4, (1979): 76–9; Adrienne Rich, "Compulsory Heterosexuality and Lesbian Existence," in Ann Snitow, Christine

Stansell, and Sharon Thompson, eds, *Powers of Desire: The Politics of Sexuality* (New York: 1983), 177–205; Bonnie Zimmerman, "On Writing Biography of Lesbians," *Sinister Wisdom* 9 (1979): 95–7. For critiques of this approach, see especially Leila Rupp, "Imagine My Surprise," *Frontiers* 5, 3 (1981): 61–70; Gayle Rubin, "Thinking Sex: Notes for a Radical Theory of the Politics of Sexuality," in Carole S. Vance, ed., *Pleasure and Danger: Exploring Female Sexuality* (Boston: 1984), 267–319; and Alice Echols, "Taming of the Id," in Vance, ed., *Pleasure and Danger*, 50–72.

3 Among those who draw on Foucault's theoretical contribution are John D'Emilio, "Capitalism and Gay Identity," in Snitow, *et al.*, eds, *Powers of Desire*, 100–16; D'Emilio, *Sexual Politics, Sexual Communities: The Making of a Homosexual Minority in the United States, 1940–1970* (Chicago: 1983); Jeffrey Weeks, *Coming Out: Homosexual Politics in Britain from the Nineteenth Century to the Present* (London: 1979); Estelle Freedman, "Uncontrolled Desires: The Response to the Sexual Psychopath 1920–1960," *Journal of American History* 74, 1 (1987): 83–106; Robert Padgug, "Sexual Matters: On Conceptualizing Sexuality in History," *Radical History Review* 20 (1979): 3–23; Jeffrey Weeks, "Movements of Affirmation: Sexual Meanings and Homosexual Identities," *Radical History Review* 20 (1979): 164–79; George Chauncey, "Fairies, Gay Men and the Reorganization of Male Homosexual Categories in Twentieth Century NYC," unpublished paper delivered at the International Scientific Conference on Gay and Lesbian Studies (Dec. 1987), Free University of Amsterdam; Kenneth Plummer, ed., *The Making of the Modern Homosexual* (London: 1981).

4 Rubin, "Thinking Sex," in Vance, ed., *Pleasure and Danger*, 307–9.

5 George Chauncey, "From Sexual Inversion to Homosexuality: Medicine and the Changing Conceptualization of Female Deviance," *Salmagundi* 58/59 (1982/3): 123.

6 Frank S. Caprio, *Female Homosexuality: A Psychodynamic Study of Lesbianism* (New York: 1954), 11.

7 W. Beran Wolfe as quoted in Caprio, *Female Homosexuality*, 266.

8 Caprio, *Female Homosexuality*, 90.

9 George W. Henry, *All the Sexes: A Study of Masculinity and Femininity* (New York: 1955), 527.

10 Ibid., 530, 581.

11 Jess Stearn, *The Grapevine* (New York: 1964), 59.

12 Caprio, *Female Homosexuality*, 265.

13 Henry, *All the Sexes*, 245.

14 Harvey E. Kaye, Soll Berl, Jack Clare, *et al.*, "Homosexuality in Women," *Archives of General Psychiatry* 17 (1967): 631–2.

15 Henry, *All the Sexes*, 286–7.

16 Ibid., 528–9.

17 Richard Robertiello, *Voyage from Lesbos: Psychoanalysis of a Female Homosexual* (New York: 1959), 103.

18 Ibid., 136.

19 David A. Ward and Gene G. Kasselbaum, *Women's Prisons: Sex and Social Structure* (Chicago: 1965), 85.

20 Ibid., 105.
21 Ibid., 113.
22 Stearn, *The Grapevine*, 300.
23 Howard S. Becker, "Deviance and Deviates," *The Nation* 201, 8 (20 September 1965): 117.
24 Massachusetts Society for Social Hygiene, report on *Commercialized Prostitution Conditions in Boston, Massachusetts and Environs*, April 1959 (Schlesinger Library, Radcliffe College), 7.
25 *Commercialized Prostitution Conditions in Boston, Massachusetts and Environs*, October 1960 (as in n. 24), 8.
26 Joan Nestle, *Restricted Country* (Ithaca, NY: 1987); Elizabeth Kennedy and Madeline Davis, "Oral History and the Study of Sexuality in the Lesbian Community: Buffalo, NY, 1940–60," *Feminist Studies* 12, 1 (1986): 7–26; Esther Newton, "Mythic Mannish Lesbian: Radclyffe Hall and the New Woman," *Signs* 9 (Summer 1984): 557–75.
27 Quoted in Caprio, *Female Homosexuality*, 240. Hall's now classic lesbian novel was the subject of an obscenity trial and sparked widespread controversy.
28 D. Griffin, "The President's Message," *The Ladder*, 1, 2 (November 1956): 3 (reprinted by Arno Press, 1975).
29 "MZB," *The Ladder*, 1, 8 (May 1957): 20–1; "LHN", *The Ladder*, 1, 8 (May 1957): 26–8.
30 "MZB," *The Ladder*, 21.
31 Interview with "Dusty," conducted by Donna Penn, 18 January 1990 (in author's possession).
32 Interview with "LB," conducted by Chris Czernik, November 1984.
33 Ibid.
34 See especially George Chauncey, "Christian Brotherhood or Sexual Perversion," this volume, 72.

Part II

WORK AND CONSUMPTION IN VISUAL REPRESENTATIONS

6

ART, THE "NEW WOMAN," AND CONSUMER CULTURE

Kenneth Hayes Miller and Reginald Marsh on Fourteenth Street, 1920–40

Ellen Wiley Todd

Ellen Todd uses art to reveal the shifting discourse of womanhood in the 1920s and 1930s. Examining the paintings of two urban realists, Kenneth Hayes Miller and Reginald Marsh, Todd finds a typology of female figures that both echo and remake contemporary images of womanhood. Like Christina Simmons, Todd uses these cultural representations to uncover contemporary debate about the sexual revolution and its revisions of gender. Moreover, Miller's and Marsh's paintings provocatively suggest the intertwining of the debates about the sexual revolution, the New Woman, and consumer culture. Miller's matronly shopper suggests resistance to the feminist claims of his time; his female figures have a certain look of modernity, but they participate in public life solely through the contained and limited role of shopping. Marsh's sirens embody a bolder version of modern womanhood and, at times, suggest a critical stance: Marsh comments on the manipulation of the erotic in advertising and film, and the shifting terms of sexual exchange and negotiation.

Feminist art historians have contributed to the emerging history of gender by arguing that visual images play an important part in reproducing and revising cultural constructions of manhood and womanhood. They interpret paintings not simply as objects of aesthetic value and demonstrations of artistic skill, but as cultural texts that rely on prevailing ideas of gender. This method of interpretation recognizes the special character and conventions of art works, but it also emphasizes that paintings – like books, movies, comic books, or advertisements – are produced and viewed within a larger culture. Skeptical of a view that romanticizes the artist as individual genius, these critics take up the assumptions of a social history of art, depicting artists as historical actors who are shaped by their society even as they influence it. Todd and other revisionist art historians, then, interpret the traditional sources of art history – "fine arts" painting and sculpture – within a larger visual and cultural landscape. She discusses Miller's and Marsh's work as part of a tradition of art history, finding sources of their imagery in Renaissance painting. She also sees these painters, however, as observers of the contemporary scene and compares their imagery to the representations of women in advertising, movie posters, and journalism.

* * *

In the 1920s and 1930s, several urban realist painters from a group later called the Fourteenth Street School fashioned a new iconography of urban types that included women shoppers, retail sales clerks, and office workers pictured as pedestrians on city streets. The artists, among them Kenneth Hayes Miller and his student Reginald Marsh, found these subjects near their studios located in the commercial district on Fourteenth Street and Union Square just north of New York City's Greenwich Village. Known as "the poor man's Fifth Avenue," the Fourteenth Street neighborhood housed bargain clothing stores, cheap movie theaters, small offices, banks, and insurance companies which provided goods, services, and jobs for the immigrant and working-class population of New York's Lower East Side.

Although their reputations faded in the post-Second World War era with the growing interest in modern abstract art, Miller and Marsh were well known in their day. Their works were widely exhibited and purchased by major museums and frequently discussed in mainstream art journals and newspapers. The artists worked from two traditions of urban realism, one European, one American. Like the mid-nineteenth-century French Realists and Impressionists, they adopted Baudelaire's belief that artists must be of their own time, painting the contemporary spectacle of commerce and leisure at the heart of the city. Like the turn-of-the-century American Ashcan School artists, they found their subjects among the lower middle and working classes. Ashcan realists like Robert Henri and John Sloan claimed that these subjects gave the viewer a more authentic experience of city life than the depictions of aristocratic men and women at home or on the uptown boulevards – paintings that formed the accepted canon of American art in the early years of the twentieth century. Although they inherited their realist beliefs from the earlier artists, Miller and Marsh also came to realism from different artistic experiences that in turn shaped their female imagery. Miller, who was born in 1876, retained a strain of academic practice from years of painting the monumental female nude in the tradition of Renaissance artists. He only became interested in the contemporary scene in the early 1920s. Marsh came to New York in 1920 as a Yale art school graduate. In contrast to Miller, he worked as a cartoonist and illustrator of city life for a range of publications, from the *New Yorker* and *Vanity Fair* to the tabloid *Daily News*, before turning to painting. As realists – whose art by definition offers some mediated window onto contemporary experience – and as artists working from different practices with different conventions for portraying the figure, Miller and Marsh offer revealing glimpses of changing images of women in their art.

Thus, in examining the art of these two artists, I ask *how* their images of shoppers or working women reinforce or undermine contemporary ideologies that molded women's lives in the interwar period.[1] Each of the new female "types" created by the artists engages some aspect of the debates surrounding women's lives. All these images embody features of a revised "New Woman," a representation of womanhood that emerged in the mid-1920s to modify perceptions and typologies and to critique experiences and choices that had characterized the older "New Woman" since the turn of the century. To place these images within this broader discourse of new womanhood I combine a close examination of the paintings and the reconstruction of the artists' personal and professional lives with a study of different kinds of historical texts: recent histories on women's domestic and working lives and on the feminist movement between the wars, new studies and early debates on consumer culture, shopping guides, and advice literature to women on how to behave in the workplace. In addition, recent concerns in feminist art history, feminist theory, and women's history have shaped my questions and methods of analysis and informed my own position as a viewer and interpreter of the paintings. I envision new womanhood and other representations of women as socially constructed and historically shifting categories. There is no single image of womanhood in this or any other period, as these two different typologies demonstrate. Visual representations of women are produced by historically situated makers, under specific historical and institutional circumstances. Many realist paintings in the 1930s, for example, followed the prevailing artistic injunction to paint the daily lives of average American men and women. Such images reflected but also informed perceptions of changing social reality, including the lives of women.

Viewers of Miller's and Marsh's paintings found a modern generation of urban women, different from their middle- to upper-middle-class predecessors. Turn-of-the-century commentators, observing the bourgeois woman's growing engagement with educational, political, and occupational pursuits outside the home, began to characterize her as the "New Woman," an independent person with a public role. Around 1900, for example, the new woman had a college education, campaigned for the vote, became a social worker in the spirit of Progressive era reform and frequently remained single. By the teens, the emergence of a modern discourse on feminism and debates about sexuality sharpened discussions about the new woman. Successive generations of men and women from various political and social perspectives invoked the phrase "New Woman" in analyzing and celebrating the changing behavior of modern women – or abhorring and condemning it. Although "New Womanhood" most often referred to middle-class experience and types, by the First World War the designation "New Woman" cut across class and occupational boundaries and encompassed a variety of stereotypes. Whether she was characterized as a tough spinster feminist, a fast-dancing flapper, a free-love Greenwich Village bohemian, an avid careerist, a working mother, or a "charity girl" (a poor factory worker who occasionally exchanged sexual favors for "treats"), the typologies of new womanhood exemplified women's increasing engagement with social spaces that were public, urban, and modern.[2] Moreover, as Carroll Smith-Rosenberg has argued, the New Woman challenged existing gender relations and the distribution of power.[3]

From the late 1920s through the first years of the Depression there was a fresh outpouring of literature on feminism and the new woman. Some commentators argued that feminism was outmoded, having served its purpose of bringing women out of their separate sphere into the modern world; others, fearing feminism's utopian projection of a genderless world, countered by invoking the importance of the family to social cohesion.[4] In 1927 journalist Dorothy Dunbar Bromley proclaimed the "Feminist – New Style" in a *Harper's Monthly* article that exemplified this new formulation. Bromley approvingly described the post-franchise woman who set aside political demands for equality, caricaturing past and present feminists as "either the old school of fighting feminists who wore flat heels and had very little feminine charm, or the current species who antagonize men with their constant clamor about maiden names, equal rights, woman's place in the world, and many another cause. . .*ad infinitum*."[5] Bromley's new woman believed in being chic, and preferred "to keep the intonations of her voice and the quality of her gestures purely feminine, as nature intended them to be."[6] Indeed she preferred to work with men because their methods were more direct than women's and she found it "amusing" to flirt. Fond of men and frankly heterosexual, she was interested in a full life that included interests outside the home as well as marriage and children. Acknowledging the new sexual mores, she condemned the promiscuity of Greenwich Village rebels as simply impractical, but conceded the passionate premarital affair that would be left "courageously" at its conclusion. Moreover, her husband "must satisfy her as a lover and a companion," along with passing on mental and physical traits she admired to her children.[7] Finally, Bromley accepted women's right to work for wages, to attempt the difficult combination of career with marriage, and to participate in the democratic process. But the revised 1920s "feminist" emphasized individual rather than collective goals and embraced female and domestic occupations. This shift from political engagement to self-involvement was also touched by and reflected the division in the postfranchise women's movement. Moderate feminists, the majority, espoused a view of gender differences and sought reform to protect women as future mothers. More militant feminists pressed for full equality, most notably in the National Woman's Party.[8] Although I do not identify the Fourteenth Street School's shoppers as members of a specific feminist constituency, they do share features of the revised new woman as that type is articulated in the 1920s and 1930s.

Two recurring female types illustrate Miller's and Marsh's participation in interpreting and remaking contemporary gender ideology. Analyzed in conjunction with selected dialogues about women's roles and behavior in the new consumer culture, these paintings show the artists' selective use and revision of available images of women. Kenneth Hayes Miller's matronly shopper, described by art critics as a mature and "robust" woman of the people who was "maternal and companionable," resembles the newly created professionalized homemaker of the 1920s.[9] This version of the new woman promoted the housewife to expert manager and consumer – no more domestic drudge, but a professional in the home. Advertisers and business spokespersons (usually male) joined female home economists in fashioning tools and strategies to continue the rationalization of housework begun at the turn of the century. The federal government established the Bureau of Home Economics in 1923, signaling a recognition of women's issues beyond the franchise for many of the women's groups supporting home economics. Many women used the new science to claim professional employment as home economists, to redefine their unpaid work in the home, and to refashion the domestic sphere through the new ideology of consumption.[10] Reginald Marsh's voluptuous shopper, modeled on the mysterious femme fatale or the wisecracking blond bombshells like Mae West or Jean Harlow, was defined in her Fourteenth Street guise by another 1930s art critic as a woman of the humbler class, "gaudy, full-bosomed and hungry for pleasure, yet immensely appealing."[11] This sultry siren of movie and fashion fame eagerly consumed fashion and beauty products designed to help her attract a man. Both artists used their pictorial strategies to articulate these new and supposedly liberated models of womanhood. Occasionally their works also suggest critical commentary on consumer culture and an awareness of feminist claims. These paintings, then, offer a glimpse of the renegotiation of womanhood as Marsh and Miller worked with and revised prevalent images.

In a 1928 painting called simply *Shopper*, 1928 (fig. 6.1), Miller's archetypal shopper is both old style and new style, modern and traditional. Poised before a Fourteenth Street hat display, she wears all the latest middle-class fashions – a snugly fitting cloche hat, the straight dress softly belted at the hips, and a choker of big beads. But Miller's matron seems dumpy and round, not sleek and streamlined like the art deco style fashion models that filled the pages of high-style magazines such as *Vogue*. In the shopper's full-bodied proportions – echoed formally throughout the picture in rounded hats and columnar backdrop – and in her balanced pose, we recognize a long line of Renaissance beauties and classical goddesses. By connecting his up-to-date woman with a tradition of idealized goddesses in art, whose pose and proportions symbolized enduring models of nurture, beauty, and fertility, Miller elevates the shopper and transforms her into a goddess of commerce.

Other signs of the coexistence of traditional and modern womanhood appear in this and other shopper images. The demure, self-protective pose of the modest Venus only partially masks the shopper's sexuality, revealed in her ample proportions, the coy sidelong glance and the umbrella as phallus held between her legs. Phallic columns frame or tower above the shopper here and in other Miller images. Such symbols of power allude to the noticeably absent male for whom she shops – men rarely appear in Miller's works – whether in her role as homemaker or to present a more attractive self. The use of such overt phallic references in his work came from Miller's intellectual and social preoccupation with Freud's theories of sexuality; the artist regularly told students that he wanted to put "Freudian things" into his work.[12]

The Miller shopper as modern goddess of commerce appears in other situations. In *The Fitting Room*, 1931 (fig.6.2), the group of three women on the left recall the Three Graces as the central woman takes a pose that is at once contemporary and reminiscent of Old Master painting. The 1930s viewers of Miller's painting might well have recognized in the pose Hollywood publicity shots of movie stars and the presentation of a potent sexual self. In *Sidewalk Merchant*, 1932/1940 (fig.6.3), Miller re-enacts the first beauty contest, the Judgment of Paris. For Venus, Juno, and Minerva – goddesses who, in the mythical account, competed for a golden apple inscribed "to the fairest" – Miller substitutes the three foreground shoppers posed again like the Three Graces. Paris, the judge, now becomes the Hawker, proffering packaged goods that will transform the recipient into "the fairest." Apart from using iconographic precedents and

Figure 6.1 Kenneth Hayes Miller, *Shopper*, 1928.

devices that suggest an old style/new style woman, Miller placed women in settings whose formal designs enhance their womanliness and stabilize or contain them. As in so many of his works, Miller orchestrated his design around curves and countercurves that exaggerate the women's roundness and femininity. They are often framed by the curved columns, enfolded within the design by the curved forms: sometimes umbrellas, the rounded cloche hats, and enveloping furs. In *The Fitting Room*, flat architectural pilasters anchor the women in place while furs connect them and bind them together.

While Miller's women in the public arena appear reasonably up-to-date if somewhat contained or controlled by their settings, his other images reveal his full affirmation of a more traditional ideology of wifehood and motherhood. In one *Mother and Child* image of 1927, the mother sports a contemporary bobbed haircut and wears a fashionable dressing gown widely advertised in clothing catalogs of the mid-1920s. Yet his use of the prototypical Renaissance Madonna and Child imparts a sacred quality to modern motherhood. Similarly, Miller's use of bathing Venuses as models for his many images of nude matrons at their toilette ritualizes self-beautification and again elevates the status of its practitioner to domestic goddess.

The more striking contrast between Miller's matronly shopper/homemaker and the new woman comes when we compare his women with the flapper, the most popular version of the new woman type as immortalized by the illustrator John Held (fig.6.4). Held's flapper was young, savvy, and independent; she comfortably sported daring clothes and engaged in pastimes that undermined all previous notions of genteel womanhood – dancing, and petting on unchaperoned dates in automobiles which aided her new-found freedom. Nurtured by a climate of rising affluence calling for increased consumption of fashion and beauty products, by Freudian psychology, by advertising and the movies, the flapper also came to symbolize women's independence for those who saw the 1920s as a decade of women's liberation.[13]

Miller's approximation of the flapper appears in his *Party Dress*, 1928 (fig. 6.5). This model wears the latest in skimpy dress with her short hair closely cut and shingled in a new permanent wave. But she appears self-consciously uncomfortable in her costume. She sits primly, eyes modestly lowered,

Figure 6.2 Kenneth Hayes Miller, *The Fitting Room*, 1931.

Figure 6.3 Kenneth Hayes Miller, *Sidewalk Merchant*, 1932–40.

Figure 6.4 John Held, dancing flapper, *McClure's* cover, c. 1926.

contained by the chair which surrounds her. Apart from her dress, she bears little resemblance to the brazen Held flapper doing the Charleston. Here, freedom is manifested in far-flung gestures, jutting chin, and jagged hemlines. Assertive angles define the independence of the Held figure, while soft curves express the vulnerability and matronly potential of Miller's feminine lady. The title of Miller's painting is also telling. *Party Dress* describes the commodity by which the young woman has made herself elegant and contemporary. But under this dress whose daring cut symbolizes freedom from constraint is a young woman tied by pose, demeanor, and romantic dream to a vision of womanhood which holds that her independence should be but temporary. She is reflective and attendant; clutching a boutonniere she waits for the absent man who will give her status and identity. Moreover, as historian Christina Simmons points out (see pp. 31–2, this volume), the flapper remained a youthful innocent, not yet able to claim a fully developed sexuality no matter what her independent stance and, as a consequence, ripe for male attention.

Compared with the flapper model, much of Miller's 1920s imagery provides evidence that the new look only masks ongoing cultural tensions between an older female ideal of nurture, companionability, and stabilizing docility and the newer image of self-centeredness, vitality, independence, and sexuality. Miller's matrons wear the flapper's fashions – outward signs of equality and liberation – but thanks to the Old Master conventions, Miller's affirmation is more overtly qualified, and conventional stereotypes of maternal femininity remain in force. The image affirms independence as a temporary youthful interlude to be followed by conventional domesticity.

Miller's matronly shopper can also be seen as a version of the revised new woman in her specific role as the professionalized homemaker and consumer of the 1920s. We can understand her appearance and persona as part of the dialogue that emerged in the 1920s, under the rubric of what one spokeswoman for the American Home Economics Association called a "back to the home movement." At that time, home economists, sociologists, psychologists, and business spokespersons began to redefine homemaking to take into account economic, technological, and political changes that had altered women's lives.[14] While the overt aims of this back-to-the-home movement were to restabilize

Figure 6.5 Kenneth Hayes Miller, *Party Dress*, 1928.

the family and reaffirm marriage in ways that recognized the new woman's postfranchise equality, the covert ideology was a homebound conception of womanhood which now made consumption a central part of her role. Miller's matronly shopper echoes this new conception of woman – one that combined modernity with domesticity.

Whether active proponents of the back-to-the-home movement or general advocates of renewed family stability, writers and advertisers found ways to reactivate the joys of domestic life and modernize the homemaker. Recognizing that the new woman had often worked before marriage and had higher expectations of herself, many sought new strategies for simplifying household activities. Advertisers and illustrators found ways to suggest that housework was challenging, fantastic, or even sexual, as *Life Magazine's* blissfully smiling kitchen witch astride a soaring vacuum cleaner makes clear (fig. 6.6). Numerous studies borrowed managerial rhetoric and streamlined housework through complicated flow charts. Such writers elevated the housewife to "home executive" or "domestic engineer" and made her a member of the household "board of directors," an equal partner with her spouse.[15] Most important for our understanding of the matronly shopper, they made proper consumption the key to family stability. Ignoring the fundamental inequality of woman's economic dependence on her spouse, writers argued that by consuming correctly she could produce more wealth, ensure family happiness, and even contribute to national well-being. In the introduction to his 1929 publication, *The Shopping Book*, written ostensibly to underscore the helplessness of the woman consumer against fully rationalized businesses, William Baldwin nevertheless granted the shopper an extraordinary level of power and responsibility:

> Running homes is the greatest single business in America, towering above steel production, transportation, the motor industry, and other familiar yardsticks of power and size. The shopper is paramount. On the one hand she controls the comfort and attractiveness of the home – the standard of living as it is actually applied; On the other hand she holds the destiny of great industries.[16]

The Miller image can be seen as icon of the professionalized homemaker. In a work like *Sidewalk Merchant*, the women

Figure 6.6 F. A. Leyendecker, "A Modern Witch", *Life Magazine* cover, 1923.

emerge from the store, crowded with other happy shoppers, some carrying packages. Miller emphasized the congruence between the shopper and consumption in compositional terms, rhyming simplified shapes that define both her and her purchases. Miller never used models when he painted. He developed instead a standard female type, like a mass-produced product. The cast and character of his women's heads are echoed in the mannequin's features in store window displays. The central figure imitates and consumes that which is displayed; and she shares that value with a community of like-minded women behind her, dressed in a manner like her own. Her upward-turned face, like that of a baroque saint in ecstasy, is suffused with a glow which indicates the joy of successful consumption, which some recent historians have argued became a substitute for traditional religion.[17]

Miller's shopper was thus basically a middle-class woman rather than a downtrodden one. Throughout the Depression, even though the painter was surrounded by more radical constituencies on Fourteenth Street who protested regularly against capitalism, Miller, consistent with his own conservative politics, rarely modified his contented matronly type formed in the 1920s – though he often showed her hunting for bargains, or occasionally coarsened her features. By contrast, artists and cartoonists working for the radical *New Masses* often exaggerated the girth of the fat shopper to symbolize the greedy capitalist, well-off and well-fed at the expense of others. Miller's paintings of stable, full-bodied matrons signified prosperity and familial well-being. Within the context of the Depression this image implied that in spite of hard times, financial stability would re-emerge, consumption would continue, and society would prosper. Such attitudes are embodied in an idealized model of substantial and nurturing womanhood, taken from earlier artistic sources. The choice of an Old Master model itself implies the value placed on continuity and tradition over radical cultural change. The image dovetails with the ideology of the back-to-the-home movement, revealing in pictorial form the ways in which artistic culture accommodated to shifts in economic and social patterns while adhering to and perpetuating cherished values.

Several years after he began instructing Reginald Marsh in the art of painting, Miller wrote to the younger artist, "You are a painter of the body and sex is your theme."[18] Miller was undoubtedly referring to Marsh's depiction of sexually provocative young women, modeled on the popular siren stereotype as opposed to his own use of classical Venuses and Renaissance madonnas. Though she emerged in the 1920s alongside the flapper, the siren dominated the popular imagination throughout the Depression; her looks and behavior projected a new ideal of mysterious and alluring femininity. This model, codified by a host of advertisers and movie producers, became so powerful that women appropriated features of it for their own purposes, as they had with the flapper. Young working-class women imitating the siren's look became the subject of Marsh's paintings.

Marsh's voluptuous model of womanhood looks and behaves very differently from the Miller matron. In contrast to the Miller type, an image of clarity and stability rendered in simplified figure compositions and settings, Marsh's voluptuous shopper is often trapped in a texture of confusion and uncertainty. Marsh's crowds, like those pictured in *In Fourteenth Street*, 1932 (fig. 6.7), are chaotic, with figures woven together into an all-over surface matrix of blurred bodies. Only a few sharp colors break out from his limited palette of Old Master browns, golds, and grays. He uses a flickering, patchy chiaroscuro created by a jittery brushwork to exaggerate the motion and confusion we often find in his pictures. Unlike Miller's shopper, who remains a homemaker and is pictured in comfortable middle-class settings when not shopping, Marsh's shopper never appears with children or at home. Instead this siren-style woman, whom Marsh's critics subsequently named the Marsh girl, is a Coney Island beach bather, a burlesque queen, or a taxi-dance hall girl, offering herself for ten cents a dance. Or she works as a live store model, tantalizing the viewer like a stripper on a burlesque runway, as in *Hudson Bay Fur Company*, 1932 (fig. 6.8). The Marsh Girl was a working-class woman, caught up in popular forms of mass entertainment that attracted many members of her social class in the early years of the Depression. For her, consumption was both a form of popular entertainment and a means of transformation – never part of a homebound womanhood.

For all their dissimilarities, Marsh's siren, like Miller's professionalized homemaker, embodied an American ideal of womanhood,

Figure 6.7 Reginald Marsh, *In Fourteenth Street*, 1934.

Figure 6.8 Reginald Marsh, *Hudson Bay Fur Company*, 1932.

144

an alluring sexualized model that accommodated only superficially to feminist ideals of equality and independence. But Marsh's image of the siren shopper is not merely presented as a packaged screen idol, a potent, depersonalized object of sexual desire. Nor is she simply a performer in an enticing consumer culture to be preyed upon, desired, and eventually acquired by the viewer's (and specifically the implicit male viewer's) gaze – though she is that in part. Instead, Marsh's paintings function as part of a larger discourse in which commentators perceived the siren not just as a victim of male desire and consumer culture, but also as a powerful individual, liberated by consumer choice. Moreover, in the depressed economic climate of the 1930s, displays of her provocative power recall the earlier Homeric meanings of the siren figure – part monster and dangerous to men. At a time when traditional masculine prerogatives seemed compromised by unemployment and the resulting inability to support a family, an energetic sexualized female figure could be interpreted as a defiant threat to masculine claims to social and economic power. Marsh's paintings reveal an ambivalent view of the siren through pictorial strategies that combined forms and subjects from popular culture and from Old Master paintings. His works suggest the contradictory qualities of power and passivity, desirability and unattainability that were part of the siren's persona.

Though often part of a crowd, Marsh's sirens receive dramatic focus. Isolated pictorially, they are often placed in larger pockets of space so that they pop out at the viewer like cut-out fantasies when compared to other crowd members. They wear bright-colored clothes and makeup, standing out as cheerful antidotes to the frequently dingy scenes that surround them. His siren is also a goddess, set apart from other women as if on a pedestal to be worshiped for her aloof and mysterious beauty. In fact these attributes of Marsh's siren were all part of a siren myth as packaged and sold by advertisers and the Hollywood film industry. Journalist Mildred Adams also described her as liberated. In her 1929 *New York Times* article, "Now the Siren Eclipses the Flapper," Adams instructed the "New Woman" to abandon the boisterous energetic behavior practiced by the flapper because all her rights were now won. The siren was to renew her convenant with femininity and strive to nurture and please men rather than competing with them. The new 1930s model should

145

be seductively serene and ladylike, wear clothes "molded to her figure to accentuate every line and curve," and behave with charm and that mysterious allure that would allow her to retain a reserve of power over men. Eventually, Adams argued, through "devious ways of courtship" women would achieve marriage and security – still the same goals. But women would also perform a valuable social function that feminists and flappers had wrongfully avoided. Beauty and charm cushioned everyone from the onslaughts of a "grimy hardworking world" much the same way that Marsh's siren sparkles against the tawdry backdrop of Fourteenth Street or Coney Island.[19]

Like publicists who elevated the homemaker, Adams assured the aspiring siren of her "independence" and her ability to manage her life with this new look and behavior. In reality, Adams's assertions masked an antifeminist rhetoric that advocated subservience to men. Her notions of liberation were conciliatory and limited to a belief that superficial changes in social conventions meant full-scale equality. Furthermore, Adams ignored demands for economic and political equality and urged women to use charm to make themselves into objects of male pleasure. Like the professionalized homemaker, the siren put male needs ahead of her own; the power of her sexuality would be traded for domesticity once she got her man.

Marsh's rendition of the siren suggests the artist's ambivalence about such openly sexual women. Pictorially, the Marsh girl displays her power by making herself desirable, yet also unattainable. More lovely by far than other figures in her neighborhood, she becomes an object of desire even as she remains aloof, an unrevealing stereotype rather than an individualized woman. Finally, throughout his work, Marsh frequently places the siren adjacent to emotionally or physically crippled men to suggest the relationship between her potency as an object of desire and her unattainability. In *In Fourteenth Street* the baby-doll blonde under the ladder and a cripple move past one another in opposing directions. In images of New York's seedy Bowery, the siren strides purposefully past helpless drunks. At dance marathons, she frequently supports exhausted men. At the burlesque or from the elevated store window in *Hudson Bay Fur Company* she towers above her helpless admirers.[20]

The siren's call to consumption was distributed to the kinds of working-class women who appear in Marsh's paintings through movies, beauty advertisements, and cheap film magazines. Advertisers who marketed the means to siren-style beauty recognized the advantage of using women's real and culturally orchestrated desire for male love and protection to sell their products. The belief that beauty could be bought and that a woman had "power" over her purchases became a mainstay of interwar advertising, along with strategies of making a woman anxious about her ability to please a man. One ad for Irresistible perfume featured a Jean Harlow-type model and was accompanied by a text that promised "no longer need you envy her choice, for now with Irresistible perfume, you can give yourself that indefinable charm. . .that has attracted men the world over."[21] As beauty and charm became purchaseable, they displaced older notions of character as yardsticks of personal success, as Lois Banner has demonstrated.[22] By transforming his women into stereotyped icons of beauty with ruby lips, painted nails, bleached hair, and heavily shadowed eyes, Marsh's siren image demonstrates the movement toward a purchased ideal of womanhood and its accompanying promises and a shift away from an ideal of individuality and independence that pre-franchise feminists had sought to promote.

Recent historians are divided in their assessments of the relation between working-class women, consumer culture, and changing sexual ideology. Kathy Peiss portrays consumption as one aspect of working-class women's new independence and their exuberant resistance to bourgeois prescriptions for women. Joanne Meyerowitz (see page 63, this volume) sees these women as more independent than their middle-class counterparts, a source of new images of sexuality and womanhood. Stuart Ewen and Elizabeth Ewen are less sanguine about the resistance and agency of women in the face of consumer culture. Along with a number of 1930s sociologists they have suggested that the kinds of immigrant and working-class women who came to Fourteenth Street to shop were particularly susceptible to both the myths and the values projected by ads and movies.[23] Movie magazines of the 1930s advertised dress patterns while other new mechanisms in consumer culture made film stars' wardrobes available to the eager shopper. For example, a chain store called The Cinema Shop opened in the 1930s and sold copies of stars' gowns from specific movies at moderate prices.[24] In Fourteenth Street bargain stores, where

Marsh's sirens shopped, cheap versions of high-style fashions were available no more than a week after their expensive counterparts appeared uptown at Saks Fifth Avenue.[25] Historical evidence suggests that women used these purchased models of beauty in different ways and to a variety of ends, from establishing personal autonomy to gaining greater social esteem.

The Marsh girl can be read in multiple registers of signification. As a taxi dancer or a strip-tease store model she confronts the viewer with sexual assurance. She uses exaggerated makeup and tight clothes as defiant challenges to the traditional complementary relationship between female passivity and male power. In a number of his other paintings, however, Marsh employed pictorial strategies that suggest his awareness of tensions between the siren image and reality for the actual Fourteenth Street shoppers. For example, in *Show Window*, 1934 (fig. 6.9), we look through an Ohrbach's display window filled with siren-style mannequins to find two window shoppers looking over the cluttered array of goods. The real shoppers in the lower right-hand corner of the image virtually mirror the look of the plastic 1930s Venuses, as passive and unreal as their inanimate counterparts. All of the objects line up close to and parallel to the picture plane. All are treated with the same loose, sketchy brushwork and limited palette that was typical of Marsh's style, imparting an overall surface similarity that blurs the distinction between real and fabricated womanhood. Within the overwhelming display of consumer goods, it becomes difficult to disengage one object from another, the real woman from the mannequin. Finally, the real shoppers are almost out of the picture; compositionally relegated to the lower right-hand corner, they defer to the mannequin who beckons seductively to them from her commanding position. In their achievement of siren-style beauty, Marsh seems to suggest, the shoppers have given themselves over to an advertised stereotype, sacrificing their individuality to become objects of consumption. As if to underscore this view, Marsh placed a price tag directly over the genitals of the central mannequin. Given Marsh's treatment of these women as powerless in the face of these institutions, it is no wonder that one close friend and critic characterized the Marsh girl as "an automaton – a tremendous fantasy."[26]

Paintings with movies as their subject also relate to

Figure 6.9 Reginald Marsh, *Show Window*, 1934.

Fourteenth Street images and consumer culture, and in a number of them, Marsh continues to expose the way alluring mass cultural stereotypes exploited female consumers. In *Paramount Pictures*, 1934, a young woman stands directly in front of a movie marquee, her image emerging from the nurturing breasts of a larger-than-life poster image of Claudette Colbert as Cleopatra. Compositionally enmeshed with an advertisement, the "real" woman is the advertisement's alter ego, her own appearance dependent on the glamorous fantasy depicted in the poster. In facial features, makeup, and hairstyle, the two women clearly resemble one another so that reality and fantasy, moviegoer and movie siren merge. At the same time, they remain distinct. Colbert is the archetypal siren, before whose alluring and all-knowing gaze an adoring Antony melts. The real woman, however, waits alone outside the movie. In her article on this painting, Erika Doss has observed that the figure's red and tired eyes may be the result of too long a working day, a sign that the fantasy she has purchased has failed to fulfill its promise.[27]

As opposed to the defiance or seductive power we observe in some of Marsh's images, the ultimate powerlessness of the voluptuous shopper and her fellow consumers is revealed in Marsh's *In Fourteenth Street*. Here, Marsh has borrowed motifs from Michelangelo's *Last Judgment* in the Sistine Chapel to subvert the otherwise lively shopping routines and to suggest the bewildered and exploited consumer caught in a swirling maelstrom of lost souls. The central hawker in the crowd, posed like Christ in the Last Judgment, raises his sinister left hand instead of his right and offers seduction over salvation by tempting the innocent consumer with fraudulent goods.[28] The mysterious figure standing with her arms folded at the upper center of the picture resembles the Virgin Mary; withdrawing into herself, like the Virgin who assumes a twisted, self-protective pose, she cannot overrule the hawker's behavior and remains powerless to control the unfolding chaos. The blond in the lower left is burdened by heart-shaped angels' wings inscribed with advertisements for beauty bargains. And the voluptuous siren, floating above the mass of shoppers with modern halo and angels' wings, promises redemption through beauty but then strides toward the picture's center to join the other lost souls in hell.

Marsh's multilevel exploration of the voluptuous shopper in consumer culture can also be seen as part of a larger social debate about the impact of mass culture. Marsh's counterparts were those contemporary social scientists, psychologists, and consumer advocates who analyzed how advertising and film were changing patterns of behavior and creating new values. By the 1930s, many of the new shopping guides for consumers touched on the theme of the victimized consumer lost in a visually chaotic world. Stuart Chase, for example, opened his popular 1927 work *Your Money's Worth: A Study in the Waste of the Consumer's Dollar* with the caveat "We are all Alices in a Wonderland of conflicting claims, bright promises, fancy packages, soaring words and almost impenetrable ignorance."[29] Other consumer advocates saw advertising as another form of social control and frequently discussed the irrationality of bargain-hunting crowds. One writer summed up the situation when he wrote, "[a]dvertising is big business. Advertisers are not philanthropists who are out to make us happy and secure. They aim to make a profit."[30]

In his paintings, Marsh dramatized what historian Richard Fox has defined as a central tenet of consumer ideology – that people are irrational and prey to whichever institution gets to them first.[31] The paintings show that ads and movies could change the individual into an unreasoning automaton – like the voluptuous shopper. At the same time, the pictures' energy and movement also convey a love for the city and its excitement – which we know Marsh, an avid consumer of popular culture himself, deeply felt. But the pictorial activity is often intense or disquieting. The angelic or provocative siren appears both powerful – able to choose her role as siren – and passive – lost in a confusing world.

Both Miller and Marsh mined contemporary images of womanhood and used consumption as a recurring theme in their paintings. Miller's matronly shopper embodied a back-to-the-home ideology that acknowledged sexual liberation and political gains without altering basic perceptions of what a woman's role should be. Through informed consumption, this model shopper provided businesses with an ally to keep the economy running both before and after the crash and stabilized family and community to counteract the fragmentation of modern society.

Marsh's siren shopper, a complex and ambivalent figure of cosmeticized beauty, could be read as declaring the new woman's sexual liberation. In that guise, she expressed, on the one hand, male anxiety about unleashed female sexuality. On the other hand, her stereotyped looks signaled an acceptance of consumer culture's model of womanhood, one that seemed to reinstate more reassuring distinctions between masculinity and femininity. Although these easel paintings were addressed to a relatively small viewing audience, they appropriated models of a wider visual culture and were among the most successful mainstream paintings of their day. As a consequence, with other representations, the paintings articulated and shaped femininity for a wider audience; no longer part of a circumscribed American art history, these works participated in the production of gendered identities in the interwar period. For all their bows to modernity, both images embodied widely shared desires for stability and old traditions.

NOTES

1 This article is based on research and interpretations that are developed in more detail in Ellen Wiley Todd's forthcoming book, *The "New Woman" Revised: Painting and Gender Politics on Fourteenth Street* (Berkeley: 1993).

2 Leila J. Rupp, in "Feminism and the Sexual Revolution in the Early Twentieth Century: The Case of Doris Stevens," *Feminist Studies* 15 (1989): 289–309, points out the variety within the new woman typology. For a discussion of the early emergence of the flapper, see James R. McGovern, "The American Woman's Pre-World War I Freedom in Manners and Morals," *Journal of American History* 55 (September 1968): 315–33. For the charity girl see Kathy Peiss, *Cheap Amusements: Working Women and Leisure in Turn-of-the-Century New York* (Philadelphia: 1986), 110–13.

3 Carroll Smith-Rosenberg, "The New Woman as Androgyne: Social Disorder and Gender Crisis, 1870–1936," in Smith-Rosenberg, ed., *Disorderly Conduct: Visions of Gender in Victorian America* (New York: 1985), 245.

4 Estelle Freedman, in "The New Woman: Changing Views of Women in the 1920s," *Journal of American History* 61 (September 1974): 374, demonstrates that between 1927 and 1933 there was a proliferation of literature on the new woman unequaled until the early 1960s. For a discussion of the stances toward feminism at the end of the 1920s, see Nancy Cott, *The Grounding of Modern Feminism* (New Haven, CT: 1987), 271.

5 Dorothy Dunbar Bromley, "Feminist – New Style," *Harper's Monthly*

Magazine 155 (October 1927): 554.

6 Ibid., 557.

7 Ibid., 556, 558.

8 Alice Kessler-Harris, *Out to Work: A History of Wage-Earning Women in the United States* (New York: 1982), 205–10.

9 Lloyd Goodrich, *Kenneth Hayes Miller* (New York: 1930), 12; and Walter Gutman, "Kenneth Hayes Miller," *Art in America* 18 (February 1930): 92.

10 For a discussion of the home economics movement see Glenna Matthews, *"Just a Housewife": The Rise and Fall of Domesticity in America* (New York: 1987), 145–71.

11 Thomas Craven, "A Paean for Marsh," *Art Digest* 11 (1 December 1936): 10.

12 Letter from Edward Laning to Isabel Bishop (9 August 1974), Edward Laning Papers, Archives of American Art, Washington, DC. Miller's fascination with Freud can also be traced in his letters to his cousin Rhoda Dunn, beginning in about 1915. The relationship is a complex one which lasted well into the 1930s. In the teens, Miller met frequently with psychiatrists and worked on trying to discover the ties between Freud's theories of the unconscious and the creative process. He was also interested, at a somewhat irksome level, if his onetime student Rockwell Kent is to be believed, in trying to "ferret out what he alleged to be erotic symbolism in the work of the greater masters of the past," to which he attached great significance.

13 Malcolm Cowley, *Exile's Return* (New York: 1951), 64; Frederick Lewis Allen, *Only Yesterday* (1964; reprint, New York: 1931), 79–81; Alice Shrock, "Feminists, Flappers and the Maternal Mystique: Changing Conceptions of Women and Their Roles in the 1920s" (Ph.D. dissertation, University of North Carolina at Chapel Hill, 1974), 130–3; and Pamela Warford, "The Social Origins of Female Iconography: Selected Images of Women in American Popular Culture, 1890–1945" (Ph.D. dissertation, Washington University, St. Louis, 1979), 43.

14 M. D. Davis, "Nineteen-Twenty: An Editorial," *Ladies Home Journal* 38 (1 January 1920): 3; and Shrock, 124–6.

15 Shrock, 201; and Amey Watson, "The Reorganization of Household Work," *The American Academy of Political and Social Science Annals* 160 (March 1932): 170–1.

16 William Baldwin, *The Shopping Book* (New York: 1929), preface.

17 T.J. Jackson Lears, "From Salvation to Self-Realization: Advertising and the Therapeutic Roots of the Consumer Culture, 1880–1920," in *The Culture of Consumption*, ed. Richard Wightman Fox and T.J. Jackson Lears (New York: 1983), 3–38.

18 Reginald Marsh, "Kenneth Hayes Miller," *Magazine of Art* 45 (April 1952): 171.

19 Mildred Adams, "Now the Siren Eclipses the Flapper," *New York Times*, 28 July 1929, sec. 5, pp. 4–5.

20 Marilyn Cohen, *Reginald Marsh's New York: Paintings, Drawings,*

Prints and Photographs (New York: 1983), 27.

21 *Modern Screen* (September 1933): 89.

22 Lois Banner, *American Beauty* (New York: 1983), 202–8.

23 Stuart Ewen and Elizabeth Ewen, *Channels of Desire: Mass Images and the Shaping of American Consciousness* (New York: 1982); Elizabeth Ewen, *Immigrant Women in the Land of Dollars* (New York: 1985); Peiss, *Cheap Amusements*; Joanne Meyerowitz, "Sexual Geography and Gender Economy: The Furnished Room Districts of Chicago, 1890–1930," in this volume.

24 *Modern Screen* (January 1934): 70–1.

25 Robert Lynd, "The People as Consumers," in *Recent Social Trends in the United States: Report of the President's Research Committee on Social Trends*, 10th printing (New York: 1934), 878.

26 Edward Laning, *East Side, West Side, All Around the Town* (Tucson: 1969), 97.

27 Erika L. Doss, "Images of American Women in the 1930s: Reginald Marsh and *Paramount Picture*," *Woman's Art Journal* 4 (Fall 1983/ Winter 1984): 3.

28 In his 1930s bestselling novel *Union Square*, Albert Halper, who described the neighborhood in documentary fashion, described these hawkers as "the cleverest lads of all," the "fellows who sold worthless watches out of small, black leather bags, one eye out for passing suckers, the other on the policeman down the street." Halper, *Union Square* (New York: 1933), 48.

29 Stuart Chase and F.J. Schlink, *Your Money's Worth: A Study in the Waste of the Consumer's Dollar* (New York: 1927), 2.

30 Kenneth Haas, *Adventures in Buysmanship* (Ann Arbor, MI: 1937), 12–21.

31 Richard Wightman Fox, "Epitaph for Middletown," in *The Culture of Consumption*, ed. Fox and Lears, 139.

7

MANLY WORK

Public art and masculinity in Depression America

Barbara Melosh

From the public monuments of Washington, DC, to the walls of small-town post offices, the New Deal left its mark in an ambitious public art program. Many of those works featured muscular, working-class versions of masculinity. This essay explores the recurring features and settings associated with the manly worker and interprets the figure as it participates in the gendered discourses of the state even as it reveals contemporary discourses of gender. The special conditions of this government-sponsored art create unusual opportunities for cultural historians, and this essay uses those sources to interpret the image through evidence of its production and reception. On one hand, the manly worker was a species of New Deal propaganda, an emblem of the enduring values of manhood and work in the face of economic depression, and a symbol of the state itself. On the other hand, the type of the manly worker was also found in labor union and radical rhetoric; as the historical record shows, it was interpreted in various ways by different audiences. This multiplicity may have accounted for its wide appeal, the essay suggests; the figure played on widely shared anxieties about masculinity that in turn expressed many Americans' concerns about changes in work and family life.

* * *

Worker (fig. 7.1), installed in a small West Virginia post office in 1941, illustrates the version of masculinity sponsored by the New Deal's Treasury Section of Fine Arts, a program that funded more than 1,400 art works for federal buildings across the nation. Bare-chested and heavily muscled, the figure

155

Figure 7.1 Albino Cavallito, *Worker*, 1941.

stands in a confident pose, one strong hand resting on a powerful thigh as the other grasps a sledgehammer. Around this central figure, four smaller motifs represent local industries. Trees signify lumbering; a locomotive and steamboat denote the town's links to the region; a kiln pays tribute to the local ceramics factory. Albino Cavallito's sculpture celebrated work as mastery, the ability to reshape the material world and to make one's own destiny. The human figure stood triumphant, master of the human resources and technological achievements arrayed around it. Tellingly, that figure was masculine.

What is the relationship between the painted or sculpted image and the complex and multifaceted society within which art is produced and viewed? Cultural historians have long been concerned about the limitations of interpretations that rely solely on reading the image. How do we know what its maker intended, or what contemporary viewers saw when they looked at an image? Social historians of art and literature emphasize a reading of the image that considers the conditions of its production and reception and interprets a given *text* within the *context* of other representations. The production of an image can influence its form, from the inadvertent alterations of slipped chisel or brush, an imperfect weave of canvas or flawed block of wood, to the market pressures of gallery owners, museum curators' preferences, or demanding patrons. Many, perhaps most, images provoke different responses from different viewers, as attested in the conversations in movie theater lobbies and art galleries as well as in published reviews. My research on the manly worker of New Deal public art reveals this multiplicity: different spectators interpreted this figure in different ways. At the same time, historical evidence also reveals the boundaries of interpretation – the grounds upon which spectators met, the assumptions they shared about what it meant to be a man.

The focused cultural intentions of the Treasury Section of Fine Arts make it an especially significant case study of gendered images, for the Section sought self-consciously to promote an art of American subjects with broad popular appeal. The public art produced under the Treasury Section offers a revealing window into the era's complex renegotiations of gender. I read these images of manhood as one expression of a larger crisis of masculinity between the world wars. Traditional ideals of manhood faltered in the wake of World War I and in the face of economic depression, even as many resisted the feminist demand for sexual equality. The New Deal established an era of sweeping liberal reform – the only such period not accompanied by a resurgence of feminism.

Images of manhood and womanhood figured prominently in Section-sponsored public art. These representations operated as cultural prescriptions – statements of the proper place of men and women – and as metaphors, allegories of the nation's history and future. The New Dealers who administered the Section used these images as propaganda for the New Deal and as inspirational figures for Depression-era Americans. Meanwhile, artists and audiences brought their own agendas and interpretations to public art; their readings of the manly worker disclose the multiple meanings associated with the figure.

In operation from 1935 until 1943, the Section was the first federally funded program of its kind. It promoted public art as a public good and as a legitimate use of taxpayers' money, and sought (unsuccessfully) to achieve permanent status as a federal bureau. Administrators saw themselves as arbiters of taste and as public servants accountable to a broad audience. They identified themselves self-consciously with American scene art – that is, they participated in the 1930s movement to work with American subjects and to acclaim a distinctively American style, turning away from the European models that had inspired many American writers and artists in the 1920s. Section administrators sought to create an art that would celebrate American possibility and achievement at a time of doubt. Although they sometimes failed spectacularly, they sought to sponsor art that would please local viewers. They enjoined artists to consult their audiences, to select subjects that viewers approved, and to use images and styles that ordinary citizens would recognize.

The procedures of the Section and the dutiful record keepers of the New Deal left a paper trail that creates unusual opportunities for cultural historians. Public sponsorship opened the production of art to bureaucratic scrutiny and intervention; public accountability meant that administrators documented their work and sought to discover and satisfy audience preferences. The process was far from seamless. Rather, the records reveal negotiation among artists, administrators, and audience that was punctuated and occasionally derailed by misunderstandings, differences, and conflict. In these records we can discern popular aesthetics and ideas of gender, along with artists' and administrators' notions of art.

Archival records document the process of producing a painting or sculpture for a post office, from awarding the commission to filing the local newspaper's review of the finished work. Though often confused with the Works Progress Administration's Federal Art Project, the Section was not a relief project; instead, it awarded commissions on the basis of anonymous competitions. Artists from a designated area could submit sketches to local juries, whose recommendations were reviewed (and usually accepted) by the five administrators in the Section's Washington office. Commissions were funded by an executive order that reserved 1 per cent of the construction budgets of the Public Buildings Administration for "embellishments" – murals and sculptures sponsored by the Section. Thus awards varied depending on the scale of the facility. Commissions for small town and rural post offices typically ran from $600 to $800; in more elaborate buildings, one per cent of the construction budget could amount to considerably more – $2,000, $5,000, even $25,000. Artists received payments for their commissions in three stages, documented in a file of correspondence between artist and administrators. First the artist sent in preliminary sketches and worked on revisions in consultation with the Section. When the subject had been settled to the satisfaction of Section and artist, the first installment was awarded. The artist then submitted color sketches or sculptural models documenting the further progress of the work. Next, he or she would submit detailed cartoons of planned murals or photographs of a sculpture in progress; when the Section administrator judged the work half-finished, the artist received the second payment. Final payment was awarded once the postmaster had confirmed that the art work was installed satisfactorily in the building. At this point, the Section also asked the postmaster to clip articles that appeared in the local newspaper and to report comments by postal patrons. Many complied, and their replies and clippings were filed along with other correspondence on that commission.

The celebration of working men and manly labor pervaded Section public art. In the face of widespread unemployment and changes in work that threatened traditional skills, public art presented work as a domain of male control and camaraderie. Several hundred Section murals and sculptures portray work through compositions containing only male figures, often accentuated with monumental or heroic gestures; by contrast, fewer than a dozen public art works feature women alone or accompanied only by other women. The selective representation of work emphasized the male domains of craft and heavy industry, rendering women's paid work invisible. Moreover, the core ideal of the manly worker relied on a complementary image of female dependence. The masculinity of work rested not only on the autonomy of craft skill or visibly productive labor, but on the wage earner's place in the family. The cultural ideology and social fact of the male breadwinner and the family wage* meant

* The "family wage" refers to the nineteenth- and twentieth-century labor movement's argument that men should earn enough to support a family adequately. This tactic rested, in turn, on an enduring nineteenth-century ideology of separate spheres, which assigned men to the public world of paid work and politics and relegated women to the domestic or private sphere of home and family. Women's paid labor, in this view, was seen as a badge of shame for the male

that manliness was defined in part by women's exclusion from paid labor. In Section art, that ideology manifests itself in a significant absence: in sharp contrast to frontier and rural scenes, which commonly feature family groups or men and women working side by side, women are seldom seen in representations of paid work. By associating wage labor with manhood, the manly ideal tacitly validated men's mastery over women: in a market economy, men's greater access to money ensured their dominance in family and social life.

Heroic workers embodied two aspects of democratic ideology: individual autonomy and collective endeavor. In Cavallito's image, the single figure of the worker signaled independence and autonomy. Many other examples reveal a similar vocabulary of manly work, as in the heroic full-length portraits of workers that punctuate the narratives of work and community in the Coit Tower mural project in San Francisco.[1] Heinz Warneke's worker (fig. 7.2) echoes the conventions of the manly worker, even as it alerts us to the racial codes that governed the New Deal's celebration of manhood. Warneke used a bare-chested worker with strongly muscled body, posed with gears and tools, emblems of his labor; however, his manly worker is African-American. Though black figures were not uncommon in Section public art, they were seldom featured in monumental roles; typically, they appeared as field workers bent over their tasks and laboring under the supervision of a white overseer. Warneke's manly worker was done for the Harlem-Macombs Housing Project, New Deal-sponsored public housing in a primarily black neighborhood of New York, a site that likely explains its deviation from the usual racial casting. In addition, the figure kneels – a common posture in artistic representations of black people and a posture of subordination that is at odds with the manly worker's usual commanding stance.

Another common theme extolled the camaraderie of shared labor, as in dozens of renderings like William Zorach's *Shoemakers of Stoneham [Massachusetts]*, where three men ply their trade side by side. Significantly, this theme can be found not only in depictions of traditional crafts, but also in artistic representations of highly industrialized factory labor. Section art ignored contemporary concerns about jobs lost through mechanization

breadwinner; for reformers, it was an indictment of a wage system that paid men too little.

of work, instead celebrating technology as an instrument of human mastery and manly control. Howard Cook's *Steel Industry* (fig. 7.3), for example, in Pittsburgh, Pennsylvania, shows men intent on the shared tasks of heavy industry. The composition shows a harmonious integration of men and machinery; decisive lines suggest the workers' purposeful action, and the human forms fit smoothly around the machines. Similarly, William Gropper's mural for a post office in Detroit, Michigan, casts automobile workers in the heroic mold of manly work. In *Automobile Industry* (fig. 7.4), Gropper's characteristic figure drawing accentuates the powerful upper body associated with the image of the manly worker. Concentrating on their tasks, the figures face away from the viewer. Though we see parts moving on a track on the right, suggestive of the assembly line, Gropper's composition places human figures in the foreground, dominating the industrial machinery of the factory. By the 1930s, the assembly line of automobile production was a widely used symbol of the exhausting pace of work, the displacement of skilled workers by new technology, and unemployment that resulted when machines took over much of the labor of unskilled workers. It is all the more striking, then, that Gropper used the narrative of heroic labor to portray the operations of the automobile industry. Notably, too, in these two murals as in other Section-sponsored art, the artists depict work shared among equals; we do not see the foremen and supervisors who would have appeared in actual industrial workplaces.

In Section correspondence, artists and administrators referred to figures of workers as recognizable types, assuming a widely shared heroic symbolism of labor. Sculptor Leopold Scholz, enthusiastic about his design for Chattanooga, Tennessee, wrote Section administrator Edward Rowan, "I must say it interests me tremendously. . . . In fact, it is just the sort of powerful figure of labor I always enjoy doing. . . ."[2] In an interview for the local newspaper, Paul Mays articulated the symbolic intention of his workers, painted for Norristown, Pennsylvania: "I wished to express the meaning of strength – the force and vitality of the working people in this valley of factories and furnaces."[3] When Rowan criticized the "unduly exaggerated" posture of a male figure wielding a shovel in a sketch by Jack J. Greitzer, the artist defended his sketch by invoking the symbolism of labor: "I purposely treated the figure in this manner to impart an heroic and idealistic feeling to him and to the work he represents, namely, civic improvement."[4] With characteristic irreverence, artist Waldo Peirce mocked the typecast manly workers he had included in his sketch of paper mill operations: "the semi machine and heroic cleanshaven mug etc. so dear to muralists. . .these dam machine hercules."[5] For painter Jac T. Bowen, work represented progress. His mural recorded the diversified industry of Higginsville, Missouri; the artist concluded his description of the mural with a lyrical encomium to labor. "Work made the town – work is building the town – and work will be the song of the future; the song of their machines, their minds and their hands."[6]

With few exceptions, images of the manly worker won warm receptions from administrators and public alike. Such figures effectively deployed widely approved ideas about masculinity in a political rhetoric that addressed a range of significant concerns. The imagery of work contained elements that spectators might readily identify with several different sources and narratives. Because this image could and did evoke multiple associations, we need to be cautious about how we read any single representation of the manly worker. At the same time, the diverse ideas associated with the image also make it an especially significant representation, and perhaps this very diversity helped to account for its wide appeal. Viewers might readily attach a number of different meanings to the manly worker, and thus make it their own.

The American labor movement was one source for the iconography of the manly worker.[7] As historian David Montgomery has argued, "manliness" was a powerful image that summed up workers' aspirations for control of work, dignified labor, and a living wage.[8] In the "turbulent years" of the 1930s, as workers challenged managers and owners in strikes and surged into the labor movement, confrontational politics heightened other connotations of manliness – courage, physical strength, defiance of unjust authority. It spoke to widespread anxieties about worklessness: the male role of the breadwinner took on a newly charged symbolism as families faced unemployment.

At the same time, figures of workers recalled the heroic images of an insurgent left: Mexican muralists, European leftists, and a wave of socialist realists in the Soviet Union celebrated the

Figure 7.2 Heinz Warneke (with Richmond Barthe), *Black Worker*, n.d.

Figure 7.3 Howard Cook, *Steel Industry*, 1936.

working class in images that closely resembled the working men in Section public art. Closer to home, radical artists – including some, such as William Gropper, who executed commissions for the Section – used the manly worker in widely circulated graphics, posters, and political cartoons.

On the other hand, artists might also draw on genre scenes of work found in popular illustration and easel painting; such images idealized manual labor, but without the critical intentions of the labor movement or the left.[9] One might – and actual spectators did – interpret murals and sculpture of the manly worker as monuments to rugged individualism; as endorsements of the New Deal; as paeans to the labor movement; as celebrations of working-class solidarity and harbingers of class struggle.

Section administrators sought to exploit the broad appeal of the manly worker and, at the same time, to contain its more subversive associations. The image of the manly worker served as propaganda for the New Deal. The figure used venerable cultural ideals of individualism and self-sufficiency to celebrate the expanding role of the state, a rhetoric that justified political innovation in the name of tradition. By singling out industrial workers, this image acknowledged working-class constituencies of the New Deal. Meanwhile, the insistent gendering of the image provided an appeal that reached across class lines: its particular version of manliness spoke to a crisis of masculinity experienced by both working-class and middle-class audiences.

164

Figure 7.4 William Gropper, *Automobile Industry*, 1941.

Public decorations in Washington, DC, illustrate the Section's version of the New Deal's common man. The manly worker of New Deal public art stands out in startling relief against sculptures of statesmen, military heroes, and classical maidens.[10] Instead, artists gave heroic treatment to emblematic American men in simple work clothing. Over one entrance to the Federal Trade Commission, for example, Chaim Gross's *Construction* depicts two burly figures facing one another as they drive rivets into a steel beam between them. The figures fill the frame of the bas relief, conveying a sense of concentrated and cooperative work. Figures like these declare the honor of daily labor, and streamlined modeling asserts simplicity and modernity against the elite tradition of classical or academic art.

The Section openly acknowledged the celebratory role of public art in the capital when it instructed artist Ben Shahn to incorporate a quotation from Franklin Delano Roosevelt into his murals for the Social Security Building. Shahn complied, and as his correspondence reveals, he shared the Section's view of the purpose of public art in the capital: "The building itself is a symbol of perhaps the most advanced piece of legislation enacted by the New Deal, and I am proud to be given the job of interpreting it, or putting a face on it, or whatever you want to call it."[11] He realized that intention through the rhetoric of manly labor. In the central hallway of the Department of Health and Human Services (formerly the Social Security Building), Ben Shahn's two panels dramatize manhood lost and regained. In the first painting, dejected, idle figures sit on the skeleton of an abandoned construction project. Subdued greys and browns convey a mood of despair. In the foreground, the bent figure of a man on crutches represents the broken men who have lost their jobs. Across the hall, the companion panel, *Social Security*, glows with the hope and renewal of purposeful work. Against a light-filled blue sky, energetic workers construct the frame of a new building. The painting's lines sweep upward, following the yellow boards and the workers' uplifted arms. Labor redeems manhood; and manly work is a force for social progress.

In Symeon Shimin's *Contemporary Justice and the Child* (fig. 7.5), the New Deal's state power is allegorized in an image of strong masculine hands. Located in the stairwell of the Department of Justice, the mural contains a dramatic focal image of a woman with a young boy framed by her supporting arms,

Figure 7.5 Symeon Shimin, *Contemporary Justice and the Child*, 1940.

which seem to offer him to the spectator. He looks out imploringly to the viewer, while her gaze is turned slightly to the side, her expression sober and contemplative. In the foreground, two strongly modeled hands grasp a drafting triangle and compass, familiar symbols of planning. The painting suggests that the New Deal, figured as the manly defender of the weak, will rescue the demoralized men and women in the breadline on the left; and that New Deal planning will shape the bright future imagined on the right side of the mural.

Conflicts over the depiction of the manly worker reveal the different political intentions associated with this figure. Rhetorics of liberal democracy, class, and labor – sometimes overlapping but sometimes conflicting – all used the brawny industrial laborer as symbol of their cause (and all competed for working-class support). When the manly worker emerged as a dominant theme in the nation's most visible commissions, the Section did not demur. But administrators did intervene to shape the figure in ways that emphasized the rhetoric of liberal democracy – and muted its associations with oppositional politics.

The most telling of such interventions focused on the race and ethnicity of the manly worker. Commissions for the Department of the Interior offer several examples of contested definitions of the "typical" American, and, as other correspondence makes clear, Section administrators acted on directives from Secretary of the Interior Harold Ickes. Rowan cautioned painter Nicolai Cikovsky that "The figures. . .should be typically American."[12] Ickes commended John Steuart Curry for figures that were "truly American and not Oriental."[13] As sketches and finished murals reveal, "typical" was a code for white males of northern European ethnicity.

Artist Ernest Fiene directly challenged the definition of "typical" when Ickes complained that "There was not an American type in the entire series [of Fiene's four proposed murals]."[14] Fiene defended himself to Rowan by arguing, ". . .the men in the mural represent a variety of American types. Even westerners are descendants of many races or nationalities. The only one that remains pure to his source, is the man holding the flag. . . . He is of Mexican origin. . . ." But Fiene's reply also inadvertently reveals the power of Ickes's notion of the typical American, for he defended his Americanism by shifting to Ickes's ground:

Without wishing to project my virtues too much, I may say that my mural "Paul Revere as an Industrialist" for the Canton, Massachusetts, post office is perhaps one of the most typically American murals produced under the sponsorship of your Department.[15]

Fiene prevailed: his finished mural reveals a group of men whose features and coloring suggest Latino and Asian origins. Fiene was one of the signers of the call to organize the American Artists' Congress, a Popular Front group committed to socially engaged art and to the promise of a more equitable society offered by the Soviet Union, a model for many 1930s artists and intellectuals.

Ickes's interventions on race recall the Section's own brand of white liberalism. No simple nativist, Ickes seemed to share Section administrators' concern about racial caricatures when he asked artist James Michael Newell to revise African-American figures with features that were "too coarse."[16] He appealed to authenticity in demanding revisions to make Gifford Beal's figures look more "Oriental," as befitted this painter's subject of Hawaii.[17] And Ickes went well beyond the Section's liberalism on race when dealing with American Indians. He demanded substantial representation of native peoples in the building, emphasizing the Interior Department's Bureau of Indian Affairs. In addition, Ickes rejected the painter commissioned by the Section, a white, instead requiring the Section to employ American Indian artists for these decorations. Though he intervened repeatedly as Millard Sheets designed his four panels on black Americans, he never proposed that such paintings had no place in his Department. Still, Ickes's interventions on behalf of the manly worker illustrate the limitations of his liberalism. He had no objection to the representation of non-Anglo-Americans in specific and contained contexts; indeed, he actively supported such subjects in the case of American Indians and in his acceptance of the subject matter assigned to Sheets. But when artists cast such figures in the monumental role of the manly worker, Ickes demurred.

During the stormy course of Interior Department commissions, administrators were often at loggerheads with the "Old Curmudgeon"; Ickes scrutinized proposed designs and exercised a peremptory veto to the considerable annoyance of his fellow bureaucrats in the Section. But Section administrators apparently acquiesced in his views of the typical American; at least, the records contain none of the grumbling or rebellious commentary that accompanied many of Ickes's other pronouncements.

Neither Section administrators nor Ickes himself can fairly be described as racists. If they were not entirely free of stereotypical views of black Americans, nonetheless they were committed liberals with genuine concerns about extending the reach and inclusiveness of American democracy. Although the evidence does not allow firm conclusions about the conflicts over race at the Interior Department, I suggest tentatively that the debates about the manly worker were shaped by the New Deal's anti-Communism. The image of the manly worker was identified with radicalism in many contemporary contexts – and radicals stood out from New Deal liberals in their critique of American racism and their advocacy on behalf of black Americans.

The boundaries between New Deal liberalism and radicalism were often blurred. In 1935, the Communist Party made common cause with liberal democracies in the Popular Front and declared its support for Roosevelt and the New Deal. Earl Browder, head of the Communist Party–USA, proclaimed, "Communism is twentieth-century Americanism," and many liberals and intellectuals apparently agreed as they lent broad support to Popular Front activities in the 1930s. Still, the litmus test of racial views distinguishes liberal from radical whites with some reliability. With few exceptions (Eleanor Roosevelt was the most prominent), white New Deal liberals did little to challenge racial segregation. In contrast, racial integration had been a priority of the Communist Party–USA, and though Popular Front coalition politics eroded this commitment,[18] it remained important for individual radicals. And perhaps most significant for this discussion, it remained a code for radical politics. Whether or not individual artists had radical intentions, when spectators saw images of blacks and whites together they often assumed a radical message. Ickes never referred to political motivations in his criticism. And yet it is difficult to explain the intensity of his response except in the context of the New Deal's opposition to communism and radicalism.

The Section was equally vigilant in monitoring the political connotations of masculinity in commissions outside the capital. The manly worker of public art drew on imagery widely used in the labor movement, but administrators deliberately suppressed references to labor conflict. Labor organization flourished during the period under the crucial enabling legislation of the Wagner Act.[19] Nevertheless labor unions still carried a subversive connotation for many Americans, who associated collective action with radicalism. Moreover, the bitter strikes of the period revealed an aspect of American life that the Section preferred to avoid: inequality, conflict, and violent confrontations between workers and police or militia had no place in the Section's vision of a harmonious community of individuals. The history of miners' struggles captured the imagination of artist James Daugherty as he did his research for a mural commission in Virden, Illinois. He wrote,

> It seems that Virden's pastoral life once blazed out into history with a smear of blood in the strike and bloodshed of the miners' stand for an eight hour day. Can you tell me why this should be Virden's shame instead of pride? Obviously the postmaster so considered it in his letter. And it is my sad premonition that you will tell me to forget it as a mural incident.[20]

He was right. Rowan vetoed the subject and counseled, "A capable artist can do as much with a pleasant subject as with any other kind."[21] Daugherty complied with *Illinois Pastoral*, an idyll of frontier democracy.

Another artist used the figure of the manly worker to deflect associations of labor struggle, an intention that reveals the multiple meanings of the image. He wrote Rowan,

> As you are undoubtedly aware, the subject of miners in the pit presents an idealogical [sic] as well as a technical problem. Ideologically I have carefully avoided any of the negative overtones that frequently occur in the pictorial handling of this subject. I have, on the contrary emphasized the strength and dignity of the man and his labor.[22]

When Section administrators perceived "negative overtones" in other proposed art works, they called for revisions. They criticized any suggestion of idleness. In one example, administrators edited out a worker leaning on a shovel, fearful that the image would recall the caricature of government makework widely used by critics of WPA projects.[23] At the same time, Section administrators discouraged images that might suggest oppressive working conditions. In reviewing jury recommendations for Moline, Illinois, Rowan advised that Edward Millman's figures should be "made a little less aggressive in action. In the sketch, they are presented very strongly, as though they were battling with their machinery rather than being actually part of it."[24] The sculptor assigned to the post office in Jenkins, Kentucky, described his intention to convey "a more intense and industrialized feeling in the figures to reflect the intensified scale of Jenkins mining." Section administrator Forbes Watson asked him to tone it down: "In the case of the Miner the 'feeling' has got somewhat out of hand. . . ."[25] Through such interventions, the Section sponsored images of labor that affirmed a mythic nineteenth-century work ethic of productive and unalienated[*] labor.

Public audiences had their own critiques to offer, as I explore at length in the book from which this essay is taken. One example provides a rare glimpse of black spectators – one of just two places where these viewers made themselves heard in Section records. Their response suggests that, like audiences elsewhere, they echoed the Section's preference for inspirational public art. In the course of Heinz Warneke's commission for the Harlem-Macombs Housing Project, local spectators objected to the sculptor's designs for the black figure (*Black Worker*, fig. 7.2). Their original criticism is not in the Section files, but the artist's response, in a letter to administrator Olin Dows, reveals its terms. Warneke wrote, "If he [the figure] is brutish, I shall by the same token hate to emasculate him"; but assured Dows, "I can see the point about the supersensitive feelings involved in the situation – and do my best. Anyway I have a great sympathy for the negroes and should not care to offend them." In another letter, Dows summarized a community meeting on the subject and noted black spectators' desire for a more "hopeful" figure.[26]

At the same time, their criticism also hinted at the racially charged connotations attached to black masculinity. Without direct evidence about the concerns of black viewers, it is difficult to interpret their response definitively. However, the word "brutish," which they apparently did use, suggests that they might have also found the figure disturbingly forceful – at least Warneke interpreted their concern that way, when he countered

---

* In Marxist theory, work (and the worker) becomes alienated under capitalism, when work is done for wages and owners control the process to generate profits for themselves. "Unalienated work" is done for one's own benefit and pleasure.

that he did not want to "emasculate" his figure. Although the image of the manly worker included a heroic representation of physical strength, the history of race and racism lent different connotations to this element of masculinity. Black viewers would have been all too well aware of the notorious stereotype that white Americans had long used to justify lynching: the image of black masculinity as savage and sexually uncontrolled.[27] This exchange, only partially preserved and difficult to interpret conclusively, nonetheless offers suggestive evidence about the manly worker as an image that constructed race as well as gender.

The figure of the manly worker embodied nostalgia for an imagined past of individual dignity lost in the modern world of work. Public art emphasized traditional crafts and industrial work, a significantly skewed representation of the actual world of paid work. With few exceptions, Section-sponsored versions of manly labor excluded middle-class men and white-collar work. Professional work with its touted autonomy might seem to embody the self-determination that was part of the ideal of manly work, and yet professionals are notably under-represented in public art. Physicians, scientists, and engineers did appear, gaining exemption from the general blackout of the professions because of the New Deal's reverence for the rationality of science and planning. Lawyers, clergymen, and college professors, often ridiculed or vilified in 1930s drama and fiction, are absent altogether. We see scarcely a glimpse of a whole layer of white-collar work: sales, advertising, middle-management – precisely those jobs that were assuming new importance in a growing service economy. And tellingly, in the many murals and sculptures of industrial work, artists focused on workers but framed out the foremen, supervisors, and owners.

Finally, masculinity is inscribed in the Section's image of labor by the pervasive erasure of women's paid work. On rare occasions, public art depicted women's wage labor, but without exception, wage-earning women are excluded from the monumental and heroic imagery associated with the manly worker. That absence is dramatized by its abrupt reversal only a few years later, when a brawny *Rosie the Riveter* would appear in popular magazines and recruiting posters.[28] Although clerical work was far more common than industrial production as a locus for women's wartime labor, designers appropriated the stylistic conventions of the manly worker for home-front propaganda. In contrast, in rare

173

depictions of women's industrial work, Section art presents women workers as bit players in straightforward documentations of industrial processes; we see them bent over sewing machines, sorting fruit in a processing plant, or making candy.[29] Nowhere does women's paid work stand as emblematic of a community, and wage-earning women never assume monumental proportions. Public art contains barely a trace of the service occupations that dominated women's paid work: clerical work, domestic service, nursing, teaching, and food service are rarely glimpsed.

Section art affirms the ideological divide of home and work, with women associated with the family and men with paid labor. Nearly absent from images of paid work, women appear prominently in scenes of the self-sustaining family on the frontier and farm. Images of the manly worker, by contrast, rarely include family members. When women and children do appear, they are usually presented in ways that focus attention on the male breadwinner. In some works, women or children bring lunch to a man on the job, a narrative that casts family members as supporting characters of the central activity of wage-earning men.

The Steel Worker and Family (fig. 7.6), a sculpture by Mildred Jerome, presents a partial exception. Done for Blawnox, Pennsylvania, the relief casts the whole family in the familiar monumental conventions of manly work. Yet even here, the male figure is subtly dominant. His right arm encircles his wife's shoulder in a protective and confident gesture, and his left hand embraces his daughter, leaning dependently on his leg. The female figure shares the mass and strong modeling of the male figure, but her right hand is open at her side in a subtle gesture of vulnerability. Meanwhile, the child at her feet sits slightly apart, a gesture of autonomy that contrasts with the little girl's dependence on her father and that encourages us to read this figure as a little boy.[30] The work's title underlines the separation of work and domesticity: *Steel Worker and Family* identifies the male figure through his work and names the other figures according to their familial identity.

Several artists indicated that they used images of family to avoid conflict. Designing for the coal-mining town of Staunton, Illinois, artist Ralf Hendricksen wrote Rowan, "In choosing my subject matter, 'A Miner's Family,' I feel I have portrayed a subject of interest to all, with least cause for disturbance politically or otherwise."[31] Edwin Boyd Johnson used a family subject to appease a suspicious postmaster. He wrote,

Figure 7.6 Mildred Jerome, *The Steel Worker and Family*, 1941.

At the first the postmaster was not very enthusiastic about the idea of having a mural placed in the building because of an article he had once read about some post office murals containing communistic and socialistic propaganda. I assured him that he need not worry on this score, and that I would strive to create a design that would be in harmony with the ideology of the community.[32]

The Old Days, the completed mural, was a nostalgic scene of a farmer and his wife at the railroad station. In all these cases, artists interpreted "family" as an alternative to work, erasing women's domestic labor, and they used domesticity to represent harmony, submerging family conflict.

As Karal Ann Marling has observed, the murals' representations of work were a reverse image of 1930s America. Often showing those crafts and occupations most crippled by the Depression – the building trades, mining, industrial work – the murals proclaimed the strength of America at work to banish the haunting specters of idle plants, unemployment, farm depression.[33] The insistent gendering of work, I would argue further, was a crucial element in the construction of this reverse image. The association of work and manhood pervaded social life as well as these artistic representations. The classic sociological works of the Depression recorded men's and women's anguish over unemployment in ways that repeatedly invoked gender ideology. Investigators brought their own biases and anxieties to their studies: in a classic example, Ruth Shonle Cavan and Katherine Howland Ranck's *The Family and the Depression* used the loss of male authority as the measure of family disorganization.[34] But as their informants spoke through the investigators' framing questions, many seemed to share the preoccupation with a manhood threatened or destroyed by the loss of work. One man told sociologist Mirra Komarovsky, "It is awful to be old and discarded at forty. A man is not a man without work."[35] Contemporary interviews reveal women's bitterness about men who had failed as breadwinners. One woman told Komarovsky, "When a husband cannot provide for the family and makes you worry so, you lose your love for him," and another said, "Of course I hate my husband for bringing hardships upon the family."[36] E. Wight Bakke's *Citizens Without Work* likewise recorded the deep personal humiliation that

176

unemployed men experienced.[37] His informants did not share Bakke's own view of the Depression as a broader social and economic problem, but rather blamed themselves and described their worklessness as a failure of manhood. The manly worker of public art bracketed the shame of unemployment by putting it out of public sight, replacing it with the enduring ideal of labor.

In addition to bolstering the image of productive manhood in the face of unemployment, the ideal of the manly worker spoke to a broader crisis of masculinity. The myth of craft independence expressed longing for an autonomy that was rapidly receding from most Americans' experience of work. Blue-collar workers were hard-pressed even before the Depression, as mechanization and the reorganization of work eroded craft skill and began to cut away jobs.[38] Meanwhile, the expanding service sector fundamentally changed the character of middle-class and white-collar work. Men increasingly moved into jobs that required traditionally feminine skills: salesmen and ad men schooled themselves in the unmanly arts of persuasion.[39] As corporations grew and reorganized to address national markets, an expanding and elaborated bureaucracy blurred managers' authority. The old image of the entrepreneur gave way to the perceived diminishment of individual authority associated with new forms of corporate management. Bureaucratic organization proved an unsatisfactory setting for middle-class white men's individualist ideologies, and by the 1920s literary and journalistic comment derided the stock figure of the businessman in caricatures like Sinclair Lewis's best-selling novel *Babbitt* (1922). Professional work too had surrendered much of its touted autonomy to the bureaucracies that increasingly bounded middle-class men's work.

In part, the manly worker was propaganda for the New Deal, and the figure can be taken as a measure of the extent and limits of that administration's brand of liberal democracy. Section art offers, on the one hand, a dramatic testament to New Deal-era populism. Peopled by figures of ordinary Americans at work and at rest, this art still stands out, instantly recognizable in a fine arts tradition that has seldom included working-class subjects and also an anomaly in public art, which more often features heroic famous men or allegorical figures based on classical myth. Public art also included modest revisions of race and

177

gender, including a heroic imagery of women as mothers and wives along with representations of men and women of southern and eastern European ancestry, Asian-Americans, African-Americans, American Indians, and the like. "Working men" in public art were a rainbow of American types. Significantly, though, the monumental rendition of the working man, the figure of the manly worker, was almost exclusively reserved for white men of northern European ethnicity. In its definition of masculinity, New Deal public art innovated by elevating the working-class man to heroic stature, but it conserved other existing hierarchies of race and gender.

More generally, we need to ask what part the manly worker played in the cultural construction of gender. Public art was only one piece of a complex cultural landscape, and to answer this question fully we would need to read its visions of masculinity against representations of men in other forms, from documentary photography and advertising to campaign speeches. Nonetheless, the wide appeal of the manly worker suggests that we can use the Section's visual and archival evidence to trace the outlines of the cultural history of masculinity in the United States between the wars. I have argued that it constituted one response to the social upheavals of war, economic depression, and changing structures of work, a reformulation of masculinity that both revised and conserved older representations of class, race, and gender.

Moreover, the Section's manly worker also offers a provocative example of the explicitly ideological uses of gender. Through this figure of idealized masculinity, administrators sought to promote the New Deal, to offer an inspirational view of American life, and to create a distinctively American art. As we have seen, administrators did not hesitate to intervene, working vigorously to shape the image to their purposes. However, the huge correspondence of the Section demonstrates the limits as well as the power of the state to shape the construction of gender. Section artists and administrators were constrained by their audiences, both because they wanted to please viewers and because they had to – the program existed, ultimately, on the sufferance of taxpayers and of Congress. They did not invent the manly worker, but selected from, and selectively revised, representations of masculinity that were already available to audiences. In this way the history of the Section can serve as a paradigm for the production of cultural meaning more generally – a complex negotiation among unequal players, whose outcome is shaped not only by power but also by conflict and consent.

NOTES

This article is a revised and condensed version of Chapter 4 in *Engendering Culture: Manhood and Womanhood in New Deal Public Art and Theater* (Washington, DC: 1991). Used by permission of Smithsonian Institution Press.

1 The Coit Tower was decorated under the sponsorship of the Public Works of Art Project, predecessor to the Section (and organized by the Section's chief administrator, Edward Bruce). For illustrations of these paintings, see Masha Zakheim Jewett, *Coit Tower, San Francisco: Its History and Art* (San Francisco, CA: 1983).
2 Leopold Scholz to Edward Rowan, 29 June 1937. 121/133, Chattanooga, Tennessee. Numbers refer to Record Group 121, series 133, at the National Archives and Record Administration, Washington, DC; Section correspondence is filed by location of commission – e.g state, city, building.
3 Quoted in *Norristown Times Herald*, 16 November (or 26 November; date unclear) 1936. In 121/133, Norristown, Pennsylvania.
4 Rowan to Jack J. Greitzer, 11 December 1937; Greitzer to Rowan, 13 March 1938. 121/133, Wauseon, Ohio.
5 Waldo Peirce to Rowan, 20 June 1936. 121/133, Westbrook, Maine.
6 Jac T. Bowen to Edward Rowan, 17 June 1941. 121/133, Higginsville, Missouri.
7 For examples, see Philip S. Foner and Reinhard Schultz, *The Other America: Art and the Labour Movement in the United States* (London and West Nyack, NY: 1985).
8 David Montgomery, *Workers' Control in America* (Cambridge, UK: 1979), 13–14.
9 See Marianne Doezema, *American Realism and the Industrial Age* (Cleveland, OH: 1980); Smithsonian Institution Traveling Exhibition Service, *The Working American* (Washington, DC: 1979). For a discussion of the ambiguous intentions of genre scenes of work, see Thomas H. Pauly, "American Art and Labor: The Case of Anshutz's *The Ironworkers' Noontime*," *American Quarterly* 40, 3 (Sept. 1988): 333–58.
10 See George Gurney, *Sculpture and the Federal Triangle* (Washington, DC: 1985).
11 Ben Shahn to Rowan, 6 November 1940. 121/133, Social Security Building, Washington, DC.
12 Rowan to Nicolai Cikovsky, 20 July 1937. 121/133, Interior, Washington, DC.
13 Assistant Secretary of the Interior Burlew to Rowan, 9 December 1939. 121/133, Interior, Washington, DC.

14 Rowan quotes Ickes's review in his letter to Ernest Fiene, 24 October 1938. 121/133, Interior, Washington, DC.

15 Ernest Fiene to Rowan, 26 October 1938. 121/133, Interior, Washington, DC.

16 E. K. Burlew to Rowan, 25 March 1938. 121/133, Interior [Newell], Washington, DC. (Burlew was Ickes's assistant and conveyed his directives.)

17 Rowan reported Ickes's criticism in his letter to Gifford Beal, 17 May 1940. 121/133, Interior [Gifford Beal], Washington, DC.

18 See Mark Naison's excellent *Communists in Harlem during the Depression* (Urbana, IL: 1983).

19 For the classic treatment of the New Deal-era labor movement, see Irving Bernstein, *The Turbulent Years; A History of the American Worker, 1933–1941* (Boston: 1970).

20 James Daugherty to Rowan, 16 December 1938. 121/133, Virden, Illinois.

21 Rowan to James Daugherty, 7 January 1939. 121/133, Virden, Illinois.

22 Michael Lenson to Rowan, 24 April 1942. 121/133, Mount Hope, West Virginia.

23 Intraoffice memo, Rowan to Hopper, 16 November 1939. 121/133, Meyersdale, Pennsylvania.

24 Rowan to Daniel C. Rich (head of Art Institute of Chicago and chairman of Moline, Illinois, competition committee), 17 September 1936. 121/133, Wood River, Illinois.

25 [Mr.] F. Jean Thalinger to Forbes Watson, 16 May 1942; Watson to Thalinger, 22 May 1942. 121/133, Jenkins, Kentucky.

26 Heinz Warneke to Olin Dows, 25 July 1936; Dows to Edwin Forbes, 4 August 1936. 121/133, New York City/Harlem Housing Project. Unfortunately these two letters contain the only references to the conflict in the fragmentary correspondence in this file.

27 See Gail Bederman's discussion of the stereotype of the black rapist in "Civilization, the Decline of Middle-Class Manliness, and Ida B. Wells's Anti-Lynching Campaign, 1892–1894," this volume.

28 See Melissa Dabakis, "Gendered Labor: Norman Rockwell's *Rosie the Riveter* and the Discourses of Wartime Womanhood," this volume.

29 These examples can be found in Gordon K. Grant's mural series painted on four walls of the post office in Ventura, California; Domenico Mortellito's *Life Saver Factory*, one of a series of panels on industries of Port Chester, New York; and Frederick Knight's murals in Johnson City, New York, including female operatives at sewing machines in a shoe factory. Notably, all three examples are found in commissions for mural series; women's paid work is contained within a larger subject and shown as one piece of a varied local economy.

30 Erving Goffman notes that advertisers often use a boy and a girl to constitute the family, a selection that mobilizes the full range of gender and generational relationships. Though he is writing about

advertisements from the 1960s and 1970s, I would argue that this convention holds for other twentieth-century representations of family. See Goffman, *Gender Advertisements* (New York: 1976), 37–40.
31 Ralf Hendricksen to Rowan, 29 May 1939. Rowan at first accepted the design but then reported the Section's reservations; one member had pointed out a number of very similar designs. Rowan enclosed Harry Sternberg's design for Ambler, Pennsylvania, to make his point, and a chagrined Hendricksen redesigned. See Rowan to Hendricksen, 25 September 1939, 121/133, Staunton, Illinois.
32 Edwin Boyd Johnson to Rowan, 30 July 1940. 121/133, Tuscola, Illinois.
33 Karal Ann Marling, in *Wall-to-Wall America: A Cultural History of Post-Office Murals in the Great Depression* (Minneapolis: 1982), 161–81.
34 Ruth Shonle Cavan and Katherine Howland Ranck, *The Family and the Depression* (Chicago: 1938).
35 Mirra Komarovsky, *The Unemployed Man and His Family* (New York: 1940), 133.
36 Ibid., 45.
37 E. Wight Bakke, *Citizens Without Work* (New Haven, CT: 1940); see, for example, responses on p. 176.
38 For a broad treatment of changes of work in the 1920s, see Irving Bernstein, *The Lean Years; a history of the American worker, 1920–1933* (Boston: 1960).
39 Roland Marchand offers a persuasive analysis of the admen's crisis of masculinity; see his *Advertising the American Dream: Making Way for Modernity* (Berkeley: 1985); see especially pp. 25–51.

8

GENDERED LABOR

Norman Rockwell's *Rosie the Riveter* and the discourses of wartime womanhood

Melissa Dabakis

With the mobilization of the home front during the Second World War, plucky women in overalls appeared in advertisements, films, and posters. This startling new image cast women in the heroic industrial roles formerly reserved for the manly worker. Orchestrated by the propaganda bureaus of the wartime New Deal, this rapid transformation offers dramatic evidence for the economic and political motivations of gender ideology. Urgently in need of workers to replace men who had gone to war and to propel the expanded industrial production of war, the government turned to women. Recruitment campaigns produced a deluge of words and images touting women's abilities and exhorting them to join the war effort. But government propaganda also pointedly solicited women's participation only "for the duration," shoring up ideologies of domesticity even as women were encouraged to do "men's" jobs in the work force.

Norman Rockwell's Rosie the Riveter, *on the cover of* Saturday Evening Post *(29 May 1943), became one of the most widely circulated representations of the wartime worker. Melissa Dabakis examines the Rockwell figure as it embodied a wartime discourse on working women. Rosie suggests an uneasy and partial endorsement of women's participation in paid labor, Dabakis argues. Rockwell revises gender conventions in his approving depiction of a woman in work clothing and "male" job, but at the same time he uses the codes of femininity to qualify Rosie's work identity. Finally, Dabakis takes up the representation of the body as a discourse of class (and race) as well as gender, as she explores the significance of wartime representations of female strength, delicacy, and conventional femininity.*

* * *

Visual representation played a large role in the construction of wartime femininity, a social construction rife with contradictions as it sought simultaneously to encourage and limit women's participation in paid work.[1] This essay will examine imagery primarily from 1943, the year that marks the height of wartime industrial and ideological production. Wartime visual imagery in general, and Norman Rockwell's *Rosie the Riveter* in particular, have received little critical attention within the myriad of articles and books devoted to women's wartime experience.[2] The complex problem of *how* visual representation signifies meaning to a diverse audience will be the focus of my argument. Rockwell's *Rosie the Riveter* conveys a fascinating and complex system of signification which fractured any coherent class or gender position. Although normally considered propaganda for the war effort, this popular image registered the contradictions embodied in official wartime ideology and exposed the diversity of women's experiences in the paid work force.

Rockwell's *Rosie the Riveter*, which appeared on the cover of the *Saturday Evening Post* on 29 May 1943, portrays a mature (perhaps 30-year-old) white woman, dressed in overalls with upturned face mask and goggles resting on her forehead (fig. 8.1). She holds an industrial riveting tool on her lap while relaxing during lunch. Her feet trample a copy of *Mein Kampf* – her contribution to the war effort clear. Her heroic and monumental presence is enhanced by her frontal pose, elevated position with respect to the viewer, and patriotic backdrop of the American flag. Two weeks after Rockwell's *Rosie* appeared on the cover of the *Post*, a real-life Rosie appeared in the press. On 8 June 1943 at the Eastern Aircraft Company in Tarrytown, New York, Rose Hicker and her partner drove a record number of rivets into a wing of a Grumman "Avenger" Bomber and became an instant media success.[3] The coincidence of these images and events constructed an ideological frame through which women's wartime experience would be presented to an American public.

Visual representation helped to define a wartime culture even as it revealed the contradictions within any effort to present a unified image of home-front America. In times of crisis, such as war, representation revealed ruptures and fissures normally concealed by the processes of ideology. The demands of the

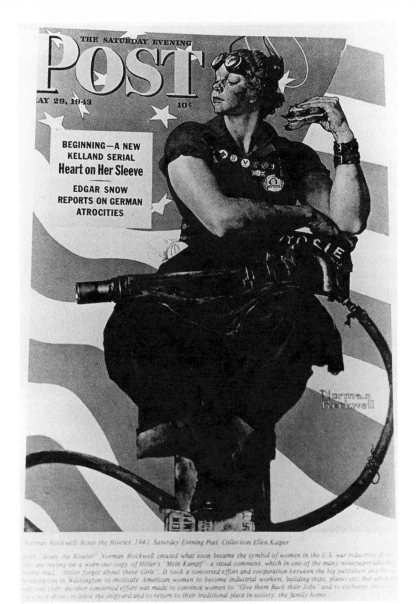

Figure 8.1 Norman Rockwell, *Rosie the Riveter, Saturday Evening Post* cover, 1943.

home front and the disruption of war unsettled gender roles and class structures.[4] Within cultural expression, Rockwell's *Rosie the Riveter* exposed such ruptures in gender and class codes. Moreover, wartime needs dictated a new alliance between state power and cultural production.[5] As we shall see, posters, movies, and magazines presented images designed to support the home-front effort – some explicitly staged and managed by the federal government.

"Rosie the Riveter" was a new construction, a mythic regime, which attempted to control and direct the changing possibilities that the home front presented to women. It formed part of a discourse, a constellation of beliefs, images, and representations, which did not simply reproduce the experience of women but sought to shape that experience.[6] Women responded quite diversely to such mythic constructions as "Rosie the Riveter" – according to the intersecting axes of class, ethnicity, marital status, and number of children. This paper looks at visual representation as one avenue of influence over women's experiences, acknowledging a myriad of possible responses to this wartime imagery.[7]

Norman Rockwell's *Rosie the Riveter* invites a multiplicity of readings. As a cultural text, the image acknowledges both middle-class and working-class women's experiences in industrial jobs through its ability to juxtapose the signs of these women's different wartime experiences. Moreover, the image unfixes traditional gender roles across class lines, providing an uneasy space for women in the male-dominated workplace. Thus, the image served various purposes. As propaganda for the war effort, it urged middle-class women to join the work force "for the duration," blending masculine and feminine signs to suggest the extraordinary nature of women's participation in the labor force. As a symbol of women's working lives, the image inscribed the signs of class upon the female body – Rosie's powerful arms signaled working-class origins – and empowered women whose lives were defined by labor outside the home rather than by domesticity. There is little doubt that Rockwell produced a commanding image of a working woman whose powerful presence affirmed, at least in part, some women's experience in the work force. However, I shall argue that embedded in this image are representational strategies that contain and undermine women's power as workers. Fluctuating and unstable in its meaning, Rockwell's *Rosie the Riveter* gave visual form to the contradictions embedded in wartime ideology.

The historical circumstances of the home front informed both the production and consumption of Rockwell's *Rosie the Riveter*. The new war economy shifted into high gear after the bombing of Pearl Harbor on 7 December 1941. With the need for extensive wartime production and the scarcity of men in the workplace (as many men between the ages of 18 and 40 enlisted or were drafted), "marginal" workers – women, minorities, older people, even disabled people – became targets of recruitment campaigns. Eighteen million women entered the work force during the war years, six million for the first time. Three million women worked in defense plants, but the majority worked in traditional women's occupations.[8] Of women workers, 50 per cent had at least five years' experience, 30 per cent ten years'.[9] What was clear from these figures was that most women had already been in the work force and had converted to wartime jobs; what was new was the influx of middle-class married women into the workplace. Women who performed skilled industrial tasks, among them welding and running a drill press, were small in number and among the elite. They formed a special cadre of women workers whose skilled status and high pay made them clearly visible to the American public. Most women, however, worked in tedious and poorly paid jobs, such as room clerk, waitress, elevator operator, maid, and cook. With women occupying these jobs, men were freed either to fight in the war or to take better-paying war jobs.[10]

Although recruitment campaigns addressed white middle-class women, there was enormous diversity among the women war workers: young, old, African-American, Latina, Anglo, single, married, student, housewife. In major war production centers, such as New York, Los Angeles, and Detroit, the proportion of minority women in the female work force increased from 10 per cent to 19 per cent.[11] In posters and advertisements, however, women of color were invisible – white middle-class women served always as the norm.

Despite employment gains, women war workers were consistently conceived as auxiliary, as temporary replacements for men, and their needs came second to those of men. Job segregation continued during the war years with women's assignments often at the whim of male supervisors.[12] Despite promises of equal pay, often the same job was designated "light" or "heavy" depending on who was in it: if a man occupied it, it was "heavy" and the pay was more; if a woman, the designation was "light" and the pay less.[13] Ultimately the policy of equal pay for equal work protected men who feared that cheap female labor would usurp their jobs.[14] Moreover, women were groomed to participate in the labor force "for the duration." Some were laid off after the war, directed to re-enter the home and "manage consumption."[15] Most women, in fact, remained in the work force but returned to low-paid women's jobs. The common slogan "The woman behind the man behind the gun" adequately expressed a wartime hierarchy that remained prominently in view even as some women crossed traditional gender boundaries at work.[16]

On Columbus Day in 1942, President Roosevelt remarked in a speech: "In some communities employers dislike to hire women. In others, they are reluctant to hire Negroes. We can no longer afford to indulge such prejudice."[17] Wartime mobilization expanded the federal apparatus of the New Deal, and new agencies generated a plethora of studies, images, and exhortations aimed at building wartime production and morale. In April 1942, the government formed the War Manpower Commission (WMC) and, in August 1942, the Woman's Advisory Committee to the WMC.[18]

By far the most influential department was the Office of War Information (OWI), formed in the summer of 1942. This commission exerted influence over private industries that discriminated in hiring and orchestrated an outpouring of home-front propaganda. To accomplish these ends, the OWI entered into an alliance with business and advertisers. Advertising agencies, in need of work because consumer industries had converted to wartime production, created slick messages for the government. In ad campaigns for business, agencies promoted individual companies as patriotic and committed to the war effort.[19] To support this alliance, the Treasury Department announced that advertising in "reasonable" amounts constituted a legitimate wartime business expense and was tax deductible.[20]

The Eureka Vacuum Cleaner Company of Detroit was one of the most active in promoting itself through advertising. In a

1943 *Saturday Evening Post* ad, "Uniform, slacks, or kitchen apron," three women proudly serve in the war effort (fig. 8.2).[21] The copy states: "Right here at Eureka we have a constant reminder of the good fight you're making. For more than 70 percent of those who *man* [emphasis added] Eureka's assembly lines today are women – enlisted in war production. . . . But when victory is final and complete, you – and we – will return to our peacetime jobs." Addressed to a middle-class audience, the message reinforced women's contribution to the war only for the duration while promoting the goodwill of Eureka. It also touted a return to "normalcy" where femininity would be linked to domestic consumerism.

In such enterprises, the lines were blurred between ad copy and journalistic reportage and between war promotion and business promotion, producing an apparently seamless set of ideologically gendered images. The period 1941 to 1945 was a unique moment in the history of representational forms in America as virtually every vehicle of communication and entertainment joined in promoting the war aims of the state.[22] For example, many movies depicted women as war workers – *Swing Shift Maisie* of 1943 with Ann Sutherland as an aircraft worker, *Meet the People* of 1944 with Lucille Ball as a defense plant worker, and *Since You Went Away* of 1944 with Claudette Colbert as a welder, among many others.[23] Songs and even a Broadway play entitled *Rosie the Riveter* achieved popularity.

"Rosie the Riveter," as a wartime image, was a product of this creative collaboration. Federal policy makers, industry leaders, and war contractors deliberately formulated a middle-class identity for the war worker – a hiring strategy that assumed the temporary labor of housewives who did not "need" to work for wages. This recruitment campaign attempted to construct a monolithic category of woman, essentially middle-class and inherently domestic, which had little to do with the actual experiences of women in the work force. Woman as full-time laborer had no apparent place in this discourse. Nonetheless, certain wartime images, as we shall see, did reveal negotiation among conflicting gender ideologies.

The OWI utilized three basic strategies to attract middle-class women into the work force. First, recruitment propaganda offered women good wages and work that was "pleasant and as easy as running a sewing machine, or using a vacuum

Figure 8.2 "Uniform. . . Slacks. . . or Kitchen Apron," advertisement by Eureka Vacuum Cleaner Company, 1943.

cleaner."[24] In a 1943 *Saturday Evening Post* ad from 3M, the copy read, "Now they're sewing metal twice as fast."[25] This ad, showing a riveter at work, transferred home skills to the war industry, connecting war work to women's domestic duties and thus implicitly asserting the temporary quality of the job. Moreover, it implied that women had no experience outside the home, subtly undermining the idea that women and men could do the same work.[26] The second strategy prompted women to take war jobs to save men's lives and help end the war sooner. This message soon turned into a threat: "Every idle machine may mean a dead soldier."[27] Such a message was clearly articulated on the back of a WMC brochure of 1943 entitled "Answers to Questions Women Ask About War Work." In this photographic image, four women stand at their respective machines hard at work; one machine highlighted in red is unoccupied. In a drawn inset, a woman kisses her lover in uniform goodbye. The copy reads: "This soldier may die *unless* you man this idle machine." Such frightening messages appeared commonly in the recruitment campaign, calling women into the work force on the strength of their ties to brothers, sweethearts, husbands, and sons. In a similar strategy, Rockwell's *Rosie the Riveter*, appearing on the cover of the 1943 Memorial Day issue of the *Post*, linked women's war efforts with the war dead and provided a not-so-subtle reminder of women's responsibilities on the home front. Finally, the third strategy, in place by September of 1943, accused any woman who was not working of being a slacker.[28]

Glamour was yet another strategy that lured women into the work force. Not only was the workplace glamorized in the popular media, but the working woman enjoyed a glamorous self-image. One commentator of the war scene noted in 1942:

> Present indications are that newspaper and radio publicity have "glamorized" industrial defense work to such an extent that in some communities the flood of women applicants has been almost embarrassing to the employment offices and war industries.[29]

Glamour fixed and ensured the existence of traditional femininity, as evidenced in a 1943 ad in the *Saturday Evening Post* extolling "Woman-power" (fig. 8.3).[30] This ad was part of the OWI's "Womanpower Campaign," a propaganda effort that championed women's virtues as workers within carefully articulated limits of femininity. The ad copy opened:

> She's 5 feet 1 from her 4A slippers to her sun-gold hair. She loves flower-hats, veils, smooth orchestras – and being kissed by a boy who's now in North Africa. *But, man, oh man, how she can handle her huge and heavy press!* [emphasis in original]

Middle-class femininity was flagged by her size, her hair, her garb, and of course, her boyfriend. In this image, a "vision" of a beautiful woman, flowing blond hair and keenly made-up features, loomed behind the more palpable image of the press with the tiny, svelte woman dwarfed before it. Her hair was covered by a scarf but her hourglass figure was featured despite her denim overalls. She worked the press with the touch of a hand. The copy continued, "Women are able to work beside men on America's roaring production lines *because electricity does the heavy labor*" [emphasis in original]. This ad, sponsored by 114 electrical companies, devalued the woman's skill at the press, giving electricity the credit for wartime production. Moreover, it demonstrated that war workers did not lose their true spirit of womanhood: femininity, marked by glamour, coexisted with the work uniform of overalls and bandanna. As a discursive strategy, "woman-power" strictly regulated female labor, insured its temporary status, and "feminized" necessary job skills.

Allusions to stylish dress and attractive appearance surfaced everywhere for the working woman. For example, the Lockheed Aircraft plant sponsored Victory Fashion shows during lunch breaks in which two-piece work outfits were modeled for the women.[31] Cosmetics were also featured prominently. A photograph of a glamorous model, posed as an ideal worker before a Red Cross backdrop, accompanied a lengthy 1943 article in the *Saturday Evening Post* entitled "Right Face" by author Pete Martin.[32] The article posited the essential nature of cosmetics to women's lives and boldly stated that "The War Face isn't a Battleax." Martin commented on "a fact about women that is one of the strangest stories of the war. They can take bombings and bloodshed, they calmly accept shortages of food or clothing, but a feeling of uneasiness grips them the moment their noses acquire the first faint glimmerings of a shine." He concluded

Figure 8.3 "Woman-power!" advertisement sponsored by
Electrical Companies Under American Business Management, 1943.

that face powder, lipstick, and deodorant (in that order) were necessary ingredients to a woman's sanity during the war years. As Kathy Peiss has argued, powder and paint came to function as essential signs of femininity beginning in the early twentieth century. Cosmetics defined the outward appearance of femininity as massive ad campaigns convinced women that cosmetics were not only respectable but, in fact, a necessary requirement of womanhood.[33]

The *Saturday Evening Post* worked closely with government agencies to promote the war effort. In June 1942, the Magazine Bureau of the OWI was formed, publishing the "Magazine War Guide" which suggested appropriate methods of stressing women's role in the war effort. In addition, "The War Guide for Advertisers," a monthly publication, identified campaign dates, objectives, and promotional methods while providing sample ad layouts for magazines.[34] These guides helped direct the *Post*'s wartime publications. Norman Rockwell, as chief cover illustrator for the *Post*, contributed his energies to the war effort by producing several covers of servicemen returning home from the war and two covers of women war workers.

Participating in a campaign to represent "Women in Necessary Civilian Jobs" on the cover of the 1943 Labor Day issue of magazines (sponsored by the OWI and WMC), Rockwell produced a humorous image of a woman war worker. Bedecked in the red, white, and blue of the American flag, she was shown performing all the jobs necessary to civilian life. Striding across the page with vigor, she held gardening implements and milk bottles to be delivered; she donned telephone operator's gear around her head and a change counter for buses around her waist; she carried an oil can and machinery parts. She could do it all – except no sign of motherhood was apparent. This striking absence complied with OWI guidelines that dictated that any conflict between women, work, and family be minimized in wartime images.

In addition to popular imagery, a proliferation of high-art images during the war years, particularly photographs, captured women in industrial labor. Although women's paid work has varied, the high-art tradition has tended to emphasize the domestic and the clerical, as in the nineteenth-century representations of laundresses by Honoré Daumier and Edgar Degas and the twentieth-century images of women in low-paid clerical or sales jobs by John Sloan and Isaac Soyer. Women's industrial work, usually in the form of unskilled labor, entered the lexicon of visual imagery primarily through the photographs of mill workers and sweatshop workers by Lewis Hine which served as critical commentary during the era of Progressive reform. Moreover, New Deal programs sponsored artists and photographers who produced thousands of images, many representing men and women at work.

The photographer Dorothea Lange, who worked for *Fortune Magazine* in 1942 documenting the expanding wartime industry in California, produced fascinating images of women war workers which, like Rockwell's *Rosie the Riveter*, expressed complex messages about women and labor. She was assigned to photograph the life of shipyard workers at Richmond, an industrial town near San Francisco.[35] In these photographs, she often featured women, as in *Shipyard Worker, Richmond, California* of 1942 (fig. 8.4). Resisting a strict regulation of gender difference, this image challenged prevailing notions of femininity through the signification of body, glance, and dress. Rather than petite with hour-glass form, this figure displays a sturdy and strong body. Rather than posing as coy and shy in demeanor, this woman stares directly into the lens of the camera. And dressed in dirty denim pants, work boots, button-down workshirt, jacket, and hair hidden by a bandanna, she conceals most traditional signs of femininity. Three other figures descend the stairway in the background dressed in slacks, the possibility of assigning gender definitions thwarted. Nonetheless, she stands with dignity on the steps, resting her hand gracefully on the railing in emulation of an elite portrait tradition. Lange dignified her model by creating a visual world that refused to acknowledge conventional sexual difference and class bias.[36]

Unlike the propaganda images disseminated by the OWI which encoded femininity into industrial work, Lange's worker lacked signs of womanhood and thus participated in the transgressive behavior of cross-dressing. Since the nineteenth century, a woman dressing like a man signaled a threat – the demand for male privileges and power.[37] Described as "The New Amazons" by one journalist writing during the war, women war workers became subtly implicated within the discourse of lesbianism, thus perceived, on one level, as a threat to

Figure 8.4 Dorothea Lange, *Shipyard Worker, Richmond, California*, 1942.

gender stability.[38] Dorothea Lange, quite consciously I believe, worked outside the limits of ideological production with these images. Norman Rockwell, on the other hand, had a difficult time managing ideological coherence in his image. As we shall see, he conflated the rhetoric of femininity espoused by the OWI with the potentially subversive signs of cross-dressing. His image conveyed double-edged messages to its varied audience – messages of resistance as well as submission, empowerment as well as containment.

In depicting the woman war worker, Rockwell resisted traditional conventions of representation that signaled the feminine. He borrowed from well-known visual precedents, basing his imagery upon Michelangelo's prophets and sibyls from the Sistine Chapel ceiling. The posture of Rockwell's *Rosie* is nearly identical with that of the *Prophet Isaiah* (fig. 8.5). Both are seated frontally, with head turned to the right, left arms raised, right arms reaching across their bodies, and ankles crossed. The *Cumean Sibyl*, a female figure also from the Sistine Chapel, revealed a similar massive (masculinized) body type, particularly apparent in the exaggerated size of the arms. Rockwell imbued his image of "Rosie" with a monumentality and power characteristic of Michelangelo's androgynous figures, utilizing (whether consciously or unconsciously) such famous "masterworks" as precedents to legitimate the instability in gender construction that his image demonstrated. "Rosie's" swelling muscles, denim work clothes, and phallic riveting tool across her lap marked the masculine order into which she transgressed. Such characteristics of heroic masculinity (which signified resistance and empowerment) were rivaled by and existed in an uneasy collusion with attributes of femininity (which signified submission and containment) – the necklace of merit buttons and industrial identification tags across her denim bodice, the halo-like ring formed by the upturned face shield, the lipstick and rouge which adorned her face, and finally her lace hanky and compact peeking from her overalls pocket.

"Rosie's" femininity is further emphasized through her association with food – the domestic replaces the industrial as the focus of her attention. "Rosie" is shown relaxing over lunch: her left hand holds a ham sandwich directed toward her face and her right hand rests protectively upon her lunchbox, inscribed in white letters with her name. Within this image,

Figure 8.5 Michelangelo, *The Prophet Isaiah*, n.d.

woman, food, and nurturance form a signifying chain which posits "Rosie's" world firmly in the orbit of traditional femininity. These associations are underscored by a 1943 ad for the *Ladies' Home Journal*, "Never Underestimate the Power of a Woman."[39] In this cartoon, two women war workers, bandannaed and bowed, act as civilizing agents to the coarse and crude masculine nature. In the top strip, the gruff and unmannered workers chomp at their lunches; in the bottom strip these same men remove their hats, comb their hair, and eat politely with knives and forks when accompanied by women.

Although Rockwell portrays his figure at the workplace, "Rosie" is at rest, not riveting. She sits poised with a very large automatic riveting hammer sprawled across her lap. Positioned in the exact center of the image, the machine demands the viewer's attention. Its size, shape, and position make the association with the phallus unmistakable. However, it lies unattended; "Rosie" does not handle it and thus reveals no agency. In this representation, Rockwell has neutralized the power that women potentially wield in the work force.

Furthermore, the magazine cover presents a highly veiled image of maternity, a sublimated message that promoted women's return to domesticity after the war. The image suggests yet another work by Michelangelo, *The Pietà*, in which a powerful maternal figure cradles the body of her dead son. Alluding to Michelangelo's figural composition, "Rosie's" over-sized lap holds her jacket upon which the large tool rests. Both the riveting hammer (symbol of the phallic order) and the power hose (allusion to an umbilical cord) construct femininity through coded signs of maternity. As woman, "Rosie" reproduces the masculine order in the sign of the riveting hammer but does not participate in the making of that order. Woman is relegated to the realm of reproduction rather than that of production.

In the configuration of "Rosie's" body, Rockwell departs from the images of middle-class war workers that dominate OWI propaganda and many other wartime representations. Through her name and prominent Irish facial features (red cheeks, turned-up nose, prominent jaw), "Rosie" is identified as ethnic and working class.[40] Her strong and powerful arms are also important signifiers of class in their exaggerated size and dominant position within the image. She is presented as a worker rather than as a middle-class housewife working "for the duration." "Rosie" wears no wedding ring but sports a large leather band around her wrist which supports her muscles in heavy labor, protecting her arm from the harsh jolts of the riveting gun. Thus, labor is made visible in the sign of the arm.

This image shared with many other war posters an emphasis on arms. In a poster produced by the War Production Co-ordinating Committee, "We Can Do It," a young, pretty, white woman looks directly out at the viewer, flexing her biceps while rolling up her sleeves (fig. 8.6). Her gesture proclaims her proud determination and commitment to the war effort. The OWI poster of 1942 by David S. Martin, "Strong in the Strength of the Lord," also focused upon arms and hands. Three over-lifesized arms comprise the composition: a gloved workman's hand holding a large pipe wrench, a soldier's hand holding a rifle whose bayonet moves directly out into the viewer's space, and a woman's hand holding a smaller (clearly more delicate) open-end-shaped wrench – her sex signaled by her ornamented shirt sleeve and decorative hand tool. Although the smallest of the three, her arm is large and muscular with little sign of feminine delicacy (except for the rickrack on her sleeve). Her strength is nearly equal to that of the men – a strength kept in check by feminine attributes at both ends of her arm. In the sign of the arm, the contradictions implicit in the rhetoric of women and labor were exposed. These are not the bodies of middle-class women whose dainty and delicate arms, wrists, and hands performed such detailed domestic labor as needlework. These images represented the bodies of (unsexed) workers, their femininity only partially asserted.[41]

Many wartime images openly contradicted the rhetoric addressed to working women in contemporary documents, such as OWI pamphlets and ad copy. In these publications, women's abilities were defined and limited by their arm reach and the delicateness of their hands. For example, in an article entitled "Engineers of Womanpower" of 1943, sexual difference was clearly articulated:

> On certain kinds of operations – the very ones requiring high manipulative skill – women were found to be a whole lot quicker and more efficient than men. Engineering womanpower means realizing fully that women are not only different from men in such things as lifting power and

Figure 8.6 "We Can Do It!" poster produced by the War Production
Co-ordinating Committee, n.d.

arm reach [emphasis added] – but in many other ways that pertain to their physiological and their social functions. To understand these things does not mean to exclude women from the jobs for which they are peculiarly adapted, and where they can help to win this war. It merely means using them as women, and not as men.[42]

In this literature, women were groomed for jobs that required dexterity rather than strength. Moreover, women war workers were defined as women first and foremost, and as laborers second. The OWI pamphlet *War Jobs for Women* presented a similar description of women's work: "High-pressured production for two years has proven that women *excel in the tasks that require sharp eyes, suppleness of wrist, delicate touch, repetitive motion, exactness*" [emphasis in original].[43] Although such tasks were not typical of women's industrial work, this rhetoric linked women's work outside the home to domestic pursuits.[44] Rockwell's *Rosie the Riveter* as well as other wartime imagery remained inconsistent with this rhetoric; portraying "Rosie's" strength, Rockwell seemed to acknowledge women's (at least temporary) increased power in the work force.

Rockwell's *Rosie the Riveter* did not articulate a unitary message. Middle-class and working-class signs as well as feminine and masculine signs coexisted in an uneasy tension. Appearing on the cover of the *Saturday Evening Post* with its markedly middle-class readership, this image presented a powerful, competent, and highly skilled worker, an image whose purpose was to lure middle-class women into the work force. But at the same time, this competent worker inhabited a body marked as working class – heavy, ponderous, and muscular. Delicacy and refinement (often characteristics of middle-class glamour) had been abandoned and femininity was reconstituted in terms of strength. Both complicitous with and resistant to dominant wartime constructions of femininity, Rockwell's *Rosie the Riveter* embodied contemporary renegotiations of gender on the home front.

NOTES

1 This paper was first presented at the Eighth Berkshire Conference on the History of Women, Douglass College, New Brunswick, New

Jersey in June of 1990. I would like to extend my particular thanks to Ellen Furlough, Barbara Melosh, Tim Quigley, Ellen Todd, and Cécile Whiting for their close reading and useful criticisms of this paper. Many other friends and colleagues heard this paper in a variety of settings – my appreciation for their insightful comments is extensive.

2 Two scholars, Maureen Honey and Michael Renov, have addressed problems of visual representation in differing ways. In *Creating Rosie the Riveter* (Amherst, MA: 1984), Honey provides a very useful class analysis of the differing strategies used by middle-class and working-class journals to construct a wartime experience for their female readership. Although she illustrates certain wartime magazine ads, visual representation is not the focus of her study. Michael Renov, a film theorist, engages in a cultural analysis of wartime films (see specific citations below).

3 Pamela Warford, "The Social Origins of Female Iconography: Selected Images of Women in American Popular Culture, 1890–1940," Ph.D. dissertation, Washington University, 1979, 104–5.

4 Margaret R. Higonnet, Jane Jensen, Sonya Michel, and Margaret C. Weitz, eds, *Behind the Lines* (New Haven, CT: 1987). See especially "Introduction," 5; and Margaret R. Higonnet and Patrice L.-R. Higonnet, "The Double Helix," 41, in that volume.

5 Michael Renov, "The State, Ideology and *Priorities on Parade*," *Film Reader* 5 (1982): 217.

6 Denise Mann, "Rosie the Riveter – Construction or Reflection?" *Quarterly Review of Film and Video*, 11, 1 (1989): 117–18.

7 Denise Riley has argued for a complex historical reading of women's wartime experience, asserting that women's needs and desires had never been fully articulated (even to themselves) as members of the wartime social formation. Thus as historians, she warned, we cannot expect to reconstruct a reality which had never existed in any clarity. See Denise Riley, "Some Peculiarities of Social Policy Concerning Women in Wartime and Postwar Britain," in Higonnet, *et al.*, eds, *Behind the Lines*, 270.

8 Miriam Frank, Marilyn Ziebarth, and Connie Field, *The Life and Times of Rosie the Riveter* (Emeryville, CA: 1982): 15–16.

9 Honey, *Creating Rosie the Riveter*, 14.

10 Michael Renov, *Hollywood's Wartime Women: Representation and Ideology* (Ann Arbor, MI: 1988), 39.

11 Frank, *et al.*, *The Life and Times of Rosie the Riveter*, 17.

12 Ruth Milkman, *Gender at Work* (Urbana, IL: 1987), 56.

13 Frank, *et al.*, *The Life and Times of Rosie the Riveter*, 19; Milkman, *Gender at Work*, 60.

14 Office of War Information, Magazine Section, *War Jobs for Women*, (Washington, DC: 1942), 19.

15 Michael Renov, "Advertising/Photojournalism/Cinema: The Shifting Rhetoric of Forties Female Representation," *Quarterly Review of Film and Video* 11, 1 (1989): 6.

16 Higonnet, *et al.*, eds, *Behind the Lines*, "Introduction," 6.

17 Quoted in Sheila Berger Gluck, *Rosie the Riveter Revisited* (New York: 1987), 10.
18 Leila J. Rupp, *Mobilizing Women for War* (Princeton, NJ: 1978), 86–9.
19 Honey, *Creating Rosie the Riveter*, 28–32.
20 Renov, *Hollywood's Wartime Women*, 30.
21 *Saturday Evening Post* 215 (26 June 1943): 93.
22 Renov, "Advertising/Photojournalism/Cinema," 3.
23 Warford, "The Social Origins of Female Iconography," footnote 15, 125.
24 Rupp, *Mobilizing Women for War*, 96.
25 *Saturday Evening Post* 215 (26 June 1943): 99.
26 Honey, *Creating Rosie the Riveter*, 129.
27 "Preliminary Supplement (A) to the U.S. Government Campaign on Manpower," March 1943. Quoted in Rupp, *Mobilizing Women for War*, 96.
28 Rupp, *Mobilizing Women for War*, 96–7.
29 Helen Baker, *Women in War Industries* (Princeton, NJ: 1942), 10.
30 *Saturday Evening Post* 215 (12 June 1943): 55.
31 Gluck, *Rosie the Riveter*, 11.
32 *Saturday Evening Post* 215 (13 March 1943): 21ff.
33 Kathy Peiss, "Making Faces: The Cosmetics Industry and the Cultural Construction of Gender, 1890–1930," *Genders* 7 (Spring 1990): 143–69.
34 Honey, *Creating Rosie the Riveter*, 33–9.
35 Milton Meltzer, *Dorothea Lange* (New York: 1978), 247; and Karin Becker Ohrn, *Dorothea Lange and the Documentary Tradition* (Baton Rouge, LA: 1980), 148–9.
36 Other Lange images attempt a dismantling of prevailing gender and class codes. See also, for example, *Shipyard Construction Workers, Richmond, California*; and *End of Shift, Richmond, California*. All photos date from 1942.
37 The most useful readings on cross-dressing are in Carroll Smith-Rosenberg, *Disorderly Conduct: Visions of Gender in Victorian America* (New York: 1985), 245–97; Simone de Beauvois, *The Second Sex*, trans. and ed. H. M. Parshley (New York: 1974), especially 470–1; Judith Butler, *Gender Trouble: Feminism and the Subversion of Identity* (New York: 1990); Marjorie Garber, *Vested Interests: Cross-Dressing and Cultural Anxiety* (New York: 1992); and Judith Roof, *A Lure of Knowledge: Lesbian Sexuality and Theory* (New York: 1991).
38 Max Lerner, "The New Amazons," in *Public Journal: Marginal Notes on Wartime America* (New York: 1945), 19. "The New Amazons" was written on 11 February 1943. For fascinating discussions on lesbianism and cross-dressing in the early twentieth century, see Esther Newton, "The Mythic Mannish Lesbian: Radclyffe Hall and the New Woman," *Signs* 9 (Summer 1984): 557–75; and Sandra M. Gilbert, "Costumes of the Mind: Transvestism as Metaphor in Modern Literature," *Critical Inquiry* (Winter 1980): 391–417.
39 *Saturday Evening Post* 215 (16 January 1943): 91.
40 See L. Perry Curtis, Jr., *Apes and Angels: The Irishman in Victorian*

Caricature (Washington, DC: 1971) for a discussion of the tradition of caricaturing the Irish. My thanks to Eugene Dwyer for his thoughts on this matter.

41 Throughout the history of art, such visual conventions have come to mark the bodies of female servants and working-class women. In a very striking historical example, Jacques-Louis David's *Brutus* of 1789, the servant, firmly relegated to the feminine realm of the painting, was set apart from the other women by her body. Her arms were large, muscled, and masculine and the strength of her body rivaled the delicacy of Brutus's wife who mourned the death of her young sons condemned by their father for treason. In a more recent example from *The Harriet Tubman Series* of 1939–40, Jacob Lawrence presented a monumental image of a black woman at work. Tubman's large and powerful arms and hands, emerging from her large squared shoulders, performed the heavy task of sawing wood. Lawrence inscribed the status of slave upon Tubman's body while simultaneously marking her with superhuman (masculinized) strength.

42 *Automotive War Production* 2 (October 1943): 4–5, quoted in Milkman, *Gender at Work*, 59.

43 Office of War Information, *War Jobs for Women*, 21.

44 Milkman, *Gender at Work*, 61.

Part III

GENDER AS POLITICAL LANGUAGE

9

CIVILIZATION, THE DECLINE OF MIDDLE-CLASS MANLINESS, AND IDA B. WELLS'S ANTI-LYNCHING CAMPAIGN (1892–94)

Gail Bederman

Gail Bederman explores the connections of gender, class, and race in her interpretation of Ida B. Wells, black reformer, whose campaign against lynching hinged on her challenges to prevailing rhetorics of manliness. First, Wells countered the stereotype of the black rapist – the African-American man as the emblem of uncontrolled lust and sexual violence – with evidence of white men's abuse of black women. Then she portrayed lynching as the work of cowardice, debunking white apologists who depicted lynching as manly defense of white women's purity. Wells's rhetoric embodied a shrewd understanding of contemporary discourses of masculinity, Bederman argues. Using Chicago's 1893 Columbian Exposition as a cultural text, Bederman interprets the images of manliness and the middle-class racial ideals that it included. By the late nineteenth century, she argues, definitions of middle-class manhood were threatened by social and economic shifts; in response, ideals of manliness drew more heavily on a notion of civilized white men in contrast to racial "others."

Bederman concludes her essay by challenging critics of poststructuralist theory who have argued that it directs us away from political action and political understanding. On the contrary, Bederman counters, Wells's campaign shows that the analysis of discourse may serve the cause of social change.

* * *

For, if civilization means anything, it means self-restraint; casting away self-restraint the white man becomes as

207

savage as the negro—Ray Stannard Baker, "What is a Lynching?"[1]

It is the white man's civilization and the white man's government which are on trial.—Ida B. Wells, *A Red Record*[2]

All England's congenital meddlers and busybodies are forming societies for civilizing us, and express themselves about our social state in language which Samoan natives would resent.—*New York Times*, 19 August 1894[3]

In March 1894, Ida B. Wells sailed to England in order to agitate against the rise of racial violence in the United States. She left a country where lynching was rarely mentioned in the white Northern press; where she herself was unknown to most whites. In June 1894, she returned a celebrity, villified as a "slanderous and nasty-minded mulatress"[4] by some papers and lauded by others. Above all, she returned to an America where lynching was widely discussed as a stain on American civilization.

Wells's success in bringing lynching to the attention of the Northern middle class was due, in large part, to her ingenious manipulations of the Northern middle class's widespread fears about declining male power. By playing on Americans' anxiety about gender dominance, she was able to raise the stakes among middle-class Northern whites, who had previously tolerated lynching as a colorful, if somewhat old-fashioned, Southern regional custom (e.g., the *New York Times* humorously editorialized in 1891, "the friends of order [in Alabama] have been in pursuit of a negro. . . . If they catch him they will lynch him, but this incident will not be likely to add to the prevailing excitement" of the more "serious" moonshining problem).[5] Historians have long recognized Wells's successful debunking of the myth of the black rapist, but this was only part of her larger strategy of playing on the 1890s' gender tensions.[6] As the epigraphs suggest, Wells brilliantly and subversively manipulated dominant middle-class ideas about race, manhood, and civilization in order to force white Americans to address lynching. Wells, in short, convinced nervous whites that lynching imperiled American manhood.

To understand how Wells played upon white Northerners'

fears about dwindling manhood, we need to understand the centrality of Victorian manliness to 1890s middle-class identity. From the time the middle class had begun to form itself as a class, gender had been a crucial element of middle-class self-definition.[7] Between 1820 and 1860, as increasing numbers of men had begun to earn comfortable livings as entrepreneurs, professionals, and managers, the middle class had become increasingly conscious of itself as a class, with interests, tastes, and lifestyles different from both the very rich and from those who performed manual labor. In large cities as well as smaller towns, they and their families began to differentiate themselves from other social elements by stressing their gentility, respectability, and adherence to evangelical Christian values.[8]

Gender was central to this self-definition.[9] Indeed, according to Mary Ryan, "the American middle class molded its distinctive identity around domestic values and family practices," especially as elaborated and instituted by evangelical Protestant women.[10] The middle class celebrated true women as pious, maternal guardians of virtue and domesticity, and contrasted pure, domestic middle-class women with working-class women, whose evident willingness to neglect domestic duties made them appear un-Christian and morally deficient.[11]

Manhood was equally crucial to middle-class identity. Middle-class constructions of both manliness and womanliness centered around willful control of sin.[12] Yet the middle class believed that men, unlike "naturally good" women, were beset by powerful gusts of sinful desires.[13] This passionate masculine nature was considered simultaneously the source of men's greatest danger and of men's greatest power. Succumbing to overwhelming emotion or sexual passion would sap a man's force, rendering him weak and degenerate.[14] Therefore, middle-class parents taught their sons to build a strong, manly "character" as they would build a muscle, through repetitive exercises of control over impulse.[15] The middle class saw this ability to control powerful masculine passions through strong character and a powerful will as a primary source of men's strength and authority. By gaining the manly strength to control *himself*, a man gained the strength, as well as the duty, to protect and direct those weaker than himself: his wife, his children, or his employees. The mingled honor, high-mindedness, and strength stemming from this powerful self-mastery were encapsulated in the term "manliness."[16] Middle-class men invoked ideals of manliness in business and domestic practices throughout the nineteenth century.

In the context of the market economy's unpredictability, a strong character built on high-minded self-restraint was seen as the rock on which middle-class men could build their fortunes. Middle-class men were awarded – or denied – credit based on others' assessment of the manly strength of their characters, and credit raters like *Dun and Bradstreet* reported on businessmen's honesty, probity, and family life.[17] Manly control over impulse also helped the middle class develop its distinctive family practices. Celebrations of manly self-restraint encouraged young men to work hard and live abstemiously, so that they could amass the capital to go into business for themselves, and to postpone marriage until they could support a family in proper middle-class style.[18] In short, by the end of the century, a discourse of manliness stressing self-mastery and restraint expressed and shaped middle-class identity.

By the 1890s, however, both manliness and middle-class identity seemed to falter. Middle-class manliness had been created in the context of a small-scale, competitive capitalism, which had all but disappeared by the 1890s. In the context of a bureaucratic, interdependent society, the manly codes of self-restraint began to seem less relevant. For example, with the growth of large-scale corporate enterprises, the proportion of middle-class men who could aspire to independent entrepreneurship dwindled. At the same time, the rapid expansion of low-level clerical work in stores and offices meant that young men beginning their careers as clerks were unlikely to gain promotion to responsible, well-paid management positions, as had clerks in their fathers' generation.[19] Under these conditions, manly self-denial grew increasingly unprofitable. Concurrent with middle-class men's narrowing career opportunities came new opportunities for commercial leisure. The growth of a consumer culture encouraged many middle-class men, faced with lowered career expectations, to find identity in leisure instead of in work.[20] Yet codes of manliness dictated they must work hard and become economically independent. The consumer culture's ethos of pleasure and frivolity clashed with ideals of manly self-restraint, further undermining the potency of middle-class manliness.[21]

Although cultural and economic changes had taken their toll, middle-class men continued to uphold manliness, for abandoning it would mean abandoning male power itself. Discourses of manliness were embedded in their very identities. They formed their sons into men by teaching them manliness. Especially in the context of challenges from the Gilded Age women's movement, abandoning familiar constructs of manliness was an unimaginable option.

Instead, middle-class men, uncomfortably confused about the nature and sources of male power, began to cast about for new ways to fortify their shaky constructions of manliness. They adopted a variety of strategies, from growing crazes for body building and college football, to warnings of neurasthenic breakdowns among overworked middle-class men.[22] A new rhetoric about maleness appeared. Contemporaries coined the new epithets "sissy," "pussyfoot," and "stuffed shirt,"[23] and began to speak approvingly about something they called "masculinity." The noun "masculinity," although rarely used until the late 1890s, would soon come into frequent parlance – precisely because it could convey new and different connotations about maleness than the more usual "manliness." These reformulations frequently were fragmented and contradictory. For example, increasing numbers of middle-class men frequented urban red light districts, yet many remained confused and ambivalent about the meaning of their illicit sexual activity. Was it an inevitable outcropping of naturally explosive masculine passions? Or was it a sordid loss of manly self-control and a sign of moral weakness?[24] In short, by the time Ida B. Wells sailed for England in 1893, middle-class manliness had taken on the character of a beloved but fragile friend, whose weakness must at all costs remain unacknowledged.

To recoup their losses and explain what made them powerful as men, many middle-class men began to focus on race and the qualities which made them powerful as "the *white* man." The 1890s were a period of virulent racism and racially conceived nativism.[25] The primarily native-born middle class gazed with distaste upon increasing crowds of eastern and southern European immigrants, and saw masses of unassimilable "races," whose unfamiliar customs and tendency to vote for "machine" Democrats challenged middle-class control of American cities. Anglo-Saxonism provided one powerful explanation of middle-class men's supremacy, by rooting white manhood in racial traits purportedly developed long ago in the forests of Germany.[26] White Americans believed the Anglo-Saxon race, as Francis Parkman put it, was "peculiarly masculine." Anglo-Saxons were described as independent, adventurous, strong of will, tenacious of purpose – as manly.[27]

The trope "the white man" also linked powerful manhood to race. When 1890s whites spoke of "the white man," they usually paired him with "the negro" or "the Indian." Referring to "the black man" or "the red man," the logical parallel construction, would mean conceding that black and red men were equally manly – thus undercutting the ideological work of the phrase "the white man." For example, in 1905 Ray Stannard Baker argued that lynching was unworthy of "the white man," because it rendered him as unmanly as "the negro": "For if civilization means anything, it means self-restraint; casting away self-restraint the white man becomes as savage as the negro."[28] But perhaps the most important thing about "the white man" – as the Baker quote also suggests – was the way it worked as a synecdoche. By referring to "the white man," contemporaries simultaneously invoked the manly white males who were "civilized" and "civilization" itself.

Affirming the manly power of the white man's "civilization" was one of the most powerful ways middle-class men found to assert their interwoven racial, class, and gender dominance. "Civilization" kept the weakness of manliness hidden by repeatedly interweaving manhood and race and affirming that white racial superiority proved white men the most manly in the world. Since Wells built her entire English anti-lynching tour around resistance to this discourse of "civilization," we need to spend some time examining it.

In the Darwinist 1890s, "civilization" had become a racial concept. Rather than simply meaning "the west" or "industrially advanced societies," "civilization" denoted a precise stage in human evolution – the one following the more primitive stages of "savagery" and "barbarism." Human races progressed in historical steps from simple and less valuable "savagery," through "barbarism," to advanced and more valuable "civilization." But only whites had, as yet, advanced to the civilized stage. In fact, people believed "civilization" was itself a *racial* trait, *inherited* by all Anglo-Saxons and other "advanced" white races.[29]

Gender was an essential component of civilization, for extreme sexual difference was seen as a hallmark of civilization's advancement. Savage (that is, nonwhite) men and women were almost identical, but civilized races had evolved the pronounced sexual differences celebrated in the middle-class's doctrine of "separate spheres." Civilized women were "womanly" – spiritual, motherly, dedicated to the home. And civilized white men were the most manly ever evolved – firm of character, self-controlled, protectors of women and children.[30]

But the power of "civilization" stemmed from the way it *interwove* middle-class beliefs about racial and gender hierarchy. "Civilization" portrayed white male power as natural; male dominance and white supremacy were products of human evolutionary development. Harnessing manliness to white supremacy, and celebrating both as essential to human progress, "civilization" temporarily revitalized middle-class Victorian manliness.

To understand how the discourse of civilization reinforced the power of manliness, let's consider a familiar example: Chicago's 1893 Columbian Exposition. In authorizing the Exposition, Congress had called for "an exhibition of the progress of civilization in the New World."[31] In order to exhibit "the progress of civilization," the organizers divided the World's Fair into two areas.[32] The civilized section, known as the "White City," celebrated advanced, masculine technology. Its focal point was the majestic "Court of Honor," a formal basin almost a half-mile long, surrounded by massive white *beaux arts* buildings. "Honorable," according to an 1890 dictionary, was a synonym for "manly," and contemporaries would not have missed the court's association with manhood.[33] The seven huge buildings framing the Court of Honor represented seven aspects of the highest civilized advancement (Manufactures, Mines, Agriculture, Art, Administrations, Machinery, and Electricity), all presented as the domain of civilized white *men*. These buildings housed thousands of enormous engines, warships, trains, machines, and armaments. The White City also glorified middle-class men's familiar world of commerce, exhibiting the most advanced products and manufacturing processes – "dynamos and rock drills, looms and wallpaper" – and housing these exhibits in magnificent white temples.[34] In short, by celebrating "civilization," the White City celebrated the power and perfection of Victorian manhood, and poets hailed it as "A Vision of Strong Manhood and Perfection of Society."[35]

Woman's place in the "advancement of civilization" was represented in the White City by the smaller, much less formidable Woman's Building. Despite the feminist intentions of its board of Lady Managers, visitors were impressed mostly by the Woman's Building's softness, compared to the masculine dynamos and technological marvels of the rest of the White City. Said the *New York Times*, "the achievements of man [are] in iron, steel, wood, and the baser and cruder products. . . [while] in the Woman's Building one can note. . . more refined avenues of effort which culminate in the home, the hospital, the church, and in personal adornment."[36] Its location underlined women's marginality: Not only was the Woman's Building located at the very edge of the manly White City, it was also situated immediately opposite the White City's only exit to the uncivilized Midway. On the border between civilized and savage (as befit women who, according to modern science, were more primitive than men), the Woman's Building underlined the manliness of the white man's civilization.[37]

In contrast, the Midway, the Exposition's uncivilized section, provided spectacles of barbarism – "authentic" villages of Samoans, Egyptians, Dahomans, Turks, and other exotic races.[38] Guidebooks advised visitors to visit the Midway only after visiting the White City, in order to fully appreciate the contrast between the civilized White City and the uncivilized native villages.[39] Where the White City spread out in all directions from the Court of Honor, emphasizing the complexity of manly civilization, the Midway's attractions were organized linearly down a broad avenue, providing a lesson in racial hierarchy. Visitors entering the Midway from the White City would first pass the German and Irish villages, proceed past the barbarous Turkish, Arabic, and Chinese villages, and finish by viewing the savage American Indians and Dahomans. "What an opportunity was here afforded to the scientific mind to descend the spiral of evolution," enthused the *Chicago Tribune*, "tracing humanity in its highest phases down almost to its animalistic origins."[40]

Where the White City stressed the manliness of the white

man's civilization, the Midway's villages depicted the absence of manliness among uncivilized, nonwhite races. In the Persian, Algerian, Turkish, and Egyptian villages, for example, unmanly dark-skinned men cajoled customers to shed manly restraint and savor their countrywomen's sensuous dancing.[41] Male audiences ogling scantily clad belly dancers could have it both ways, simultaneously relishing the dances' suggestiveness and basking in their own sense of civilized superiority to the swarthy men hawking tickets outside, unashamedly vending their countrywomen's charms.[42] Those who had just visited the White City would be especially conscious of their own racially superior manliness.

Least manly of all the Midway's denizens, according to many commentators, were the savage Dahomans, who seemed to lack gender difference entirely. The *New York Times* described "The Dahomey gentleman (or perhaps it is a Dahomey lady, for the distinction is not obvious), who may be seen at almost any hour. . .clad mainly in a brief grass skirt and capering nimbly to the lascivious pleasings of an unseen tom-tom pounded within. . . . There are several dozen of them of assorted sexes, as one gradually makes out. . ." The columnist then ridiculed African-American spectators for imagining themselves more civilized than the Dahomans.[43]

The bifurcation of the Columbian Exposition between civilized White City and uncivilized Midway worked only if the darkest races were always represented as insurmountably savage. Therefore, organizers rebuffed the many African-Americans who worked tirelessly to gain representation on the White City's organizing bodies. The Exposition's logic of constructing manly white civilization in opposition to savage swarthy barbarism made it impossible for the white organizers to recognize the existence of fully civilized African-Americans. Black men and women objected vociferously to their exclusion and agitated to be included in the exhibits and planning committees, but to no avail.[44]

Ida B. Wells, like most educated African-Americans, was outraged by this racist exclusiveness. Always attuned to the cultural dynamics behind whites' racism, in her counterattack she pinpointed the key discourse: the Exposition's celebrations of manly white American "civilization." Along with Frederick Douglass, she called for black Americans to fund a pamphlet, printed in English, French, German, and Spanish, in which civilized African-Americans could explain to the rest of the civilized world why the less-than-civilized Exposition organizers had excluded them. Warning that "The absence of colored citizens from participating therein will be construed to their disadvantage by the representatives of the civilized world there assembled," Wells promised her pamphlet would set forth "the past and present condition of our people and their relation to American civilization."[45]

And it did. Entitled "The Reason Why the Colored American is not in the World's Columbian Exposition," the pamphlet inverted the white organizers' depiction of manly civilization as the opposite of Negro savagery. Instead, Wells argued, the best illustration of America's "moral grandeur" and civilization would have been to exhibit the phenomenal progress African-Americans had made after only twenty-five years of freedom. For centuries, American blacks had "contributed a large share to American prosperity and civilization."[46] Why, then, was the colored American not in the World's Columbian Exposition?

The pamphlet's answer, left implicit to avoid excessive confrontation, was that the *white* American was not the manly civilized being he pretended to be. Wells's coauthor Frederick Douglass made this argument, lamenting the unfortunate necessity of speaking plainly of wrongs and outrages endured "in flagrant contradiction to boasted American Republican liberty and civilization."[47] Indeed, far from embodying high civilization, white Americans still embraced "barbarism and race hate."[48] Yet the Negro was "manfully resisting" this oppression, and "is now by industry, economy and education wisely raising himself to conditions of civilization and comparative well being."[49] Douglass concluded his chapter by insisting upon black manliness: "We are men and our aim is perfect manhood, to be men among men. Our situation demands faith in ourselves, faith in the power of truth, faith in work and faith in the influence of manly character."[50]

The balance of the pamphlet, compiled and partly written by Ida B. Wells, documented Douglass's assertion of black manhood. Since emancipation, African-Americans had demonstrated manly character, making phenomenal strides in education, the professions, the accumulation of wealth, and literature. Nonetheless, white Americans had perversely

216

attacked this youthful black manliness – through oppressive legislation, disfranchisement, the convict lease system, and the "barbarism" of lynch law. Finally, the pamphlet documented the Exposition organizers' deliberate exclusion of blacks – except, Douglass sniffed, "as if to shame the Negro, the *Dahomians* are also here to exhibit the Negro as a repulsive savage."[51] In short, the pamphlet demonstrated that excluding the African-American from the Columbian Exposition, far from glorifying American civilization, demonstrated American barbarism.

Wells and Douglass, headquartered in the White City's small Haitian Building, distributed 10,000 copies of *The Reason Why* during the three months before the Fair closed. (Debarred from representing his own nation, Douglass had been named Haiti's representative to the Exposition.) Wells received responses from England, Germany, France, Russia, and India.[52] Yet Wells's greatest success in turning the claims of "manly civilization" against white racism lay not in her World's Fair agitation, but in her 1892–94 campaigns against lynching.

In 1892, one year before Wells and Douglass published their pamphlet, Wells had been forced into Northern exile by her agitation against lynching. At 30, she was already an experienced journalist and agitator. Since March 1892, she had spearheaded black Memphis's protest against the heinous lynchings of three respected local businessmen, one of whom had been a close personal friend. Finally, in May, she wrote her famous editorial: "Nobody in this section of the country believes the old thread bare lie that Negro men rape white women. If Southern white men are not careful, they will over-reach themselves and public sentiment will have a reaction; a conclusion will then be reached which will be very damaging to the moral reputation of their women."[53] White Memphis's violent response shocked Wells: editorialists threatened her with mutilation and hanging; her presses were seized and sold; and white men watched her home, vowing to kill her on sight.

Exiled to the North, she framed new tactics for her new circumstances. While she continued to urge black Americans to boycott, vote, and agitate against white oppressors,[54] she knew these methods alone could not stop lynching. Instead, as she later recalled, she focused her efforts on "the white press, since it was the medium through which I hoped to reach the white people of the country, who alone could mold public sentiment."[55] Yet the white Northern press excluded most African-American writers. To gain a hearing in the white press, Wells was forced to create effective new arguments and tactics. To this end, she began to work to counter the middle class's interweavings of manly authority and white racial dominance.[56]

One month after Wells arrived in the North, *The New York Age*, a major black newspaper, published Wells's attack on Southern lynching, later reprinted as *Southern Horrors*.[57] This pamphlet, addressed to the American people, black and white, described dozens of gruesome, horrific Southern lynchings, each appalling enough to convince any open-minded reader that lynching must be stopped. Yet Wells had long lost faith that white Americans would be open-minded where racial justice was concerned.[58] Aware that whites would shrug off tales of tortured black men, Wells chose to invoke an issue that she knew would affect white men more viscerally: their fears of declining manliness.

Wells recognized that inherent in the "lynching for rape" scenario was a symbolic celebration of the power of Victorian manliness. Like the White City – which demanded that black men be represented as unmanly savages so that white men could embody powerful, manly civilization – the "lynching for rape" scenario represented black men as unmanly rapists, so that white men could embody powerful, manly self-restraint. As Jacquelyn Dowd Hall has argued, by constructing black men as "natural" rapists and by resolutely and bravely avenging the (alleged) rape of pure white womanhood, Southern white men constructed themselves as ideal men: "patriarchs, avengers, righteous protectors."[59]

This "lynching for rape" scenario stirred *Northern* white men too, because it dramatized the potency of traditional manliness. In this dramatization, upright character and powerful manliness (embodied in the white lynch mobs) restrained uncontrolled, unmanly, sexual passion (embodied in the Negro rapist). These noxious images permeated Northern press reports of Southern lynchings. *The Providence Journal*, reporting a Louisiana lynching in 1893, celebrated the mob's manly restraint: "Three Negroes were lynched in a quiet, determined manner by a mob of white men on Friday night. . . . The lynching was one of the coolest that has taken place in this section."[60] And the *New York Times*, describing the Memphis lynching of Wells's friends, stressed what it called the "quick and quiet" demeanor of the white men in the mob, contrasting their stern and firm behavior with that of the "shivering negroes" whom they murdered.[61] In these depictions, the black victims represented weak, unmanly passion – whether fear or lechery – while the lynch mob represented the strength of manly self-control.

In *Southern Horrors*, Wells refuted the lynching scenario by inversion. Where whites' scenario depicted black men as unmanly passion incarnate, Wells depicted black men as manliness personified. In Wells's framework, black men lynched for "rape," far from embodying uncontrolled lust, were innocent victims, seduced into having consensual sex with carnal white women. As Wells put it, they were "poor blind Afro-American Sampsons who suffer themselves to be betrayed by white Delilahs."[62] Like the Biblical Samson, these black men had been manly towers of strength until they were ensnared and destroyed by the wiles of a wicked woman. The white Delilahs who falsely cried "rape" were the real embodiments of lust, not the innocent lynch victims. To prove white women, and not black men, instigated these liaisons, Wells lists thirteen white women who willingly had sexual relationships with black men. Only upon discovery were these liaisons called "rapes." Several of these white women were prostitutes, and Wells jokes bitterly, " 'The leading citizens' of Memphis are defending the 'honor' of *all* white women, *demi-monde* included."[63]

Where whites' lynching scenario depicted lynch mob members as disciplined, manly, and restrained, Wells depicted them as vile, unmanly cowards, hiding their own rampant lusts with sanctimonious calls for chastity and excusing their brutal murders by invoking the honor of harlots. Wells argued that white Southern men, including those who formed the lynch mobs, were enthusiastic *supporters* of rape and sexual abuse – as long as the victims were *black*. Far from suppressing lust, "the white man" gloried in it. His miscegenation laws, Wells wrote, "only operate against the legitimate union of the races; they leave the white man free to seduce all the colored girls he can," knowing he need neither marry nor support the victims of his lust.[64] Furthermore, Wells charged, Southern white men were "not so desirous of punishing rapists as they pretend." If they truly reviled *rape*, they would not so readily forgive the many *white* men who raped *black* women. Again, Wells names names and gives dates, overwhelming the reader with cases of black women and little girls brutally raped by white men, with no objections from their white neighbors. Yet these solid white citizens of the South – rapists and accessories to rape – murdered black men who slept with willing white women, and proclaimed themselves defenders of chastity![65] Hypocrisy, licentiousness, and unrestrained passion – sexual lust and blood lust – characterized Southern white men, as Wells depicted them. Thus, in her account, the Southern lynch mob did not embody white manliness *restraining* black lust – it embodied white men's lust running amok, *destroying* true black manliness.

Finally, Wells attacked the idea that lynching showed the continuing power of manliness. Instead, she argued, Northern men could only regain their manliness by stopping the lynching. These ideas echoed old antislavery arguments: just as antislavery activists had warned that the slave power would spread North and contaminate free labor, so Wells warned that Southern men's unrestrained lust had spread north and corrupted Northern men's manliness. Northern white men had abrogated their manly duty to restrain vice. They had allowed white Southerners to rape, butcher, and burn black Americans alive, and this tolerance of vice had rotted their manliness. Throughout America, Wells wrote, "Men who stand high in the esteem of the public for Christian character, for moral and physical courage, for devotion to the principles of equal and exact justice to all, and for great sagacity, stand as cowards who fear to open their mouths before this great outrage."[66]

More was at stake in these tactics than mere rhetoric. In refuting this discourse of civilization, Wells was trying to stop lynching by producing an alternative discourse of race and manhood. "Civilization" positioned black men as unmanly savages, unable to control their passions through manly will. Northern whites, accepting the linkage of white civilization and manhood, believed black men were savage rapists; therefore, they tolerated the brutal actions of Southern lynch mobs. As Hazel Carby has insightfully argued, black women, including Wells, reconstructed the sexual ideologies of the nineteenth century to produce an alternative discourse of womanhood.[67] Similarly, Wells's anti-lynching propaganda constructed an alternative discourse of manhood, remaking and redefining the "truths" that whites deployed to define and limit black men's place in the world and to construct white men as powerful and manly.

In 1892, however, most whites ignored Wells's pamphlet. A few scattered anti-lynching articles in white periodicals borrowed Wells's arguments. For example, in 1892 Albion Tourgée, the period's most forthright antiracist white, wrote in the Chicago *Daily Inter-Ocean*, "[W]ithin a year half a score of colored men have been lynched for the crime of having white mistresses, while it does not seem to be thought necessary to hang or burn the white woman, nor is the white man who keeps a colored mistress in any danger of violence at the hands of his fellow citizens. . . ."[68] George C. Rowe, the sole black contributor to an 1894 symposium on lynching in *The Independent*, made a similar case.[69] But such articles were exceptional. Wells, like most blacks, could only get her articles published in the black press, which few whites read. Despite the eloquence of *Southern Horrors*, Wells's objective of reaching white Northerners remained frustrated.

By 1893, after a year of writing and speaking in the North, Wells still had no access to the white American press. When offered the opportunity to tour England, she jumped at it, recognizing that although the white American press ignored *her*, they might not ignore the British.[70] Although her first tour – in 1893 – got very little American press coverage, it laid the foundation for her 1894 tour, which got all the publicity she desired. When Wells returned, she had become notorious; and white Americans had discovered that, due to their tolerance and practice of lynching, the rest of the world's Anglo-Saxons doubted whether white Americans were either manly or civilized.

Wells shaped both tours in terms of "civilization."[71] Her speeches, her writings, and even her demeanor framed her mission as an appeal from one civilized race to another for protection from violent white barbarians. As she told one British journalist, if Britain told America "the roasting of men alive on unproved charges and by a furious mob was a disgrace to the civilisation of the United States, then every criminal in America, white or black, would soon be assured of a trial under the proper form of law."[72] Wells spoke to British audiences, but her goal was to convince Americans that their tolerance of lynching rendered them unmanly savages in the eyes of the civilized world.

Wells knew that many Americans felt a pleasurable sense of racial kinship with the English – as fellow Anglo-Saxons, the most manly and civilized of all races. By forming an alliance with British reformers, Wells attacked this smug racial empathy. As she told an audience in Birmingham (England), "America cannot and will not ignore the voice of a nation that is her superior in civilisation. . . . I believe that the silent indifference with which [Great Britain] has received the intelligence that human beings are burned alive in a Christian (?) country, and by civilised (?) Anglo-Saxon communities is born of ignorance of the true situation; and that if she really knew she would make the protest long and loud."[73]

Wells's newspaper columns from abroad, published in the white *Chicago Inter-Ocean*, described the massive support she received from the most prominent, civilized British dignitaries.[74] Wells detailed dinners given in her honor by prominent members of Parliament and intimate gatherings organized by titled aristocrats. In all her columns, these celebrities express shock at lynching's barbarity. Often she included stories of loutish white Americans whose incivility further convinced the British of American barbarism. For example, a "swell reception" was given for her at Princess Christian's Writer's Club, Wells wrote, and "The ubiquitous and (so far as I am concerned) almost invariably rude American was on evidence there. In a strident voice she pronounced my statements false. I found she had never been in the South and was a victim to her own imagination. I heard an Englishwoman remark after the encounter was over that she had seen a side of Mrs.——'s character which she never knew before."[75] In contrast, Wells always carried herself with restraint, dignity, and refinement, and Britons clearly appreciated her as a true lady.[76] By presenting herself and her mission as embodying civilized values, Wells highlighted the barbarism of white Americans.

Throughout, Wells hammered away at the myth of the black rapist. In the context of "civilization," though, her old arguments from *Southern Horrors* took on new weight. Since civilization, by definition, entailed pure womanliness and upright manliness, Wells could now show that white Americans' lasciviousness proved them uncivilized. Barbarous white American men burned innocent black men alive for the "crime" of sleeping with willing white women, while they themselves brutally and boldly raped black women. Wells also added statistics, culled from the white *Chicago Tribune*, to prove that fewer than one-third of all lynch victims had even been *accused* of rape. The unchaste white women who took black lovers, then watched them burn, were also uncivilized; but, Wells claimed, unchastity was endemic to the white South: "Why should it be impossible to believe white women guilty of the same crime for which southern white men are notorious?"[77] Why should it be hard to imagine that depraved white men, whose crimes had peopled the South with mulattoes, had depraved white daughters?

Most unmanly of all, however, were the bloodthirsty lynch mobs. Wells argued passionately that by refusing to try accused African-Americans in a court of law, and by engaging in the most horrific of tortures, lynch mobs and the Americans who tolerated them exposed themselves as barbarians.

> Make your laws as terrible as you like against that class of crime [rape]; devise what tortures you choose; go back to the most barbarous methods of the most barbarous ages; and then my case is just as strong. Prove your man guilty, first; hang him, shoot him, pour coal oil over him and roast him, if you have concluded that civilization demands this; but be sure the man has committed the crime first.[78]

Similarly, in describing an Alabama lynching, Wells ironically interweaves references to race and gender, invoking "civilization" in order to condemn Americans as manifestly uncivilized. Bitterly she writes, "the civilization which defends itself against the barbarisms of Lynch Law by stating that it lynches human beings only when they are guilty of awful attacks upon women and children" might have been expected to give these alleged *arsonists* a fair trial, especially since "one of the prisoners charged was a woman, and if the Nineteenth Century has shown any advancement upon any lines of human action, it is pre-eminently shown in its reverence, respect and protection of its womanhood." But, Wells argued, these uncivilized white men were entirely unmanly – anxious not to protect woman-hood, but to butcher it. The victims, Wells wrote, "were caged in their cells, helpless and defenseless; they were at the mercy of civilized white Americans, who, armed with shotguns, were there to maintain the majesty of American law." And these "brave and honorable white southerners. . .lined themselves up in the most effective manner and poured volley after volley into the bodies of their helpless, pleading victims, who in their bolted prison cells could do nothing but suffer and die."[79] Manliness and civilization, which stood for the rule of law, the defense of the weak, and the protection of womanhood, did not exist in the American South.

Wells's powerful tactics mobilized the British press and reformers, who turned lynching into that season's *cause célèbre*. A *Westminster Gazette* writer said he could no longer "regard our American cousins as a civilized nation."[80] The *Christian World* thought American lynch law "would disgrace a nation of cannibals."[81] The *Birmingham Daily Gazette* editorialized, "The American citizen in the South is at heart more a barbarian than the negro whom he regards as a savage. . . . Lynch law is fiendishly resorted to as a sort of sport on every possible opportunity, and the negroes are butchered to make a Yankee holiday. . . . Either they mistrust their legal institutions or they murder in wantonness and for mere lust of blood."[82]

Having convinced a large segment of the British public of American barbarism, Wells called upon the moral forces of Britain to stop it. She convinced the gatherings she addressed to pass resolutions condemning lynching as uncivilized and warning the United States that its tolerance of lynch law was lowering it in the estimation of civilized countries. She got the national conventions of major religious denominations – Baptists, Methodists, Quakers, Unitarians – to send resolutions to their counterparts in America condemning lynching as uncivilized and asking what they were doing to stop it. Individual churches and reform organizations followed suit, sending resolutions to American organizations, politicians, and publications, warning that the civilized world held all Americans – Northern or Southern – responsible for these "barbarisms."[83] For example, Liverpool's Unitarian church wrote to *The Christian Register*, America's leading Unitarian periodical, expressing its "grief and horror" upon learning of "the barbarities of Lynch Law as carried out by white men on some of the coloured citizens of the United States." They demanded to know why American Unitarians did not stop such horrific torture and brutality, which instilled into white American children the "lust of cruelty and callousness of murder." The American Unitarians were forced to agree that lynching made "the dark deeds of the dark ages seem light in comparison," and the magazine sent letters of protest to three Southern mayors and Georgia's Governor W. T. Northen.[84]

Wells ultimately convinced British reformers that they bore the responsibility of civilizing the United States. As Sir Edward Russell wrote in the *Liverpool Daily Post* (and as Wells quoted to her American readers), Americans were "horrifying the whole of the civilized world," and needed British uplift, for "when one reflects that [such things] still happen while we in this country are sending missions to the South Sea Islands and other places, they strike to our hearts much more forcibly, and we turn over in our minds whether it were not better to leave the heathen alone for a time and to send the gospel of common humanity across the Atlantic. . . ."[85] Moreover, the British were preparing to send such "missionaries." By the end of Wells's tour, prominent British reformers were organizing anti-lynching societies and planning to send representatives to the United States to investigate these atrocities first hand.[86] Such societies had been formed previously to protest Turkish and other exotic atrocities, but never to investigate fellow Anglo-Saxons.

All this British fervor finally got Wells her hearing in the white American press. Wells could be ignored; but the British were considered fellow Anglo-Saxons, racial equals qualified to pronounce upon civilized manliness. Thus, American men felt obligated to reply to their accusations.

The *Memphis Daily Commercial* attempted to discredit Wells by slandering her character. Playing on longstanding racist discourses depicting black women as especially licentious – thus unwomanly and uncivilized – it flooded England with newspapers accusing Wells of being a "negro adventuress" with an unsavory past. Yet Wells skillfully turned these slanders to her advantage by using them to prove American barbarity. Her rebuttal, circulated to newspapers throughout Great Britain, noted "so hardened is the Southern public mind (white) that it does not object to the coarsest language and most obscene vulgarity in its leading journals so long as it is directed against a negro," and pointed out that since the *Daily Commercial* could not deny the barbarity of the South's frequent lynchings, they were reduced to smearing her character. British papers were as shocked as Wells intended. The *Liverpool Daily Post* described the articles as "very coarse in tone, and some of the language is such as could not possibly be reproduced in an English journal." Since it was neither manly nor civilized to slander a lady's character, the episode served to reinforce British opinions of American barbarism.[87]

Southern newspapers typically insisted that rape justified lynching; and that "the negro" was uncivilized. The Atlanta *Constitution* argued that British agitation was futile, since "the negroes themselves are the only people who can suppress the evil, and the way for them to get rid of it is to cease committing"[88] rape. The New Orleans *Times-Democrat* opined that once Wells left Britain, she would no longer be believed, for Americans "know well that the Negro is not a model of virtue and the white man a cruel, bloodthirsty tyrant, as the Wells woman pretends. . . ."[89] A Southern educator complained, "stigmatizing [Southern men] as savages and barbarians" did no good – the real problem lay with the negro, who was "still a semi-savage, far below the white man in the science and practice of civilization."[90]

Other critics accused the British of hypocrisy, arguing that British colonists abused blacks more brutally than white Southerners did. The Democratic *Philadelphia Daily Record*, for example, countered the British and Foreign Unitarian Association's condemnations by alleging, "John Bull looks at America with one eye and at Africa with the other. His hands are bloody with recent African butcheries. . . ."[91] While plausible, these criticisms stemmed not from concern for Africans, but from resentment of meddlesome British "civilizers."

Many Northern Democrats and Southerners complained that American lynch law was none of Britain's business.[92] In this they echoed British conservatives, such as one *London Times* columnist who accused the anti-lynchers of having a "fanatical anxiety to impose our own canons of civilization upon people differently circumstanced." The *New York Times* cited the column as the sentiment of "a big majority of sensible Englishmen, who resent the meddlesome antics of a little and noisy minority," and approvingly reprinted it.[93] Governor No.then of Georgia accused Wells of being funded by a syndicate of British and American capitalists who wanted to stop British immigration to the South.[94]

The last straw for those upset about British "meddling" came in early September 1894, when the London Anti-Lynching Committee sent a small fact-finding delegation to tour the South.[95] Governor O'Ferrall of Virginia complained, "Things have come to a pretty pass in this country when we are to have a lot of English moralists sticking their noses into our national affairs," and fourteen other governors, Northern and Southern, concurred. Governor Northen accused the British of unmanly hypocrisy, suggesting the anti-lynching committee return to England and "prevent by law the inhuman sale of virtuous girls to lustful men in high places. Hang all such demons as 'Jack, the Ripper'; punish as it deserves the barbarous, wholesale slaughter of negroes in Africa by Englishmen who go there to steal their gold. . . ." Governor Turney of Tennessee agreed: "I think they had better purify their own morals before coming among a better people."[96]

Governor Turney was embarrassed, however, when several days later six black men accused of arson were lynched near Memphis; he condemned the murders and offered a reward of $5,000 for the lynchers' capture. Jeered the Northern editors of *The Independent*, "It is very unfortunate. . .that just after Miss Wells's charges had been loudly pronounced false other such atrocious cases should have occurred, as if to justify all that she had said. . . ."[97] But in Memphis, Wells's campaign had borne fruit. Although two years before, Memphis's civic leaders had destroyed Wells's presses and driven her north for protesting the three businessmen's murders, now they piously proclaimed their horror of lynch law. The *Memphis Scimitar* – the same paper that two years earlier had demanded that Wells herself be lynched – editorialized, "Every one of us is touched with blood-guiltiness in this matter, unless we prove ourselves ready to do our duty as civilized men and citizens who love their country and are jealous of its good name."[98] White Memphis merchants even demonstrated their civilized manliness by holding an indignation meeting and raising $1,000 for the murdered men's widows and orphans![99] Thirteen white men were indicted, although never convicted, for the lynchings. According to historian David Tucker, the Memphis press never again condoned lynch law; and no new lynchings occurred until 1917.[100]

Wells's campaign inspired many white Northerners to object more vocally to lynching, too. In Chicago, Brooklyn, and Santa

Cruz, whites were reported to have formed anti-lynching societies, although these organizations seem to have been ephe-
meral.[101] While some Northern papers still defended lynching
as necessary to deter rape, many others agreed with the
Cleveland Leader that "Acts of barbarism have been committed in
this country within the last twenty years by people claiming to
be civilized which would scarcely have been credited to the
cruelest and most bloodthirsty savages in Africa."[102]

In sum, Wells's British agitation had hit a nerve. White
Americans, the cheers for the Columbian Exposition still ringing
in their ears, were chagrined to discover prominent British
reformers calling them unmanly barbarians. The United States –
the glory of the civilized world, the epitome of evolutionary
progress – was the object of "missionaries"! Finally, Wells had
the attention of the white American public. Her campaign, by
enlisting the aid of British reformers, had forced indifferent
American whites to address lynching. The *Indianapolis Freeman*,
like most of the African-American press, proclaimed that Wells's
campaign had put an end to white complacency: "For the first
time since the commencement of its long debauch of crime, the
South has been jerked up to a sudden standstill; it is on the
defensive. . . . The North has at last realized that the so-called
race problem is a matter that concerns not only the South, but
the nation. . . ."[103] Wells could not force white Americans to
oppose lynching, but in 1894, they could no longer *ignore*
lynching.

How effective was Well's agitation in the long run? Wells did
not put an end to lynching. Although lynching did decline
after 1892, most historians credit factors other than Wells's
efforts.[104] The British anti-lynching committees, faced with
white Americans' vehement complaints about the London
committee's visit, cancelled further factfinding tours and restricted their activities to outraged letter-writing campaigns.[105]
Southern lynchings continued, and Wells continued to agitate
against them.

But even if Wells could not put an end to the violence, her
success in putting American whites on the defensive did force
some long-lasting, if subtle, shifts in whites' approaches to
lyncli law. White Americans had no stomach for being called
unmanly and uncivilized by the British. After 1894, most
Northern periodicals stopped treating lynching as a colorful

Southern folkway. They dropped their jokey tones and piously condemned lynching as "barbarous" – although they still implied one could do little to stop it. It became a truism that lynching hurt America in the eyes of the "civilized world."[106] At the same time, Wells's statistics forced the Northern press to acknowledge that most lynch victims had *not* been accused of rape – although the "lynching for rape" scenario retained its appeal as a dramatization of white male power, and the myth of the Negro rapist remained almost as strong as ever. Southern states began to pass anti-lynching laws – which, unfortunately, were almost never enforced.[107] While it is impossible to know whether these small changes actually deterred any prospective lynchers, in the context of the nation's overwhelming climate of racist violence, they must be seen as modest but definite victories.

To appreciate how skillfully Ida B. Wells conducted her anti-lynching campaign, one needs to understand, as Wells did, the subtle ways race, gender, and class were interwoven in the 1890s. With social and cultural change threatening middle-class dominance, middle-class men had become fearful that their manhood was at risk. In order to strengthen faltering constructs of traditional manly power, they turned to race. By envisioning themselves as "the white man," whose superior manliness set them apart from more primitive dark-skinned races, middle-class men reassured themselves that manliness remained as strong as ever. "Civilization" proclaimed manly/racial dominance as natural, the glorious result of human evolutionary progress. By celebrating "civilization," as they did at the 1893 Columbian Exposition, middle-class white men reassured themselves that they were the most powerful beings ever evolved.

Wells inverted these linkages between manhood and white supremacy. Where white Northerners imagined lynching proved white men's superior manliness, Wells argued the reverse: lynching proved black men were far more manly than whites who tolerated lynching. Where white Americans constructed elaborate pageants like the Columbian Exposition to dramatize that white men were more manly and civilized than savage dark-skinned races, Well mobilized "civilization" to demonstrate the opposite: white Americans were despicably unmanly and uncivilized.

Wells's manipulation of manliness and civilization can be seen as one example of a tactic oppressed groups have frequently adopted: mobilizing dominant discourses in subversive ways. Women's and labor historians have written about many such cases – from Cleveland unionists who turned their employers' calls for "law and order" into a potent rationale for a citywide strike,[108] to working girls in turn-of-the-century New York who parodied upper-class fashions in order to publicly assert their own working-class identities,[109] to labor and women's rights activists who found in Protestantism a potent rationale for their own liberatory projects.[110] Similarly, Ida B. Wells inverted discourses of manly civilization, which made lynching tolerable to many whites, in order to show that manliness could only be saved, and civilization advanced, by stamping out lynch law.

Unlike Cleveland's law-and-order unionists or New York's stylish working girls, who were synthesizing beliefs and identities for themselves, however, Wells was consciously working to propagandize her *oppressor*. Her effectiveness stemmed from the skill with which she manipulated cherished middle-class ideologies. Her strategy of playing on middle-class men's fears about the fragility of traditional manliness made Wells's propaganda especially effective, her accusations especially devastating.

By inverting "civilization" and challenging the links between white supremacy and manliness, Wells produced an antiracist construction of manhood. Wells recognized that behind middle-class gender lay a fundamental assumption that pure women and manly men were *white*. To attack that one point, as Wells and many of her contemporaries did, was to attack the entire edifice of middle-class identity and middle-class gender. Victorian ideologies of womanhood marginalized black women by depicting them as unwomanly harlots and contrasting them with white women, who were depicted as "real" women, high minded and sexually pure. By resisting these ideas and insisting on black women's pure womanliness, black women in effect produced an alternative discourse of womanhood, as Hazel Carby has shown.[111] In the same way, middle-class formulations of manliness marginalized black men by depicting them as unmanly rapists, whose uncontrolled sexuality contrasted with the restrained self-mastery and manliness of "the white man." By arguing that it was "the white man," and not the black man, who was lustful and uncivilized, Wells produced a less damaging formulation of gender.

Middle-class gender's racial underpinnings may seem merely ideological, but as Wells recognized, they had dire material repercussions. They legitimized both the sexual victimization of black women and the brutal murders of black men. Wells's insistence upon the womanliness of black women and the manliness of black men was meant to dismantle the ideological structure that facilitated whites' oppressive practices. By subverting whites' racist discourses of gender, Wells hoped to force an end to racial violence.

For Wells, critiquing middle-class gender was a *tactic*, not an objective. More than a theorist, Wells was a skilled journalist, a gifted publicist, a consummate activist. As such, she understood – and was gifted at – practical propaganda. Above all else, she passionately desired to end the terror black Americans faced at the hands of "Judge Lynch." She analyzed the complexities of middle-class Americans' race/class/gender system in order to forge an effective weapon for social change. Cognizant of the subtle dynamics of these discourses, she was able to manipulate them to her political ends. Her example suggests that the ability to deconstruct the discourses of race, gender, and class, more than merely an academic exercise, is an inherently *practical* political skill for those interested in effectively motivating social movements.

NOTES

First published in *Radical History Review* 52 (Winter 1992): 5–30. Used by permission of MARHO, the Radical Historians' Organization.

For helpful criticisms of earlier drafts, many thanks to Mari Jo Buhle, Ruth Feldstein, Elizabeth Francis, Kevin Gaines, Suzanne Kolm, Louise Newman, Mary Lou Roberts, Joan Scott, the audience at my Berkshire Conference panel, and Barbara Melosh and the *RHR* readers.

1 Ray Stannard Baker, "What is a Lynching? A Study of Mob Justice, South and North," *McClure's Magazine* 24 (February 1905): 429.
2 Ida B. Wells, *A Red Record*, reprinted in *On Lynchings* [1895] (Salem, NH: 1987), 98.
3 "China Cares Not to Borrow. . . If They Believe All That They Read, It Is Not Surprising English Busybodies Talk of Forming Societies to Civilize Us," *New York Times*, 19 August 1894, p. 1.
4 "British Anti-Lynchers," *New York Times*, 2 August 1894, p. 4.
5 "An Idyll of Alabama," *New York Times*, 30 December 1891, p. 4.

See also "The Cartwright Avengers," *New York Times*, 19 July 1893, p. 4.

6 Paula Giddings, *When and Where I Enter: The Impact of Black Women on Race and Sex in America* (New York: 1984), 27–9.

7 Mary P. Ryan, *Cradle of the Middle Class: The Family in Oneida County, New York, 1790–1865* (Cambridge: 1981); Leonore Davidoff and Catherine Hall, *Family Fortunes: Men and Women of the English Middle Class, 1780–1850* (Chicago: 1987). Although *Family Fortunes* discusses English, and not American, middle-class formation, many of their observations, especially about the importance of manliness in class formation, are applicable to the United States.

8 Stuart M. Blumin, *The Emergence of the Middle Class: Social Experience in the American City, 1760–1900* (Cambridge: 1989), 138–91, 298–310; Paul E. Johnson, *A Shopkeeper's Millennium: Society and Revivals in Rochester, New York 1815–1837* (New York: 1978).

9 Ryan, *Cradle of the Middle Class*, 83–151, 116–27; Davidoff and Hall, *Family Fortunes*, 71–192.

10 Ryan, *Cradle of the Middle Class*, 15.

11 Nancy F. Cott, *The Bonds of Womanhood: "Woman's Sphere" in New England, 1780–1835* (New Haven, CT: 1977); Christine Stansell, *City of Women: Sex and Class in New York 1789–1860* (New York: 1986), 63–75, 163–5.

12 Norman Vance, *The Sinews of the Spirit: The Ideal of Christian Manliness in Victorian Literature and Religious Thought* (Cambridge: 1985), 8–10; E. Anthony Rotundo, "Learning about Manhood: Gender Ideals and the Middle-Class Family in Nineteenth-Century America," in *Manliness and Morality: Middle-Class Masculinity in Britain and America 1800–1940*, ed. J. A. Mangan and James Walvin (New York: 1987), 37–40, 43–6.

13 John D'Emilio and Estelle B. Freedman, *Intimate Matters: A History of Sexuality in America* (New York: 1988), 178–82.

14 D'Emilio and Freedman, *Intimate Matters*, 68–9; John S. Haller, Jr., and Robin M. Haller, *The Physicians and Sexuality in Victorian America* (Urbana, IL: 1974), 191–234; Cynthia Eagle Russett, *Sexual Science: The Victorian Construction of Womanhood* (Cambridge, MA: 1989), 112–16.

15 On character, see Warren I. Susman, "Personality and the Making of Twentieth-Century Culture," in *Culture as History* (New York: 1984), 273–7; David I. Macleod, *Building Character in the American Boy* (Madison, WI: 1983).

16 On "manliness" see Davidoff and Hall, *Family Fortunes*, 108–13; Peter G. Filene, *Him/Her/Self: Sex Roles in Modern America*, (Baltimore: 1986; first published 1974), 70–1; Mangan and Walvin, eds, *Manliness and Morality*; and Vance, *The Sinews of the Spirit*.

17 Davidoff and Hall, *Family Fortunes*, 207–8; Ryan, *Cradle of the Middle Class*, 140–2.

18 Ryan, *Cradle of the Middle Class*, 165–85.

19 Blumin, *Emergence of the Middle Class*, 290–5; Filene, *Him/Her/Self*, 70–3.

20 Lewis A. Erenberg, *Stepping Out: New York Nightlife and the Transformation of American Culture, 1890–1930* (Chicago: 1981), 33–59; John F. Kasson, *Amusing the Million: Coney Island at the Turn of the Century* (New York: 1978).

21 Gail Bederman, "The Women Have Had Charge of the Church Work Long Enough," *American Quarterly* 41 (September 1989): 435–40.

22 On middle-class men's confusion about the meaning of manhood, see Bederman, "Church Work," 432–65; Filene, *Him/Her/Self*, 69–93; Elliott J. Gorn, *The Manly Art: Bare Knuckle Prizefighting in America* (Ithaca, NY: 1986), 179–206; John Higham, "The Reorientation of American Culture in the 1890s," in *Writing American History: Essays on Modern Scholarship* (Bloomington, IN: 1978), 73–102; Michael S. Kimmel, "The Contemporary 'Crisis' of Masculinity in Historical Perspective," in *The Making of Masculinities*, ed. Harry Brod (Boston: 1987), 121–54; Joe L. Dubbert, "Progressivism and the Masculinity Crisis," in *The American Man*, ed. Elizabeth H. Pleck and Joseph H. Pleck (Englewood Cliffs, NJ: 1980). For an opposing view, see Margaret Marsh, "Suburban Men and Masculine Domesticity," *American Quarterly* 40 (June 1988): 165–86.

23 Higham, "Reorientation," 78–9.

24 D'Emilio and Freedman, *Intimate Matters*, 178–82.

25 Thomas F. Gossett, *Race: The History of an Idea in America* (Dallas: 1963), 287–309; John Higham, *Strangers in the Land: Patterns of American Nativism 1860–1925* (New York: 1971), 131–57.

26 On Anglo-Saxonism see Stuart Anderson, *Race and Rapprochement: Anglo-Saxonism and Anglo-American Relations, 1895–1904* (Rutherford, NJ: 1981); Gossett, *Race*, 84–123, 310–38; Neil Irvin Painter, *Standing at Armageddon: The United States, 1877–1919* (New York: 1987), 149–52.

27 Anderson, *Race and Rapprochement*, 20–1; Parkman, quoted in Gossett, *Race*, 95.

28 Baker, *What is a Lynching*, 429.

29 George W. Stocking, Jr., "The Dark Skinned Savage," in *Race, Culture, and Evolution* (New York: 1968), 112–32; see especially pp. 114, 121–2. For an excellent and exhaustive analysis of the history and development of the discourse of "civilization," see George W. Stocking, *Victorian Anthropology* (New York: 1987).

30 Russett, *Sexual Science*, 144–8.

31 Quoted in Virginia C. Meredith, "Woman's Part at the World's Fair," *Review of Reviews* 7 (May 1893): 417.

32 Robert W. Rydell, *All The World's a Fair: Visions of Empire at American International Expositions, 1876–1916* (Chicago: 1984), 38–71. My discussion of the racial aspect of the Fair draws heavily upon Rydell's excellent analysis. On the cultural meaning of the Columbian Exposition, see also Kasson, *Amusing the Million*, 17–28; and Alan Trachtenberg, *The Incorporation of America: Culture and Society in the Gilded Age* (New York: 1982), 208–34.

33 *The Century Dictionary: An Encyclopedic Lexicon of the English Language* (New York: 1890), s.v. "manly."
34 "The World's Columbian Exposition – A View from the Ferris Wheel," *Scientific American* 69 (9 September 1893): 169.
35 *Chicago Daily Inter-Ocean*, 26 April 1893, Supplement. Cited in Rydell, *All the World's a Fair*, 249, n. 19.
36 "Exhibits which Prove that the Sex is Fast Overhauling Man," *New York Times*, 25 June 1893, quoted in Jeanne Madeline Weimann, *The Fair Women* (Chicago: 1981), 427. For a similar assessment, somewhat more humorously patronizing, see M. A. Lane, "The Woman's Building, World's Fair," *Harper's Weekly* 36 (9 January 1892): 40.
37 Russett, *Sexual Science*, 54–77.
38 For lists of Midway attractions, see map in "Opening of the World's Columbian exposition, Chicago, 1 May, 1893," *Scientific American* 68 (6 May 1893): 274–5; "Notes from the World's Columbian Exposition Chicago 1893," *Scientific American* 68 (27 May 1893): 323.
39 Rydell, *All the World's a Fair*, 61–2.
40 Ibid., 65.
41 "Sights at the Fair," *Century Magazine* 46 (5 September 1893): 653.
42 For contemporary commentary on this dynamic, see "The World's Columbian Exposition – A View from the Ferris Wheel," 169; and Frederic Remington, "A Gallop Through the Midway," *Harper's Weekly* 37 (7 October 1893): 996.
43 "Wonderful Place for Fun," *New York Times*, 19 June 1893, p. 9. On Dahomans as popularly seen as the most primitive savages at the Fair, see Rydell, *All the World's a Fair*, 66.
44 Elliot M. Rudwick and August Meier, "Black Man in the 'White City': Negroes and the Columbian Exposition, 1893," *Phylon* 26 (Winter 1965): 354–5; Ann Massa, "Black Women in the 'White City'," *Journal of American Studies* 8 (December 1974): 319–37.
45 Wells and Douglass's letter is reprinted in "No 'Nigger Day,' No 'Nigger Pamphlet!' " *Indianapolis Freeman*, 25 March 1893, p. 4. The *Freeman*'s editor, who was involved in a long-standing feud with Wells, accused her of washing American dirty laundry (i.e., bringing up slavery) in public, for foreign guests. Unfortunately, Wells and Douglass were unable to raise funds to cover printing full translations into four languages. Only the introduction was translated, into French and German.
46 [Ida B. Wells], "Preface," in *The Reason Why The Colored American is not in the World's Columbian Exposition* [ed. Ida B. Wells] (Chicago: 1892), no page number.
47 Frederick Douglass, "Introduction," *The Reason Why*, 2.
48 Ibid., 3.
49 Ibid., 10–11.
50 Ibid., 12.
51 Ibid., 9. Lest this sound like Douglass lacks respect for Dahomans, note that American cartoonists leapt to draw unflattering depic-

tions of impossibly thick-lipped Dahoman men, clad (like women) only in brief grass skirts, necklaces, bracelets, and earrings. See Rydell, *All the World's a Fair*, 53, 54, 70.

52 Alfreda M. Duster, ed., *Crusade for Justice: The Autobiography of Ida B. Wells* (Chicago: 1970), 117.

53 Ida B. Wells, *Southern Horrors: Lynch Law in All Its Phases*, reprinted in *On Lynchings* [1892] (Salem, NH: 1987), 4.

54 See, for example, Iola [Ida B. Wells], "Iola's Southern Field – Save the Pennies," *New York Age*, 19 November 1892, p. 2; Iola [Ida B. Wells], "The Reign of Mob Law: Iola's Opinion of Doings in the Southern Field," *New York Age*, 18 February 1893 (typescript in Ida B. Wells Papers, University of Chicago); Wells, *Southern Horrors*, 22–3.

55 Duster, ed., *Crusade for Justice*, 86, 219.

56 More complete biographical information on Wells's campaign and her beginnings as an anti-lynching activist may be found in: Duster, ed., *Crusade for Justice*; Bettina Aptheker, "Woman Suffrage and the Crusade against Lynching, 1890–1920," in *Woman's Legacy: Essays on Race, Sex, and Class in American History* (Amherst, MA: 1982), 53–76; Paula Giddings, "Ida Wells-Barnett 1862–1931," in *Portraits of American Women from Settlement to the Present*, ed. G. J. Barker-Benfield and Catherine Clinton (New York: 1991), 366–85; Giddings, *When and Where I Enter*, 19–31, 89–93; Thomas C. Holt, "The Lonely Warrior: Ida B. Wells-Barnett and the Struggle for Black Leadership," in *Black Leaders of the Twentieth Century*, ed. John Hope Franklin and August Meier (Urbana, IL: 1982), 39–50; Mary Magdelene Boone Hutton, "The Rhetoric of Ida B. Wells: The Genesis of the Anti-Lynch Movement" (Ph.D. dissertation, University of Indiana, 1975); Dorothy Sterling, *Black Foremothers: Three Lives* (New York: 1988), 61–117; Mildred Thompson, "Ida B. Wells-Barnett: An Exploratory Study of an American Black Woman, 1893–1930" (Ph.D. dissertation, George Washington University, 1979), 20–125; David M. Tucker, "Miss Ida B. Wells and Memphis Lynching," *Phylon* 32 (Summer 1971): 112–22. Hazel V. Carby deftly analyzes Wells's anti-lynching pamphlets in the context of the 1890s black women's movement in *Reconstructing Womanhood* (New York: 1987), 95–120, and in " 'On the Threshold of Woman's Era': Lynching, Empire and Sexuality in Black Feminist Theory," in *"Race," Writing, and Difference*, ed. Henry Louis Gates, Jr. (Chicago: 1985), 301–16.

57 Wells, "Preface," *Southern Horrors*, no page number.

58 For Wells's lack of faith in appealing to whites for justice, see Iola [Ida B. Wells], "Freedom of Political Action – A Woman's Magnificent Definition of the Political Situation," *New York Freeman*, 7 November 1885, p. 2; Ida B. Wells Diary 1884–1887, entry for 11 April 1887, 183, Ida B. Wells Papers, University of Chicago.

59 Jacquelyn Dowd Hall, " 'The Mind that Burns in Each Body': Women, Rape and Racial Violence," in *Powers of Desire: The Politics*

of Sexuality, ed. Ann Snitow, Christine Stansell, and Sharon Thompson (New York: 1983), 328–49; see especially p. 335. On the myth of the black rapist, see Angela Davis, "Rape, Racism, and the Myth of the Black Rapist," *Women, Race, and Class* (New York: 1981), 172–201. On Southern white men's projecting repressed sexuality onto black men, see also Jacquelyn Dowd Hall, *Revolt Against Chivalry: Jessie Daniel Ames and the Women's Campaign Against Lynching* (New York: 1979), 148; and Trudier Harris, *Exorcising Blackness: Historical and Literary Lynching and Burning Rituals* (Bloomington, IN: 1984), 1–28.

60 "Negro Lynching," *Providence Journal,* 2 February 1893, p. 5.

61 "Negroes Lynched by a Mob," *New York Times,* 10 March 1892, p. 1.

62 Wells, *Southern Horrors,* "Preface" (no page number) and 5.

63 Ibid., 7–10, quotation on 8. Emphasis in original.

64 Ibid., 6.

65 Ibid., 11–12.

66 Ibid., 14.

67 Carby, *Reconstructing Womanhood,* 6, "On the Threshold," 303–4.

68 Albion Tourgée, "A Bystander's Notes," *Chicago Daily Inter-Ocean,* 24 September 1892, p. 4.

69 George C. Rowe, "How to Prevent Lynching," *The Independent* 46 (1 February 1894): 131–2.

70 Duster, ed., *Crusade for Justice,* 77–8, 82, 85–6. Also see Wells's comments in "Idol of her People," *Chicago Daily Inter-Ocean,* 8 August 1894, p. 2.

71 *Note on sources:* Although Wells's speeches were covered extensively by the English press, they are mostly not obtainable in the USA. Hutton's dissertation, "The Rhetoric of Ida B. Wells," uses British press reports extensively to document both tours. The excerpts Hutton cites are similar in tone to interviews Wells gave to American papers immediately after returning, and to Wells's book, *A Red Record,* published early in 1895. Thus, I am using these sources, in addition to a few available English sources, to reconstruct what Wells said.

72 "A Sermon on Ibsen – A Coloured Woman In the Pulpit," *Christian World* 38 (14 March 1894): 187; quoted in Hutton, "Rhetoric," 127.

73 Ida B. Wells, "Lynch Law in the United States" (letter), *The Birmingham Daily Post* (England photocopy, n.d. [16 May 1893]) in Ida B. Wells Papers, University of Chicago. The article is reprinted and dated in Duster, ed., *Crusade for Justice,* 101, but is not accurately transcribed.

74 Significantly, Wells never explicitly discussed incidents of lynching in these columns, evidently believing that British censure would upset Northern whites far more than African-American suffering. Similarly, Wells rarely discussed the economic causes of lynching to white audiences during these years, although she regularly raised economic issues in her writings for African-American newspapers. She had a sophisticated analysis of the economic causes of lynching, catalyzed by her realization that the three Memphis

grocers had been lynched in order to stop them from competing with white merchants. Yet she nearly always stressed issues of "civilization" and downplayed economic factors for white audiences during the years of her British tours. This was probably because she did not believe most white Americans would *care* that blacks were being murdered for economic reasons, while she knew it would rankle them to be called uncivilized.

75 Ida B. Wells, "Ida B. Wells Abroad," *Chicago Daily Inter-Ocean*, 25 June 1894, p. 10. Also in Duster, ed., *Crusade for Justice*, 179.
76 "Ida B. Wells Abroad – The Bishop of Manchester on American Lynching," *Chicago Daily Inter-Ocean*, 23 April 1894, p. 10; "Against Lynching – Ida B. Wells and Her Recent Mission in England," *Chicago Daily Inter-Ocean*, 4 August 1894, p. 9.
77 Quoted in "An Anti-Lynching Crusade in America Begun," *The Literary Digest* 9 (11 August 1984): 421.
78 Ida B. Wells, *London Daily Chronicle*, 28 April 1894, p. 3, quoted in Hutton, "Rhetoric," 135.
79 Wells, *A Red Record*, 74–5.
80 "The Bitter Cry of Black America – A New *Uncle Tom's Cabin*," *Westminster Gazette* 3 (10 May 1894): 2, quoted in Hutton, 146.
81 "Lynch Law in America," *Christian World* 38 (19 April 1894): 287, quoted in Hutton, "Rhetoric," 156.
82 From a photocopy in the Ida B. Wells Papers, marked "The *Birmingham Daily Gazette*, May 18th [1893]."
83 Ida B. Wells, "Ida B. Wells Abroad," *Chicago Daily Inter-Ocean*, 25 June 1894, p. 10; Hutton, 156–9, 170–1; Duster, ed., *Crusade for Justice*, 176, 190–7; "English Feeling upon America's Lynchings," *The Literary Digest* 9 (14 July 1894): 308; "That Irish Begging Letter," *New York Times*, 9 September 1894, 12; "The Sneer of a Good Natured Democrat," *Indianapolis Freeman*, 16 June 1894, p. 4.
84 Hutton, "Rhetoric," 157–8. Quotations from Richard Acland Armstrong, "Lynching in the United States" (letter), *Liverpool Mercury*, 3 April 1894, p. 3; and "Lynch Law in the South," *Christian Register* 83 (12 April 1894): 225–6; both as cited in Hutton, "Rhetoric."
85 Quoted in Ida B. Wells, "Ida B. Wells Abroad," *Chicago Daily Inter-Ocean*, 19 May 1894, p. 16. A version is also in Duster, ed., *Crusade for Justice*, 157–8, but it is not transcribed precisely.
86 Duster, ed., *Crusade for Justice*, 215–17; Hutton, "Rhetoric," 68–9.
87 Ida B. Wells, "Ida B. Wells Abroad," *Chicago Daily Inter-Ocean*, 7 July 1894, p. 18; also in Duster, ed., *Crusade for Justice*, 183–6. For other evidence of attempts to smear Wells, see "Editor Flemming's Denial," *Indianapolis Freeman*, 28 July 1894, p. 4; and "Is it Necessary?" *Indianapolis Freeman*, 4 August 1894, p. 4.
88 Quoted in "How Miss Wells' Crusade is Regarded in America," *Literary Digest* 6 (28 July 1894): 366.
89 Quoted in "The Anti-Lynching Crusade," *Literary Digest* 6 (8 September 1894): 544.
90 Edward C. Gordon, "Mob Violence: 'The National Crime'," *The*

Independent 46 (1 November 1894): 1,400.

91 Quoted in "The Sneer of a Good Natured Democrat," *Indianapolis Freeman*, 16 June 1894, p. 4. See also "British Treatment of Negroes," *New York Times*, 20 August 1894, p. 8; and "How Miss Wells' Crusade is Regarded in America," *Literary Digest* 6 (28 July 1894): 367.

92 Since the South was solidly Democratic, Northern Democratic newspapers were more likely to defend Southern practices and politicians, while Republican newspapers were more likely to attack them. See, for instance, "An Anti-Lynching Crusade in America Begun," *Literary Digest* 9 (11 August 1894): 421–2; Editorial, *New York Times*, 16 March 1894, p. 4.

93 Reprinted as "Lessons for Busybodies," *New York Times*, 15 October 1894, p. 9; "London Week of Excitement," *New York Times*, 7 October 1894, p. 1. See also "English Criticism of the English Anti-Lynching Committee," *Literary Digest* 9 (27 October 1894): 757; and "British Anti-Lynchers," *New York Times*, 2 August 1894, p. 4. In the London *Spectator*, a debate on lynching raged in the Letters-to-the-Editor column, while the editors simultaneously condemned lynching and called on Britons to stop interfering in American internal affairs. See Editorial, *Spectator* 72 (16 June 1894): 810; W. McKay, "Lynching in Georgia: A Correction" (letter), *Spectator* 73 (28 July 1894): 111; S. Alfred Steinthal, "Lynching in America" (letter), *Spectator* 73 (4 August 1894): 142; Chas. S. Butler, "The Lynching of Negroes in America" (letter), *Spectator* 73 (25 August 1894): 240; ΒαρβαροΣ, "Lynch Law in the United States" (letter), *Spectator* 73 (8 September 1894): 303; and "Lynching in America and English Interference," *Spectator* 73 (11 August 1894): 1669–70.

94 "An Anti-Lynching Crusade in America Begun," *Literary Digest* 9 (11 August 1894): 421.

95 Although some historians have suggested that no delegations of British anti-lynching committees ever came to the United States, contemporary press reports suggest that Sir John Gorst – and perhaps a small committee – came as a representative of the London committee. See "Sir John Gorst's Report," *New York Times*, 10 September 1894, p. 8; "Governor Northen is Aroused," *New York Times*, 11 September 1894, p. 2; "Southern Governors on English Critics," *Literary Digest* 9 (22 September 1894): 601–2; and Peter Stanford, "Serious Complications – The Anti-Lynch Sentiment in England Being Cooled," *Indianapolis Freeman*, 1 December 1894, p. 1.

96 "Governor Northen is Aroused," *New York Times*, 11 September 1894, p. 2; "Southern Governors on English Critics," *Literary Digest* 9 (22 September 1894): 601–2.

97 "A Bad Week for the Lynchers," *The Independent* 46 (18 September 1894): 1,187.

98 Quoted in "The Latest Lynching Case," *Literary Digest* 9 (15 September 1894): 577; Wells, *Southern Horrors*, 5.

99 "Killing of the Six Tennessee Negroes," *New York Times*, 9 September 1894, p. 12.

100 Tucker, "Miss Ida B. Wells," 121–2.

101 "How Miss Wells' Crusade Is Regarded in America," *Literary Digest* 9 (28 July 1894): 366; "Helping Miss Wells's Crusade," *New York Times*, 11 December 1894, p. 6.

102 Quotation in "The Anti-Lynching Crusade," *Literary Digest* 9 (11 August 1984): 545. For a selection of Northern newspaper editorials in favor of and against the anti-lynch agitation, see in addition, ibid., 421–2; and "Remedies for Lynch Law: A Case in Point," *Indianapolis Freeman*, 4 August 1894, p. 4.

103 "His 'Opinion' No Good," *Indianapolis Freeman*, 29 September 1984, p. 4. See also "Remedies for Lynch Law – A Case in Point," *Indianapolis Freeman*, 4 August 1894; and Thompson, "An Exploratory Study," 116–22.

104 Edward L. Ayers, *Vengeance and Justice* (New York: 1984), 237–55; Joel Williamson, *The Crucible of Race: Black-White Relations in the American South Since Emancipation* (New York: 1984), 117–18. Tucker credits Wells's campaign with curtailing lynchings in Memphis, however; see Tucker, "Miss Ida B. Wells," 121–2.

105 James Elbert Cutler, *Lynch-Law* (New York: 1905), 229–30; Peter Stanford, "Serious Complications – The Anti-Lynch Sentiment in England Being Cooled," *Indianapolis Freeman*, 1 December 1894, p. 1.

106 See, for example, "Lynching," *New York Times*, 27 May 1895, p. 5; "Lynching in the South," *New York Times*, 14 January 1896, p. 4; compare these to "The Cartwright Avengers," *New York Times*, 19 July 1893, p. 4.

107 "Public Sentiment Against Lynching," *New York Times*, 8 December 1895, p. 32; Cutler, *Lynch Law*, 233–45.

108 Steven J. Ross, *Workers on the Edge: Work, Leisure, and Politics in Industrializing Cincinnati* (New York: 1985), 270–93.

109 Kathy Peiss, *Cheap Amusements: Working Women and Leisure in Turn-of-the-Century New York* (Philadelphia: 1986), 62–7. Christine Stansell makes a similar argument in *City of Women*, 164–5.

110 Herbert G. Gutman, "Protestantism and the American Labor Movement," in *Work, Culture & Society in Industrializing America* (New York: 1976), 79–117; Elizabeth Fones-Wolf and Kenneth Fones-Wolf, "Trade-Union Evangelism: Religion and the AFL in the Labor Forward Movement, 1912–16," in *Working Class America*, ed. Michael H. Frisch and Daniel J. Walkowitz (Urbana, IL: 1983), 153–84; Elizabeth Cady Stanton, ed., *The Woman's Bible* (New York: 1895); and Kathryn Kish Sklar, *Catharine Beecher: A Study in American Domesticity* (New York: 1973).

111 Carby, *Reconstructing Womanhood*, 6, 20–61; Giddings, *When and Where I Enter*, 82–9.

10

DISORDERLY WOMEN
Gender and labor militancy in the Appalachian South

Jacquelyn Dowd Hall

Much labor history has been resolutely masculine, focused on the experiences of male workers in sex-segregated occupations and in unions. Jacquelyn Dowd Hall revises and expands that historiography as she constructs a rich narrative and interpretation of women workers' participation in a 1929 strike in the rayon mills of Elizabethton, Tennessee. Court records, newspaper reports, letters, and regional histories provide some of her materials. Moreover, Hall adds to the historical record by conducting interviews with women who took part in the conflict, providing invaluable evidence of workers' own understandings of these events and the impact of this strike on their lives afterwards. Hall's work is labor history with a difference: gender adds a new dimension to her account of conflict and workers' consciousness. An intriguing story emerges, one that suggests working-class people's participation in new possibilities of sexual revolution and consumer culture. Defiant female strikers used a bold sexual style to taunt militia members and to proclaim their resistance to mill owners; in turn, Hall argues, the experience of labor protest reinforced and expanded new patterns of male–female relationships.

* * *

The rising sun "made a sort of halo around the crown of Cross Mountain" as Flossie Cole climbed into a neighbor's Model T and headed west down the gravel road to Elizabethton, bound for work in a rayon plant. Emerging from Stoney Creek hollow, the car joined a caravan of buses and self-styled "taxis" brimming with young people from dozens of tiny communities strung along the creek branches and nestled in the coves of the Blue Ridge Mountains of East Tennessee. The caravan picked up

240

speed as it hit paved roads and crossed the Watauga River bridge, passing beneath a sign advertising Elizabethton's new-found identity as a "City of Power." By the time Cole reached the factory gate, it was 7:00 a.m., time to begin another ten-hour day as a reeler at the American Glanzstoff plant.[1]

The machines whirred, and work began as usual. But the reeling room stirred with anticipation. The day before, 12 March 1929, all but seventeen of the 360 women in the inspection room next door had walked out in protest against low wages, petty rules, and high-handed attitudes. Now they were gathered at the factory gate, refusing to work but ready to negotiate. When 9:00 a.m. approached and the plant manager failed to appear, they broke past the guards and rushed through the plant, urging their coworkers out on strike. By 1:40 p.m. the machines were idle and the plant was closed.[2]

The Elizabethton conflict rocked Carter County and made national headlines. Before March ended, the spirit of protest had jumped the Blue Ridge and spread through the Piedmont. Gastonia, Marion, and Danville saw the most bitter conflicts, but dozens of towns were shocked by an unexpected workers' revolt.[3]

The textile industry has always been a stronghold of women's labor, and women were central to these events. The most well-known protagonist in the 1929 strikes was, and remains, Gastonia's Ella May Wiggins, who migrated from the moun-tains, composed ballads for the union, and became a martyr to the workers' cause. But even Ella May Wiggins has been more revered than explained. Memorialized in proletarian novels but slighted by historians, she has joined a long line of working-class heroines who served with devotion and died young. Elizabethton too had its heroines, cast from a more human mold. They were noted by contemporaries sometimes as leaders, more often as pathetic mill girls or as "Amazons" pro-viding comic relief. In historical renditions they have dropped out of sight. The result has been thin description: a one-dimensional view of labor conflict that fails to take culture and community into account.[4]

Elizabethton, of course, is not unusual in this regard. Until recently, historians of trade unionism, like trade unionists them-selves, neglected women, while historians of women concen-trated on the Northeast and the middle class. There were few scholarly challenges to the assumption that women workers in general and southern women in particular were "hard to organize" and that women as family members exercised a conservative pull against class cohesion. Instances of female militancy were seen and not seen.[5] Because they contradicted conventional wisdom, they were easily dismissed.

Recent scholarship has revised that formulation by unearthing an impressive record of female activism, thus broadening our definition of politics, deepening our understanding of resistance, and revealing new dimensions of women's historical agency.[6] That activism, however, must be contextualized in order to be understood fully. The Elizabethton strikers are a case in point. The nature of farm life, the structure of the work force, the global march of capitalism – such particularities of time and place conditioned women's choices and identities. Equally important were developments usually pushed to the margins of labor history. Class-inflected tensions over sexual respectability, the efflorescence of peer culture in a context of intergenerational solidarity, the incorporation of new consumer desires in a dynamic regional culture – these, too, energized women's participation. Women in turn helped to create the circumstances from which the strike arose and by their actions guided the course the conflict took.

The melding of narrative and analysis that follows has three major goals. The first is a fresh reading of an important episode in southern labor history, employing gender as a category of analysis to reveal aspects of the strike that have been overlooked or misunderstood. The second is a close look at the ways in which women used dress, language, and gesture to manipulate gender ideology for political ends. Inevitably, different observers read that body language differently, for it symbolized conflicts too tangled to be discussed overtly.[7]

The third goal is a challenge to static notions of social identity. The "disorderly women" of Elizabethton were neither traditionalists acting on family values nor market-oriented individualists, neither peculiar mountaineers nor universalistic modern women.[8] Their sexual expressiveness and political savvy explode stereotypes and illuminate the intricacies of southern working-class women's lives.

In 1925 the J. P. Bemberg Company of Barmen, Germany, manufacturer of high-quality rayon yarn by an exclusive stretch spinning process, began pouring the thick concrete floors of its first United States subsidiary. Three years later Germany's leading producer of viscose yarn, the Vereinigte Glanzstoff Fabriken, A. G., of Elberfeld opened a jointly managed branch nearby. A post-First World War fashion revolution, combined with protective tariffs, had spurred the American rayon industry's spectacular growth. As one industry publicist put it, "With long skirts, cotton stockings were quite in order, but with short skirts, nothing would do except sheer, smooth stockings. . . . It was on the trim legs of post-war flappers, it has been said, that rayon first stepped out into big business." Dominated by a handful of European giants, the rayon industry clustered along the Appalachian mountain chain. By the Second World War more than 70 per cent of American rayon production took place in the southern states, with 50 per cent of the national total in Virginia and Tennessee alone.[9]

When the Bemberg and Glanzstoff companies chose East Tennessee as a site for overseas expansion, they came to a region that has occupied a peculiar place in the American economy and imagination. Since its "discovery" by local-color writers in the 1870s, southern Appalachia has been seen as a land "where time stood still." Mountain people have been romanticized as "our contemporary ancestors" or maligned as "latter-day white barbarians." Central to both images is the notion of a people untouched by modernity. In fact, as a generation of regional scholars has now made clear, the key to modern Appalachian history lies not in the region's isolation but in its role as a source of raw materials and as an outlet for investment in a capitalist world economy.[10]

Frontier families had settled the fertile Watauga River Valley around Elizabethton before the Revolution. Later arrivals pushed farther up the mountains into the hollows carved by fast-falling creeks. Stoney Creek is the oldest and largest of those creek-bed communities. Two miles wide at its base near Elizabethton, Stoney Creek hollow points fourteen miles into the hills, narrowing almost to a close at its upper end, with only a little trail twisting toward the Tennessee–North Carolina line. Here descendants of the original settlers cultivated their own small plots, grazed livestock in woods that custom held open to all, hunted and fished in an ancient hardwood forest, mined iron ore, made whiskey, spun cloth, and bartered with local merchants for what they could not produce at home.[11]

In the 1880s East Tennessee's timber and mineral resources attracted the attention of capitalists in the United States and abroad, and an era of land speculation and railroad building began. The railroads opened the way to timber barons, who stripped away the forests, leaving hillsides stark and vulnerable to erosion. Farmers abandoned their fields to follow the march of the logging camps. Left behind, women and children did their best to pick up the slack. But by the time Carter County was "timbered out" in the 1920s, farm families had crept upward to the barren ridge lands or grown dependent on "steady work and cash wages." Meanwhile, in Elizabethton, the county seat, an aggressive new class of bankers, lawyers, and businessmen served as brokers for outside developers, speculated in land, invested in homegrown factories, and looked beyond the hills for their standards of "push, progress and prosperity."[12]

Carter County, however, lacked Appalachia's grand prize: The rush for coal that devastated other parts of the mountains had bypassed that part of East Tennessee. Nor had county farmers been absorbed into the cotton kingdom, with its exploitative credit system and spreading tenancy. To be sure, they were increasingly hard pressed. As arable land disappeared, farms were divided and redivided. In 1880 the average rural family had supported itself on 140 acres of land; by 1920 it was making do on slightly more than 52 acres. Yet however diminished their circumstances, 84.5 per cent still owned their own land. The economic base that sustained traditional expectations of independence, production for use, and neighborly reciprocity tottered but did not give way.[13]

The coming of the rayon plants represented a coup for Elizabethton's aspiring businessmen, who wooed investors with promises of free land, tax exemptions, and cheap labor.[14] But at first the whole county seemed to share the boomtown spirit. Men from Stoney Creek, Gap Creek, and other mountain hamlets built the cavernous mills, then stayed on to learn the chemical processes that made "artificial silk." Women vied for jobs in the textile division where they wound, reeled, twisted, and inspected the rayon yarn. Real-estate prices soared as the city embarked on a frenzied improvement campaign and private developers threw up houses in subdivisions of outlying fields.

Yet for all the excitement it engendered, industrialization in Carter County retained a distinctly rural cast. Although Elizabethton's population tripled (from 2,749 in 1920 to 8,093 in 1930), the rayon workers confounded predictions of spectacular urban growth, for most remained in the countryside, riding to work on chartered buses and trains or in taxis driven by neighbors and friends.[15]

Women made up a large proportion of the 3,213 workers in the mills. According to company sources, they held 30 per cent of the jobs at the Bemberg plant and a full 44 per cent at the larger Glanzstoff mill – where the strike started and the union gained its firmest hold. Between 75 and 80 per cent of those female employees were single and aged 16 to 21. But these figures underestimate the workers' youth, for the company ignored state child-labor laws and hired girls as young as 12 or, more commonly, 14. By contrast, a significant proportion of male workers were older, married men. Since no company records have survived, it is impossible to describe the work force in detail, but its general character is clear: The work force was white, drawn predominantly from Elizabethton and Carter County but also from contiguous areas of North Carolina and Virginia. Adult married men, together with a smaller number of teenage boys, dominated the chemical division, while young women, the vast majority of whom commuted from farm homes, processed the finished yarn.[16]

Whether married or single, town- or country-bred, the men who labored in the rayon plants followed in the footsteps of fathers, and sometimes grandfathers, who had combined farming with a variety of wage-earning occupations. To a greater extent than we might expect, young women who had grown up in Elizabethton could also look to earlier models of gainful labor. A search of the 1910 manuscript census found 20 per cent (97/507) of women aged 14 and over in paid occupations. The largest proportion (29.6 per cent) were cooks and servants. But close behind were women in what mountain people called "public work": wage-earning labor performed outside a household setting. Most of these (25.1 per cent) worked in the town's small cotton and garment mills. Clerks, teachers, and boardinghouse keepers rounded out this employment profile.[17]

For rayon workers from the countryside, it was a different story. Only 5.2 per cent of adult women on Stoney Creek were gainfully employed (33/638). Nineteen of these were farmers. The rest – except for one music teacher – were servants or washerwomen.[18] Such statistics, of course, are notorious for their underestimation of women's moneymaking activities. Nor do they reflect the enormous amount of unpaid labor performed by women on Carter County farms. Still, the contrast is telling, and from it we can surmise two things. The first is that industrialization did not burst upon a static, conflict-free "traditional" world. The women who beat a path to the rayon plants came from families that had already been drawn into an economy where money was a key to survival. The second is that the timber industry, which attracted Carter County's men, undermined its agricultural base, and destroyed its natural resources, created few opportunities for rural women. No wonder that farm daughters in the mills counted their blessings and looked on themselves as pioneers. For some the rayon plants offered another way of meeting a farm daughter's obligations to the family economy. But others had more complex motivations, and their route to the factory reflected the changing configuration of mountain women's lives.

Flossie Cole's father owned a tiny farm on Stoney Creek, with a gristmill built from stones he had hauled over the mountain in an ox-drawn sled. When Flossie was "two months and twelve days old," he died in a coal-mining accident in Virginia, leaving his wife with seven children to support. The family kept body and soul together by grinding corn for their neighbors and tending the farm. Cole may have been new to factory labor, but she was no stranger to women's work. While her brothers followed their father's lead to the coal mines, she pursued the two most common occupations of the poorest mountain girls: agricultural labor and domestic service in other people's homes. "We would hire out and stay with people until they got through with us and then go back home. And when we got back home, it was workin' in the corn or wash for people." When Cole lost her job after the strike, she went back to domestic service – "back to the drudge house," as she put it.[19]

Bessie Edens was the oldest of ten children in a family that had been to Illinois and back before the rayon mills arrived. Her father had found a job in a brickyard, but her mother missed the mountains and insisted on coming home. Edens dreamed of an education and begged to go to nursing school. But her parents opposed her plan. At 15 she too went to work as a servant. "Then I'd come back when Momma had a baby and wait on her, and help if she needed me in any way." When asked fifty years later about a daughter's place on a hardscrabble farm, Edens replied: "The girls were supposed to do housework and work in the fields. They were supposed to be slaves." By the time the rayon plants opened, Edens was married and the mother of two. She left the children with her mother and seized the chance to earn her own money and to contribute to her family's support.[20]

Nettie Reece's father worked for Elizabethton's Empire Chair Company while her mother kept up a seven-acre farm on the outskirts of town. Mrs. Reece also kept four or five cows, ten to fifteen hogs, and one hundred chickens – all that while giving birth to ten children, eight of whom survived. Nettie Reece earned her first fifty cents pulling weeds in a wealthy family's yard. When the German factory managers arrived, she waited on tables at their boardinghouse (although her father was indignant when she brought home "tips" and almost made her quit). At 14 she got a reeling job at the Bemberg plant. To her, work seemed an extension of school, for she was surrounded by girls she had known all her life. "We grew up together," she remembered. "We used to be called the dirty dozen. [When we went to work] it looked like the classroom was walking down the street." Movies, Chautauqua events, and above all the opportunities for courting presented by the sudden gathering of so many young people in the town – these were Nettie Reece's main memories of the eight months she spent at Bemberg before the strike began.[21]

Whether they sought employment out of family need, adventurousness, or thwarted aspiration – or a combination of the three – most saw factory labor as a hopeful gamble rather than a desperate last resort. Every woman interviewed remembered two things: how she got her first job and the size of her first paycheck. "I'll never forget the day they hired me at Bemberg," said Flossie Cole. "We went down right in front of it. They'd come out and they'd say, 'You and you and you,' and they'd hire so many. And that day I was standing there and he picked out two or three more and he looked at me and he said, 'You.' It thrilled me to death." She worked fifty-six hours that week and took home $8.16.[22]

Such pay scales were low even for the southern textile industry, and workers quickly found their income eaten away by the cost of commuting or of boarding in town. When the strike came it focused on the issue of Glanzstoff women's wages, which lagged behind those at the older Bemberg plant. But workers had other grievances as well. Caustic chemicals were used to turn cellulose into a viscous fluid that was then forced through spinnerets, thimble-shaped nozzles pierced with tiny holes. The fine, individual streams coagulated into rayon filaments in an acid bath. In the chemical division men waded through water and acid, exposed all day to a lethal spray. Women labored under less dangerous conditions, but for longer hours and less pay. Paid by the piece, they complained of rising production quotas and what everyone referred to as "hard rules."[23]

Women in particular were singled out for petty regulations, aimed not just at extracting labor but at shaping deportment as well. They were forbidden to wear makeup; in some departments they were required to purchase uniforms. Most galling of all was company surveillance of the washroom. According to Bessie Edens, who was promoted to "forelady" in the twisting room, "men could do what they wanted to in their own department," but women had to get a pass to leave the shop floor. "If we went to the bathroom, they'd follow us," Flossie Cole confirmed, "'fraid we'd stay a minute too long." If they did, their pay was docked; one too many trips and they lost their jobs.[24]

Complaints about the washroom may have had other meanings as well. When asked how she heard that a strike was brewing, Nettie Reece cited "bathroom gossip."[25] As the company well knew, the women's washroom where only a forelady, not a male supervisor, could go might serve as a communications center, a hub of gossip where complaints were aired and plans were formulated.

The German origins of the plant managers contributed to the tension. Once the strike began, union organizers were quick to play on images of an "imported Prussian autocracy." The frontier republicanism of the mountains shaded easily into post-First World War Americanism as strikers demanded their rights as "natural born American citizens" oppressed by a "latter day industrialism." In that they had much in common with other twentieth-century workers, for whom the democratic values articulated during the war became a rallying cry for social justice at home. The nationality of the managers helped throw those values into sharp relief.[26]

Above all, the fact that the plant managers were newcomers to the region made them unusually dependent on second- and third-line supervisors, few of whom could be drawn from established hierarchies of age and skill. The power that shop-floor supervisors thus acquired could cut two ways. If used arbitrarily to hire and fire, it could provoke resentment. At the same time, men and women whose primary concern was the welfare of family and friends might act more as shop stewards than as enforcers of the company will. Reduced to promoting the likes of Bessie Edens to authority over seventy-five young women from her own mountain coves, the managers strengthened their opposition.[27]

Efforts to organize the plants by local American Federation of Labor (AFL) craft unionists had begun at least as early as 1927.[28] But the strike was initiated on 12 March 1929 by women in the Glanzstoff inspection department, by what one observer called "girls in their teens [who] decided not to put up with the present conditions any longer." For weeks Margaret Bowen had been asking for a raise for herself and the section she supervised. That morning she had asked again and once more had been turned away. Christine Galliher remembered the moment well: "We all decided in that department if they didn't give us a raise we wasn't going to work." One by one the other sections sent word: "We are more important than any other department of the plant. . . . Why don't you walk out and we will walk out with you?" At 12:30 the inspectors left their jobs.[29]

On 13 March the women returned to the plant and led the rest of the work force out on strike. Five days later Bemberg workers came out as well. By then the Carter County Chancery Court had handed down two draconian injunctions forbidding all demonstrations against the company. When strikers ignored the injunctions, plant managers joined town officials in convincing the governor to send in the National Guard. The strikers secured a charter from the AFL's United Textile Workers (UTW). Meeting in a place called the Tabernacle, built for religious revivals, they listened to a Baptist preacher from Stoney Creek warn: "The hand of oppression is growing on our people. . . . You women work for practically nothing. You must come together and say that such things must cease to be." Each night more workers "came forward" to take the union oath.[30]

Meanwhile, UTW and Federal Conciliation Service officials arrived on the scene. On 22 March they reached a "gentlemen's agreement" by which the company promised a new wage scale for "good girl help" and agreed not to discriminate against union members.[31] The strikers returned to work, but the conflict was far from over. Higher paychecks never materialized; union members began losing their jobs. On 4 April local businessmen kidnapped two union organizers and ran them out of town. Eleven days later a second strike began, this time among the women in the Glanzstoff reeling room. "When they blew that whistle everybody knew to quit work," Flossie Cole recalled. "We all just quit our work and rushed out. Some of 'em went to Bemberg and climbed the fence. [They] went into Bemberg and got 'em out of there." With both plants closed by what workers called a "spontaneous and complete walkout," the national union reluctantly promised its support.[32]

This time the conflict quickly escalated. More troops arrived, and the plants became fortresses, with machine guns on the rooftops and armed guardsmen on the ground. The company sent buses manned by soldiers farther up the hollows to recruit new workers and to escort them back to town. Pickets blocked narrow mountain roads. Houses were blown up; the town water main was dynamited. An estimated 1,250 individuals were arrested in confrontations with the National Guard.[33]

As far as can be determined, no women were involved in barn burnings and dynamitings – what Bessie Edens referred to as the "rough. . .stuff" that accompanied the second strike. Men "went places that we didn't go," explained Christine Galliher. "They had big dark secrets. . .the men did." But when it came to public demonstrations, women held center stage. At the outset "hundreds of girls" had ridden down main street "in buses and taxis, shouting and laughing at people who watched them from windows and doorsteps." Now they blocked the road at Gap Creek and refused soldiers' orders that they walk twelve miles to jail in town. "And there was one girl that was awful tough in the bunch. . . . She said, 'No, by God. We didn't walk out here, and we're not walking back!' And she sat her hind end down in the middle of the road, and we all sat down with her. And the law used tear gas on us!. . .And it nearly put our eyes out, but we still wouldn't walk back to town." At Valley Forge women teased the guardsmen and shamed the strikebreakers. In Elizabethton after picket duty, women marched down the "Bemberg Highway. . .draped in the American flag and carrying the colors" – thereby forcing the guardsmen to present arms each time they passed. Inventive, playful, and shrewd, the women's tactics encouraged a holiday spirit. They may also have deflected violence and garnered community support.[34]

Laughter was among the women's most effective weapons. But they also made more prosaic contributions, chief among which was taking responsibility for the everyday tasks of the union. In this they were aided by the arrival of middle-class allies, a series of extraordinary women reformers who provided new models of organizational skill and glimpses of a wider life.

After the First World War national women's organizations long interested in working women had looked with increasing concern on the relocation of the female-intensive textile industry to a region where protective legislation was weak and unions were weaker. The National Women's Trade Union League (NWTUL) launched a southern educational campaign. The Young Women's Christian Association (YWCA) strengthened its industrial department and employed a series of talented southern industrial secretaries. In 1927 Louise Leonard left her YWCA post to found the Southern Summer School for Women Workers in Industry. The convergence of interest in the South's women workers intensified with the 1929 strikes. The strikes, in turn, raised reformers' expectations and lent substance to their strategies. Leonard, for instance, visited Elizabethton, recruiting students for the Southern Summer School. Some of those who went returned again and again, and for them the school offered an exciting political education. But the benefit ran both ways. For Leonard the strike confirmed in microcosm the school's larger hopes: The nature of southern industrialization made women the key to unionization; women had led the way at Elizabethton; once reached by the Southern Summer School (and a trade-union movement more sensitive to their needs), women would lead the way throughout the South.[35]

Unlike the YWCA-based reformers, the NWTUL was a new-comer to the region, and to most of its executive committee the South was literally "another nation." Dependent on the writings of journalists and sociologists, NWTUL leaders concluded that southern workers were crippled by poverty and paternalism and that only a roundabout approach through southern liberals would do. The Elizabethton strike persuaded them to take a fresh approach. The NWTUL's twenty-fifth anniversary convention, held in 1929, featured a "dramatic and moving" speech by Margaret Bowen and a historical tableau linking the revolt of the Lowell, Massachusetts, mill women with "the revolt of the farmers' daughters of the new industrial South today." Matilda Lindsay, director of the NWTUL's southern campaign, became a major presence at Elizabethton and at subsequent conflicts as well.[36]

Within a week after the inspectors' walkout, Matilda Lindsay set up shop in Elizabethton and began coordinating women's union support activities. Women gave out union food vouchers at L. G. Bowles's boardinghouse, where Margaret Bowen lived. They helped to run the union office. Teams of "pretty young girls" distributed handbills and took up contributions at union "tag days" in Knoxville and Asheville. A similar contingent tried to see Governor Henry H. Horton in Nashville. Failing, they picketed his home. When the strike dragged on, the union leased a boardinghouse for young women and put Lindsay in charge. At the Tennessee Federation of Labor's 1929 convention, UTW officials acknowledged Lindsay's contributions: "She was speaker, adviser, mother, sister, bookkeeper, secretary and stenographer. . . . [A]nd we are happy to say she did them all without protest and without credit." But the tribute said less about Lindsay than about the distance between the vision of women reformers and the assumptions of trade-union leaders. Whether workers or reformers, women were seen as supporting players, not the best hope for cracking the nonunion South.[37]

In any event, it was workers, not organizers or reformers, who bore the brunt of the struggle and would have to live with its results. And beneath high spirits the terms of battle had begun to change. The militancy of Alfred Hoffmann, the UTW's chief organizer at Elizabethton, matched the strikers' own. But he was hobbled by a national union that lacked the resources and commitment to sustain the strike. Instead of translating workers' grievances into a compelling challenge, the UTW pared their demands down to the bone. On 26 May, six weeks after the strike began, the union agreed to a settlement that made no mention of wages, hours, working conditions, or union recognition. The company's only concession was a promise not to discriminate against union members. The workers were less than enthusiastic. According to the strike's most thorough chronicler, "It took nine speeches and a lot of question answering lasting two and a half hours to get the strikers to accept the terms."[38]

The press, for the most part, greeted the settlement as a workers' victory, or at least a satisfactory resolution of the conflict. Anna Weinstock, the first woman to serve as a federal conciliator, was credited with bringing the company to the bargaining table and was pictured as the heroine of the event. "SETTLED BY A WOMAN!" headlined one journal. "This is the fact that astounds American newspaper editors." "Five feet five inches and 120 pounds of femininity; clean cut, even features" – and so on, in great detail. Little was made of Weinstock's own working-class origins. She was simply a "new woman," come to the rescue of a backward mountain folk. The strikers themselves dropped quickly from view.[39]

Louise Leonard had visited Elizabethton only weeks before the UTW capitulated. With her was the left-wing journalist Mary Heaton Vorse. Both were heartened by what they found. In her years of labor reporting, Vorse "had never seen anything to compare with the quality of courage and determination of the Elizabethton strikers." Leonard was impressed not only by the women's leadership but also by the strike's community support.[40] As it turned out, neither "courage and determination" nor community support was sufficient to the strikers' needs. The contest at Elizabethton was an unequal one, with a powerful multinational corporation backed by the armed force of the state pitted against workers who looked to an irresolute national union for support. But it was not so unequal in contemporary eyes as hindsight would have it. To the strikers, as to Vorse and Leonard, the future seemed up for grabs.

Observers at the time and historians since saw the Elizabethton strike as a straightforward case of labor–management strife. But the conflict appeared quite different from within. Everyone interviewed put the blame for low wages on an alliance between the German managers and the "leading citizens" of the town. Preserved in the oral tradition is the story of how the "town fathers" promised the company a supply of cheap and unorganized labor. Bessie Edens put it this way: They told the company that "women wasn't used to working, and they'd work for almost nothing, and the men would work for low wages. That's the way they got the plant here." In this version of events the strike was part of an ongoing tug-of-war. On one side stood workers, farmers, and small merchants linked by traditional networks of trade and kin. On the other, development-minded townspeople cast their lot with a "latter day industrialism" embodied by the rayon plants.[41]

Workers' roots in the countryside encouraged resistance and helped them to mobilize support once the strike began. "These workers have come so recently from the farms and mountains . . .and are of such independent spirit," Alfred Hoffmann observed, "that they 'Don't care if they lose their jobs' and cannot be scared." Asked by reporters what would happen if strike activity cost them their jobs, one woman remarked, "I haven't forgotten to use a hoe," while another said, "We'll go back to the farm."[42] Such threats were not just bravado. High levels of farm ownership sustained cultural independence. Within the internal economy of families, individual fortunes were cushioned by reciprocity; an orientation toward subsistence survived side by side with the desire for cash and store-bought goods.

Stoney Creek farmers were solidly behind the sons and daughters they sent to the factories. In county politics Stoney Creekers had historically marshaled a block vote against the town. In 1929 Stoney Creek's own J. M. Moreland was county sheriff, and he openly took the strikers' side. "I will protect your plant, but not scabs," he warned the company. "I am with you and I want you to win," he cheered the Tabernacle crowd.[43]

Solidarity flowed not only from the farm families of striking workers but also from small merchants who relied on those families for their trade. A grocer named J. D. White turned his store into a union commissary and became a mainstay on the picket line. A strike leader in the twisting room ran a country store and drove his working neighbors into town. "That's why he was pretty well accepted as their leader," said a fellow worker. "Some of them were cousins and other relations. Some of them traded at his store. Some of them rode in his taxi. All intertwined."[44]

The National Guard had divided loyalties. Parading past the

plants, the strikers "waved to and called the first names of the guardsmen, for most of the young men in uniforms [were friends of] the men and girls on strike." Even when the local unit was fortified by outside recruits, fraternizing continued. Nettie Reece, like a number of her girlfriends, met her future husband that way; she saw him on the street and "knew that was mine right there." Some guardsmen went further and simply refused to serve. "The use of the National Guard here was the dirtiest deal ever pulled," one protested. "I turned in my equipment when I was ordered to go out and patrol the road. I was dropped from the payroll two weeks later."[45]

In this context of family- and community-based resistance, women had important roles to play. Farm mothers nurtured the strikers' independence simply by cleaving to the land, passing on to their children a heritage at odds with the values of the new order and maintaining family production as a hedge against the uncertainties of a market economy. But the situation of farm mothers had other effects as well, and it would be a mistake to push the argument for continuity too far. As their husbands ranged widely in search of wage labor, women's work intensified while their status – now tied to earning power – declined. The female strikers of Elizabethton saw their mothers as resourceful and strong but also as increasingly isolated and hard pressed. Most important, they no longer looked to their mothers' lives as patterns for their own.[46]

The summer after the strike, Bessie Edens attended the Southern Summer School, where she set the group on its ear with an impassioned defense of women's rights:

> It is nothing new for married women to work. They have always worked. . . . Women have always worked harder than men and always had to look up to the man and feel that they were weaker and inferior. . . . If we women would not be so submissive and take every thing for granted, if we would awake and stand up for our rights, this world would be a better place to live in, at least it would be better for the women.
>
> Some girls think that as long as mother takes in washings, keeps ten or twelve boarders or perhaps takes in sewing, she isn't working. But I say that either one of the three is as hard work as women could do. So if they do that at home

and don't get any wages for it, why would it not be all right for them to go to a factory and receive pay for what they do?[47]

Bessie Edens was remarkable in her talent for translating Southern Summer School teachings into the idiom of her own experiences and observations. But scattered through the life histories written by other students are echoes of her general themes.[48] Read in the context of farm daughters' lives – their first-hand exposure to rural poverty, their yearnings for a more expansive world – these stories reflect the "structure of feeling" women brought to the rayon plants and then to the picket line and union hall. Women such as Edens, it seems, sensed the devaluation of women's handicraft labor in the face of cheap consumer goods. They feared the long arm of their mothers' fate, resented their fathers' distant authority, and envied their brothers' exploits away from home. By opting for work in the rayon plants, they struck out for their own place in a changing world. When low wages, high costs, and autocratic managers affronted their dignity and dashed their hopes, they were the first to revolt.

The Elizabethton story thus presents another pattern in the female protest tradition. In coal-mining communities a rigid division of labor and women's hardships in company towns have resulted, paradoxically, in the notable militancy of miners' wives. By contrast, tobacco factories have tended to employ married women, whose job commitments and associational lives enable them to assume leadership roles in sustained organizing drives. In yet other circumstances, such as the early New England textile mills or the union insurgency of the 1920s and 1930s, single women initiated independent strikes or provided strong support for male-led, mixed-sex campaigns. Where, as in Elizabethton, people were mobilized as family and community members rather than as individual workers, non-wage-earning women could provide essential support. Once in motion, their daughters might outdo men in militancy, perhaps because they had fewer dependents than their male coworkers and could fall back more easily on parental resources, perhaps because the peer culture and increased independence encouraged by factory labor stirred boldness and inspired experimentation.[49]

The fact of women's initiative and participation in collective action is instructive. Even more intriguing is the gender-based symbolism of their protest style. Through dress, language, and gesture, female strikers expressed a complex cultural identity and turned it to their own rebellious purposes.[50]

Consider, for instance, Trixie Perry and a woman who called herself "Texas Bill." Twenty-eight-year-old Trixie Perry was a reeler in the Glanzstoff plant. She had apparently become pregnant ten years before, had married briefly and then divorced, giving her son her maiden name. Her father was a butcher and a farmer, and she lived near her family on the edge of town. Perry later moved into Elizabethton. She never remarried but went on to have several more children by other men. Texas Bill's background is more elusive. All we know is that she came from out of state, lived in a boardinghouse, and claimed to have been married twice before she arrived in town. These two friends were ringleaders on the picket line. Both were charged with violating the injunction, and both were brought to trial.[51]

Trixie Perry took the stand in a dress sewn from red, white, and blue bunting and a cap made of a small American flag. The prosecuting attorney began his cross-examination:

"You have a United States flag as a cap on your head?"

"Yes."

"Wear it all the time?"

"Whenever I take a notion."

"You are dressed in a United States flag, and the colors?"

"I guess so, I was born under it, guess I have a right to."[52]

The main charge was that Perry and her friend had drawn a line across the road at Gap Creek and dared the soldiers to cross it. Above all they were accused of taunting the National Guard. The defense attorney, a fiery local lawyer playing to a sympathetic crowd, did not deny the charges. Instead, he used the women to mock the government's case. Had Trixie Perry threatened a lieutenant? "He rammed a gun in my face and I told him to take it out or I would knock it out." Had she blocked the road? "A little thing like me block a big road?" What had she said to the threat of a tear gas bomb? "That little old fire cracker of a thing, it won't go off."[53]

Texas Bill was an even bigger hit with the crowd. The defense attorney called her the "Wild Man from Borneo." A guard said she was "the wildest human being I've ever seen." Texas Bill both affirmed and subverted her reputation. Her nickname

257

came from her habit of wearing "cowboy" clothes. But when it was her turn to testify, she "strutted on the stand" in a fashionable black picture hat and a black coat. Besides her other transgressions, she was accused of grabbing a soldier's gun and aiming it at him. What was she doing on the road so early in the morning? "I take a walk every morning before breakfast for my health," Texas Bill replied with what a reporter described as "an assumed ladylike dignity."[54]

Witnesses for the prosecution took pains to contradict Texas Bill's "assumed ladylike dignity." A guardsman complained that she called him a " 'God damned yellow son-of-a-bitch' and then branched out from that." Texas Bill offered no defense: "When that soldier stuck his gun in my face, that did make me mad and I did cuss a little bit and don't deny it." Far from discrediting the strikers, the soldiers' testimony added to their own embarrassment and the audience's delight. In tune with the crowd, the defense attorney "enjoyed making the guards admit they had been 'assaulted'. . .by 16- and 18-year-old girls."[55]

Mock gentility, transgressive laughter, male egos on the line – the mix made for wonderful theater and proved effective in court as well. The judge reserved maximum sentences for three especially aggressive men; all the women and most of the men were found not guilty or were lightly fined. In the end even those convictions were overturned by the state court of appeals.[56]

Trixie Perry and Texas Bill certainly donned the role of "disorderly woman." Since, presumably, only extraordinary circumstances call forth feminine aggression, women's assaults against persons and property constitute a powerful witness against injustice. At the same time, since women are considered less rational and taken less seriously than men, they may meet less resistance and be punished less severely for their crimes.[57]

But Trixie Perry and Texas Bill were not just out of line in their public acts; they also led unconventional private lives. It was that erotic subtext that most horrified officialdom and amused the courtroom crowd. The only extended discussion of the strike that appears in the city council minutes resulted in a resolution that read in part:

> WHEREAS, it has come to [our] attention. . .that the moral tone of this community has been lowered by reason of men

and women congregating in various houses and meeting-places in Elizabethton and there practicing lewdness all hours of the night, in defiance of morality, law and order. . .

NOW, THEREFORE, BE IT RESOLVED, that the police force of the City arrest and place in the City Jail those who are violating the laws by practicing lewdness within the City of Elizabethton. . . .[58]

Union representatives apparently shared, indeed anticipated, the councilmen's concern. Worried by rumors that unemployed women were resorting to prostitution, they had already announced to the press that 25 per cent of the strikers had been sent back to their hillside homes, "chiefly young single girls whom we want to keep off the streets." The townsmen and the trade unionists were thus united in drawing a line between good women and bad, with respectability being measured not only by chastity but by nuances of style and language as well.[59] In the heat of the trial, the question of whether or not women – as workers – had violated the injunction took second place to questions about their status *as women*, as members of their sex. Had they cursed? Had they been on the road at odd hours of the day or night? Was Texas Bill a lady or a "wild man from Borneo"? Fearing that "lewd women" might discredit the organizing drive, the organizers tried to send them home. To protect the community's "moral tone," the city council threatened to lock them up.

There is nothing extraordinary about this association between sexual misbehavior and women's labor militancy. Since strikers are often young single women who violate gender conventions by invading public space customarily reserved for men (and sometimes frequented by prostitutes) – and since female aggressiveness stirs up fears of women's sexual power – opponents have often undercut union organizing drives by insinuations of prostitution or promiscuity. Fearing guilt by association, "respectable" women stay away.[60]

What is impressive here is how Trixie Perry and Texas Bill handled the dichotomy between ladyhood and lewdness, good girls and bad. Using words that, for women in particular, were ordinarily taboo, they refused to pay deference and signaled disrespect. Making no secret of their sexual experience, they

259

combined flirtation with fierceness on the picket line and adopted a provocative courtroom style. And yet, with the language of dress – a cap made of an American flag, an elegant wide-brimmed hat – they claimed their rights as citizens and their place in the female community.

Moreover, that community upheld their claims. The defense attorney chose "disorderly women" as his star witnesses, and the courtroom spectators enthusiastically cheered them on. The prosecuting attorney recommended dismissal of the charges against all the women on trial except Trixie Perry, Texas Bill, and a "hoodlum" named Lucille Ratliffe, on the grounds that the rest came from "good families." Yet in the court transcripts, few differences can be discerned in the behavior of good girls and bad. The other female defendants may have been less flamboyant, but they were no less sharp-tongued. Was Vivian King a member of the UTW? "Yes, and proud of it." Had she been picketing? "Yes, proud of that." What was a young married woman named Dorothy Oxindine doing on Gap Creek at five o'clock in the morning? "Out airing." Did Lena May Jones "holler out 'scab' "? "No, I think the statement made was 'I wouldn't be a scab' and 'Why don't you come and join our organization.' " Did she laugh at a soldier and tell him his gun wouldn't shoot? "I didn't tell him it wouldn't shoot, but I laughed at him. . .and told him he was too much of a man to shoot a lady."[61]

Interviewed more than fifty years later, strike participants still refused to make invidious distinctions between themselves and women like Trixie Perry and Texas Bill. Bessie Edens was a settled, self-educated, married woman. But she was also a self-described "daredevil on the picket line," secure in the knowledge that she had a knife hidden in her drawstring underwear. To Edens, who came from a mountain hamlet called Hampton, the chief distinction did not lie between herself and rougher women. It lay between herself and merchants' wives who blamed the trouble on "those hussies from Hampton." When asked what she thought of Trixie Perry and Texas Bill, she answered simply, "There were some girls like that involved. But I didn't care. They did their part."[62]

Nettie Reece, who lived at home with parents who were "pretty particular with [their] daughters," shared Bessie Edens's attitude. After passing along the town gossip about Trixie Perry, she was anxious to make sure her meaning was not misconstrued. "Trixie was not a woman who sold her body," she emphasized. "She just had a big desire for sex. . . . And when she had a cause to fight for, she'd fight." Reece then went on to establish Perry's claim to a certain kind of respectability. After the strike Perry became a hard-working restaurant cook. She was a good neighbor: "If anybody got sick, she was there to wait on them." The six children she bore out of wedlock did well in life, and they "never throwed [their mother] aside."[63]

Family and community solidarity were obvious in the courtroom, implicit in press reports, and confirmed by interviews. By inference, they can also be seen in the living situations of female strikers. Of the 122 activists whose residences could be determined, only 6 lived or boarded alone. Residing at home, they could hardly have joined in the fray without family toleration or support.[64]

Industrialization, as we know, changed the nature of work, the meaning of time. In Carter County it entailed a shift of economic and political power from the countryside to the town. At issue too were more intimate matters of fantasy, culture, and style.

Implicit in the conflict were two different sexual systems. One, subscribed to by union officials and the local middle class, mandated chastity before marriage, men as breadwinners, and women as housewives in the home. The other, rooted in a rural past and adapted to working-class life, assumed women's productive labor, circumscribed women's roles without investing in abstract standards of femininity, and looked upon sexuality with a more pragmatic eye.

It must be noted at once that this is uncharted territory. There are no studies of gender in preindustrial Appalachia, let alone of sexuality, and discussions of the subject have been limited for the most part to a defense against pernicious stereotypes. The mountain women who people nineteenth-century travel accounts, novels, and social surveys tend to be drudges who married young and aged early, burdened by frequent pregnancies and good-for-nothing men. Alongside that predominant image is another: the promiscuous mountain girl, responsible for the supposed high rate of illegitimacy in the region.[65] We need not dwell on the shortcomings of such stylized accounts, filtered as they are through the lenses of class and cultural "otherness." But it would also be a mistake to discount them altogether, or to oppose them only with examples of mountain folk who conformed quite nicely to outlanders' middle-class norms. The view of married women as drudges is analogous to white observations of American Indian life: Women may in fact have taken on agricultural responsibilities seen by observers as inappropriate to their sex, while men engaged in hunting, fishing, and moonshining – and later logging or coal mining – that seemed unproductive or illegitimate or that took them away from home. Similarly, stripped of moralism, observations about sexual mores in the backcountry South may contain a grain of truth. The women of Elizabethton came from a society that seems to have recognized liaisons established without the benefit of clergy or license fees and allowed legitimacy to be broadly construed – in short, a society that might produce a Trixie Perry or defend "hussies from Hampton" against the snubs of merchants' wives.[66]

This is not to say that the women of Elizabethton were simply acting on tradition. On the contrary, the strikers dressed the persona of the disorderly woman in unmistakably modern garb. Women's behavior on the witness stand presupposed a certain sophistication: A passing familiarity allowed them to parody ladyhood and to thumb a nose at the genteel standards of the town. Combining garments from the local past with fragments of an expansive consumer culture, the women of Elizabethton assembled their own version of a brash, irreverent Jazz Age style.

By the early 1920s radios and "Ford touring cars" had joined railroads and mail-order catalogs as conduits to the larger world. Record companies had discovered hillcountry music, and East Tennessee's first country-music stars were recording hits that transformed ballad singing, fiddle playing, and banjo picking into one of America's great popular-music sounds. The banjo itself was an African-American instrument that had come to the mountains with the railroad gangs. Such cultural interchanges multiplied during the 1920s as rural traditions met the upheavals of industrial life. The result was an explosion of musical creativity – in the hills of Tennessee no less than in New York City and other cosmopolitan centers.[67] Arriving for work in the rayon plants, young people brought with them the usable past of the countryside, but they quickly assimilated the speeded-up rhythms, the fashions, the popular culture of their generation's changing times.

Work-related peer groups formed a bridge between traditional loyalties and a novel youth culture. Whether married or single, living with parents or on their own, women participated in the strike in same-sex groups. Sisters boarded, worked, and demonstrated together. Girlfriends teamed up in groups or pairs. Trixie Perry and Texas Bill were a case in point. But there were others as well. Nettie Reece joined the union with her parents' approval but also with her whole "dirty dozen" gang in tow. Ethel and M. C. Ashworth, ages 18 and 17, respectively, came from Virginia to work in the plants. "Hollering and singing [in a] Ford touring car," they were arrested together in a demonstration at Watauga Point. Ida and Evelyn Heaton boarded together on Donna Avenue. Evelyn was hit by a car on the picket line, swore out a warrant, and had the commander of the National Guard placed under arrest. After the strike Evelyn was blacklisted, and Ida attended the Southern Summer School.[68]

The sudden gathering of young people in the town nourished new patterns of social life and courtship, and the strike's erotic undercurrent surfaced not only in Trixie Perry's "big desire for sex" but also in the behavior of her more conventional peers. The loyalties of the guardsmen were divided, but their sympathy was obvious, as was their interest in the female strikers. Most of the Elizabethton women were in their teens or early twenties, the usual age of marriage in the region, and the strike provided unaccustomed opportunities for courtship. Rather than choosing a neighbor they had known all their lives, under watchful parental eyes, women flirted on the picket lines or the shop floor. Romance and politics commingled in the excitement of the moment, flowering in a spectrum of behavior – from the outrageousness of Trixie Perry to a spate of marriages among other girls.

What needs emphasis here is the dynamic quality of working-class women's culture – a quality that is sometimes lost in static oppositions between modernism and traditionalism, individualism and family values, consumer and producer mentalities. This is especially important where regional history has been so thoroughly mythologized. Appalachian culture, like all living cultures, embraced continuity and discontinuity, indigenous and borrowed elements.[69] As surely as Anna Weinstock – or Alabama's Zelda Fitzgerald – or any city flapper, the Elizabethton strikers were "new women," making their way in a world their mothers could not have known but carrying with them values handed down through the female line.

Three vignettes may serve to illustrate that process of grounded change.

Flossie Cole's mother, known by everyone on Stoney Creek as "Aunt Tide," was kin to Sherriff Moreland, but that didn't keep her from harboring cardplayers, buck-dancers, and whiskey drinks in her home. Aunt Tide was also a seamstress who "could look at a picture in a catalog and cut a pattern and make a dress just like it." But like most of her friends, Cole jumped at the chance for store-bought clothes. "That first paycheck, that was it. . .I think I bought me some new clothes with the first check I got. I bought me a new pair of shoes and a dress and a hat. Can you imagine someone going to a plant with a hat on? I had a blue dress and black shoes – patent leather, honey, with real high heels – and a blue hat." Nevertheless, before Cole left home in the morning for her job in the rayon plant, Aunt Tide made sure that around her neck – beneath the new blue dress – she wore a bag of asafetida, a strong-smelling resin, a folk remedy to protect her from diseases that might be circulating in the town.[70]

Then there was Myrtle Simmerly, whose father was killed in a logging accident and whose brothers went "out West" to work, faithfully sending money home so that she could finish school. Myrtle was the first secretary hired at the rayon plant, and she used her earnings to buy a Ford roadster with a rumble seat and a wardrobe of up-to-date clothes. For all her modern trappings, Myrtle defended her "hillbilly" heritage and took the workers' side against what she called the "city fathers, the courthouse crew." Asked why she thought women played such active roles in the strike, she spoke from experience: "They grew up on these farms, and they had to be aggressive to live."[71]

Finally, there is visual evidence: a set of sixteen-millimeter films made by the company in order to identify – and to blacklist – workers who participated in the union. In those films groups of smiling women traipse along the picket line dressed in up-to-date clothes.[72] Yet federal conciliator Anna Weinstock, speaking to an interviewer forty years later, pictured them in sunbonnets, and barefooted. "They were," she explained, "what we would normally call hillbillies": women who "never get away from their shacks."[73] This could be seen as the treachery of memory, a problem of retrospection. But it is also an illustration of the power of stereotypes, of how cultural difference is registered as backwardness, of how images of poverty and backwardness hide the realities of working-class women's lives.

The strike, as we know, was defeated, but not without cost to the company and some benefit to the workers. Elizabethton set off a chain reaction across the textile South. "It was supposed to be the leading strike in the South of the textile workers," Bessie Edens explained. "It was the main key to start the labor movement in the South, is what I understood." In Elizabethton itself an autocratic plant manager was recalled to Germany, a personnel officer installed a plant council and an extensive welfare program, wages went up, and hours went down. The new company official chose symbols of hierarchy and privilege that blended more easily with the American scene. Uniforms were eliminated. At the dedication of a company athletic field in 1930, the "Bemberg-Glanzstoffband" marched around the grandstand, followed first by plant officials, then by workingmen carrying banners, and finally by "beautiful women, dressed in rayon suits and costumes of brilliant hues."[74]

To be sure, blacklisted workers suffered for their choices. The Depression, followed by the great drought of 1930–1, devastated the rural economy and put a powerful bludgeon in company hands.[75] Union support inevitably fell away. Rosa Long, for one, was a pragmatist: "I quit the Union because I didn't see anything to them. Wasn't making me a living talking." Yet a committed remnant, supported by the "Citizens Committee," kept the local alive. When the National Labor Relations Act passed in 1935, the Elizabethton plants were among the first to join the Textile Workers Union of America–Congress of Industrial Organizations. Transferring their allegiance to the UTW–AFL in the late 1930s, Elizabethton's workers formed the largest rayon workers' local in the country.[76]

In the community at large, a muted debate over development went on. The local newspaper kept publishing paeans to progress. But the Citizens Committee saw things differently: "Our sons and daughters have been assaulted, arrested and imprisoned because they refuse to bow to the management of the plants. [Concessions to the companies have] defrauded Carter County out of thousands of dollars of taxes rather than bettering the conditions of the county." In some ways at least, the Citizens Committee seems to have taken the more realistic view. The metropolis dreamed of by Elizabethton boosters never materialized. Having bargained away its tax base, the town was forced to default on its bonded debt. Unfinished streets and sidewalks meandered to an end in open fields; houses in subdivisions sat half-finished; chemical wastes from the rayon plants poured into the Watauga River, polluting the clear spring water that had been one of the site's attractions to industry.[77]

The fate of the Elizabethton women is difficult to discern. Interviews traced the road from farm to factory, then focused on the strike itself; they offered only hints of how the experience of the 1920s fit into whole-life trajectories. Still, circumstantial evidence allows at least a few observations. The first is that from the time the rayon plants reopened in the fall of 1929 until the Second World War the number of women they employed steadily declined. Perhaps female strikers were more ruthlessly blacklisted, or men preferentially rehired. Perhaps, disillusioned, women simply stayed away. In any case, shrinking opportunities in the rayon mills did not mean that women abandoned wage labor. Although most of the activists whose subsequent histories are known married and had children, they did not permanently leave the work force. Some returned to the old roles of laundress, cook, and housekeeper; others became telephone operators, saleswomen, and secretaries.[78] Still others eventually slipped back into the rayon plants. "They called back who they wanted," said Flossie Cole. "I was out eighteen years. . .I probably wouldn't ever have gotten back 'cause they blacklisted so many of 'em. But I married and changed my name and World War II came on and I went back to work." Overall, the percentage of Carter County women who were gainfully employed held steady through the 1930s, then leaped upward with the outbreak of war.[79]

But if the habit of female "public work" persisted, its meaning probably did not. Young women had poured eagerly into the rayon mills, drawn at least in part by the promise of independence, romance, and adventure. As the Depression deepened, such motives paled beside stark necessity. One statistic makes the point: The only female occupation that significantly increased during the decade from 1930 to 1940 was domestic service, which rose from 13.4 per cent of gainfully employed women to 17.1 per cent. When Flossie Cole went "back to the drudge house," she had plenty of company.[80]

Still, despite subsequent hardships, the spirit of the 1920s flickered on. Setting out to explore the strike through oral-history interviews, we expected to find disclaimers or silences. Instead, we heard unfaded memories and no regrets. "I knew I wasn't going to get to go back, and I didn't care," said Bessie Edens. "I wrote them a letter and told them I didn't care whether they took me back or not. I didn't! If I'd starved I wouldn't of cared, because I knew what I was a'doing when I helped to pull it. And I've never regretted it in any way. . . . And it did help the people, and it's helped the town and the country."[81] For those, like Edens, who went on to the Southern Summer School or who remained active in the union, the strike was a pivot around which the political convictions and personal aspirations of a lifetime turned. For them, there were intangible rewards: a subtle deepening of self-esteem, a belief that they had made history and that later generations benefited from what they had done.

The strike, of course, made a fainter impression on other lives. Women's rebelliousness neither redefined gender roles nor overcame economic dependency. Their desire for the trappings of modernity could blur into a self-limiting consumerism. An ideology of romance could end in sexual danger or a married woman's burdensome double day. None of that, however, ought to obscure a generation's legacy. A norm of female public work, a new style of sexual expressiveness, the entry of women into public space and political struggles previously monopolized by men – all these pushed against traditional constraints even as they created new vulnerabilities.[82] The young women who left home for the rayon plants pioneered a new pattern of female experience, and they created for their post-Second World War daughters an environment far different from the one they, in their youth, had known. It would be up to later generations to wrestle with the costs of commercialization and to elaborate a vision that embraced economic justice and community solidarity as well as women's liberation.

NOTES

First published in *Journal of American History* 73 (September 1986). Used by permission.

This essay is part of a larger study of southern textile workers cowritten by Christopher Daly, Jacquelyn Dowd Hall, Lu Ann Jones, Robert Korstad, James Leloudis, and Mary Murphy. It began as a collaborative endeavor with Sara Evans of the University of Minnesota, who joined me in gathering many of the interviews on which I have relied. Support for this project came from a University Research Council Grant, an Appalachian Studies Fellowship, and a Woodrow Wilson International Center for Scholars Fellowship.

1 Dan Crowe, *Old Town and the Covered Bridge* (Johnson City, TN: 1977), 32, 71; Florence (Cole) Grindstaff interview by Jacquelyn Dowd Hall, 10 July 1981 (in Jacquelyn Dowd Hall's possession). The oral history component of this essay consists of approximately thirty interviews, the most detailed of which were with pro-union activists, a National Guardsman, one of the original German managers of the Bemberg plant, a leader of a company-sponsored organization of "loyal" workers, and members of the sheriff's family. Briefer interviews with workers who remembered the strike but who had not been actively involved are also included.

2 *Elizabethton Star*, 13 March 1929; *Knoxville News Sentinel*, 13 March 1929; Margaret Bowen, "The Story of the Elizabethton Strike," *American Federationist* 36 (June 1929): 664–8; US Congress, Senate, Committee on Manufactures, *Working Conditions of the Textile Industry in North Carolina, South Carolina, and Tennessee*, 71 Cong., 1 sess., May 8, 9, and 20, 1929; *American Bemberg Corp. v. George Miller, et al.*, minute books "Q" and "R," Chancery Court minutes, Carter County, TN, 22 July 1929 (Carter County Courthouse, Elizabethton, TN).

3 For the 1929 strike wave, see Tom Tippett, *When Southern Labor Stirs* (New York: 1931); Liston Pope, *Millhands and Preachers: A Study of Gastonia* (New York: 1942), 207–330; James A. Hodges, "Challenge to the New South: The Great Textile Strike in Elizabethton, Tennessee, 1929," *Tennessee Historical Quarterly* 23 (December 1964): 343–57; Irving Bernstein, *The Lean Years: A History of the American Worker, 1920–1933* (Boston: 1960), 1–43; David S. Painter, "The Southern Labor Revolt of 1929" (seminar paper, University of North Carolina, Chapel Hill, 1974, in David S. Painter's possession); and Jesse Creed Jones, "Revolt in Appalachia: The Elizabethton Rayon Strike, 1929" (honors thesis, University of Tennessee, Knoxville, 1974, in Paul H. Bergeron's possession).

4 On Ella May Wiggins, see Lynn Haessly, " 'Mill Mother's Lament': Ella May, Working Women's Militancy, and the 1929 Gaston County Textile Strikes" and " 'Mill Mother's Lament': The Intellectual Left's Reshaping of the 1929 Gaston County Textile Strikes and Songs" (seminar papers University of North Carolina,

Chapel Hill, 1984, in Lynn Haessly's possession). Proletarian novels, in contrast to historical accounts, took the perspectives and experiences of women as their central concern. See esp. Fielding Burke [Olive Tilford Dargan], *Call Home the Heart* (New York: 1932). See also Sylvia Jenkins Cook, *From Tobacco Road to Route 66: The Southern Poor White in Fiction* (Chapel Hill, NC: 1976), 98–142. For contemporary observations on Elizabethton women, see Matilda Lindsay, "Women Hold Key to Unionization of Dixie," *Machinists' Monthly Journal* 41 (September 1929): 638–9, 684; Sherwood Anderson, "Elizabethton, Tennessee," *Nation*, 1 May 1929, pp. 526–7; *Knoxville News Sentinel*, 17 May 1929; and Florence Kelley, "Our Newest South," *Survey*, 15 June 1929, pp. 342–4. Sara Evans was the first historian to raise questions about women's roles. See Sara Evans, "Women of the New South: Elizabethton, Tennessee, 1929" (seminar paper, University of North Carolina, Chapel Hill, 1970, in Sara Evans's possession).

5 Anne Firor Scott, "On Seeing and Not Seeing: A Case of Historical Invisibility," *Journal of American History* 71 (June 1984): 7–8. The new scholarship in Appalachian studies has had little to say about gender. For this point and for a plea for "concrete, empirical, historical research" on class and gender in the region, see Sally Ward Maggard, "Class and Gender: New Theoretical Priorities in Appalachian Studies," paper presented at the Eighth Annual Appalachian Studies Conference, Berea, KY, 1985, esp. 7 (in Sally Ward Maggard's possession).

6 This scholarship has suggested that the working-class family may serve as a base for resisting exploitation. It has begun to outline the structural factors that include or exclude women from labor movements and to explore the consciousness that informs or inhibits women's collective action. See, for example, Alice Kessler-Harris, " 'Where Are the Organized Women Workers?' " *Feminist Studies* 3 (Fall 1975): 92–110; June Nash, "Resistance as Protest: Women in the Struggle of Bolivian Tin-Mining Communities," in *Women Cross-Culturally: Change and Challenge*, ed. Ruby Rohrlich-Leavitt (The Hague: 1975), 261–71; Dorothy Thompson, "Women and Nineteenth-Century Radical Politics: A Lost Dimension," in *The Rights and Wrongs of Women*, ed. Juliet Mitchell and Ann Oakley (New York: 1976), 112–38; Jane Humphries, "The Working Class Family, Women's Liberation, and Class Struggle: The Case of Nineteenth Century British History," *Review of Radical Political Economics* 9 (Fall 1977): 25–41; Carole Turbin, "Reconceptualizing Family, Work and Labor Organizing: Working Women in Troy, 1860–1890," *Review of Radical Political Economics* 16 (Spring 1984): 1–16; Elizabeth Jameson, "Imperfect Unions: Class and Gender in Cripple Creek, 1894–1904," in *Class, Sex, and the Woman Worker*, ed. Milton Cantor and Bruce Laurie (Westport, CT: 1977), 166–202; Thomas Dublin, *Women at Work: The Transformation of Work and Community in Lowell, Massachusetts, 1826–1860* (New York: 1979), esp. 86–131; Ruth Milkman, "Organizing the Sexual Division of

Labor: Historical Perspectives on 'Women's Work' and the American Labor Movement," *Socialist Review* 10 (January/February 1980): 95–150; Meredith Tax, *The Rising of the Women: Feminist Solidarity and Class Conflict, 1880–1917* (New York: 1980); Temma Kaplan, "Female Consciousness and Collective Action: The Case of Barcelona, 1910–1918," *Signs* 7 (Spring 1982): 545–66; Susan Levine, "Labor's True Woman: Domesticity and Equal Rights in the Knights of Labor," *Journal of American History* 70 (September 1983): 323–39; Linda Frankel, "Southern Textile Women: Generations of Survival and Struggle," in *My Troubles Are Going to Have Trouble with Me: Everyday Trials and Triumphs of Women Workers*, ed. Karen Brodkin Sacks and Dorothy Remy (New Brunswick, NJ: 1984), 39–60; Louise A. Tilly, "Paths of Proletarianization: Organization of Production, Sexual Division of Labor, and Women's Collective Action," *Signs* 7 (Winter 1981): 400–17; Sharon Hartman Strom, "Challenging 'Woman's Place': Feminism, the Left, and Industrial Unionism in the 1930s," *Feminist Studies* 9 (Summer 1983): 359–86; Dolores E. Janiewski, *Sisterhood Denied: Race, Gender, and Class in a New South Community* (Philadelphia: 1985), esp. 152–78; and Ruth Milkman, ed., *Women, Work and Protest: A Century of US Women's Labor History* (Boston: 1985). In contrast, Leslie Woodcock Tentler has emphasized how family values and the structure of work have encouraged female acquiescence. Leslie Woodcock Tentler, *Wage-Earning Women: Industrial Work and Family Life in the United States, 1900–1930* (New York: 1979), esp. 9–10, 72–80, 180–5.

7 Carroll Smith-Rosenberg, in *Disorderly Conduct: Visions of Gender in Victorian America* (New York: 1985), 268, makes a similar point in a different context.

8 Natalie Zemon Davis, *Society and Culture in Early Modern France* (Stanford: 1975), 124–51. For this phenomenon in the New World, see Laurel Thatcher Ulrich, *Good Wives: Image and Reality in the Lives of Women in Northern New England, 1650–1750* (New York: 1982), 191–7.

9 Jesse W. Markham, *Competition in the Rayon Industry* (Cambridge, MA: 1952), 1–38, 97, 186, 193, 209; Joseph Leeming, *Rayon: The First Man-Made Fiber* (Brooklyn: 1950), 1–82; John F. Holly, "Elizabethton, Tennessee: A Case Study of Southern Industrialization" (Ph.D. dissertation, Clark University, 1949), 123, 127–8, 133.

10 Bruce Roberts and Nancy Roberts, *Where Time Stood Still: A Portrait of Appalachia* (New York: 1970); William Goodell Frost, "Our Contemporary Ancestors in the Southern Mountains," *Atlantic Monthly* 83 (March 1899), 311; Arnold J. Toynbee, *A Study of History*, 2 vols. (New York: 1947), II, 312. For images of Appalachia, see also Henry D. Shapiro, *Appalachia on Our Mind: The Southern Mountains and Mountaineers in the American Consciousness, 1870–1920* (Chapel Hill, NC: 1978). In the 1970s regional scholars posited a neocolonial, or world-systems, model for understanding the "development of underdevelopment" in the Southern Mountains. More recently, they have begun to emphasize the role of indigenous elites, class

formation, and the similarities between the Appalachian experience
and that of other societies in transition from a semisubsistence to a
corporate capitalist economy. See, for example, John Gaventa, *Power
and Powerlessness: Quiescence and Rebellion in an Appalachian Valley*
(Urbana IL: 1980); David Alan Corbin, *Life, Work, and Rebellion in the
Coal Fields: The Southern West Virginia Miners, 1880–1922* (Urbana, IL:
1981); and Ronald D. Eller, *Miners, Millhands, and Mountaineers:
Industrialization of the Appalachian South, 1880–1930* (Knoxville: 1982).
For an approach to cultural change, see David E. Whisnant, *All That
Is Native & Fine: The Politics of Culture in an American Region* (Chapel
Hill, NC: 1983).

11 Eller, *Miners, Millhands, and Mountaineers*, 3–38; Steven Hahn, *The
Roots of Southern Populism: Yeoman Farmers and the Transformation of
the Georgia Upcountry, 1850–1890* (New York: 1983), 1–169; Holly,
"Elizabethton, Tennessee," 1–121; Alfred Hoffmann; "The
Mountaineer in Industry," *Mountain Life and Work*, 5 (January 1930):
2–7.

12 J. Fred Holly, "The Co-operative Town Company of Tennessee: A
Case Study of Planned Economic Development," *East Tennessee
Historical Society's Publications* 36 (1964): 56–69; Holly, "Elizabethton,
Tennessee," 117–20; Eller, *Miners, Millhands, and Mountaineers*, 86–
127; Rebecca Cushman, "Seed of Fire: The Human Side of History in
Our Nation's Southern Highland Region and Its Changing Years,"
typescript, n.d., pp. 142–4, North Carolina Collection (Wilson
Library, University of North Carolina, Chapel Hill); *Mountaineer*, 28
December, 31 December 1887; Nan Elizabeth Woodruff, *As Rare as
Rain: Federal Relief in the Great Southern Drought of 1930–31* (Urbana,
IL: 1985), 140–57; Ronald D. Eller, "Class, Conflict, and
Modernization in the Appalachian South," *Appalachian Journal* 10
(Winter 1983): 183–6; George F. Dugger, Sr., interview by Hall and
Sara Evans, 8 August 1979, transcript, pp. 8–14, Southern Oral
History Program Collection, Southern Historical Collection (Wilson
Library, University of North Carolina, Chapel Hill). See also David
L. Carlton, *Mill and Town in South Carolina, 1880–1920* (Baton Rouge:
1982), 1–39. The problems associated with economic change in
Carter County were exacerbated by a high birth rate and by the
enclosure of half the county's land area for a national forest reserve.
See Si Kahn, "The Government's Private Forests," *Southern Exposure*
2 (Fall 1974): 132–44; Margaret J. Hagood, "Mothers of the South: A
Population Study of Native White Women of Childbearing Age of
the Southeast" (Ph.D. dissertation, University of North Carolina,
Chapel Hill, 1938), 260–86; and Woodruff, *As Rare as Rain*, 140–1.

13 US Department of the Interior, Census Office, *Report on the
Productions of Agriculture as Returned at the Tenth Census (June 1, 1880)*
(Washington, DC: 1883), 84–5, 132, 169; US Department of
Commerce, Bureau of the Census, *Fourteenth Census of the United
States Taken in the Year 1920: Agriculture*, vol. VI, pt. 2 (Washington,
DC: 1922), 446–7.

14 The negotiations that brought the rayon company to Elizabethton

can be traced in the John Nolen Papers (Department of Manuscripts and University Archives, Cornell University Libraries, Ithaca, NY). See esp. John Nolen, "Report on Reconnaissance Survey", typescript, box 27, and John Nolen, "Progress Report and Preliminary Recommendation," typescript. See also Holly, "Elizabethton, Tennessee," 123, 133–8; Hodges, "Challenge to the New South," 543–4; and Dugger interview, 12–14.

15 Hoffmann, "Mountaineer in Industry," 3; *Elizabethton Star*, 22 March 1929; *Knoxville News Sentinel*, 14 March, 22 March 1929; Holly, "Elizabethton, Tennessee," 156, 198. For some indirect evidence of discontent with the course of events, however, see *Elizabethton Star*, 1 January, 17 January 1929.

16 Accounts of the size and composition of the work force differ widely. I am relying here on Committee on Manufactures, *Working Conditions of the Textile Industry in North Carolina, South Carolina, and Tennessee*, 95; interview with Arthur Mothwurf, *Knoxville News Sentinel*, 20 May 1929; Noel Sargent, "East Tennessee's Rayon Strikes of 1929," *American Industries*, 29 (June 1929): 10–11; and Henry Schuettler interview by Hall, n.d. [1981] (in Hall's possession). The city directory for 1930 showed only 21 married women out of 232 town-dwelling female rayon workers, whereas the figures for men were 375 out of 651. It is likely, however, that the directory underestimated married women's employment by listing only the occupation of the male head-of-household. *Miller's Elizabethton, Tenn., City Directory*, II (Asheville, NC: 1930). (City directories are extant only for 1926, 1929, and 1930. They were published more regularly after 1936.) Blacks comprised less than 2 per cent of the county's population in 1930, and few were employed in the rayon plants. This is not to say that the county's black population was unaffected by industrialization. The pull of urban growth combined with worsening conditions in the countryside drew blacks to town where they found jobs on the railroads, in construction, and as day laborers. From 1920 to 1930, the black population dropped from 569 to 528 in the county while increasing by 650 per cent in Elizabethton. US Department of Commerce, Bureau of the Census, *Fifteenth Census of the United States: 1930, Population*, vol. III, pt. 2 (Washington, DC: 1932), 909.

17 Holly, "Elizabethton, Tennessee," 108–10; "Thirteenth Census of the United States, 1910, Manuscript Population Schedule," Carter County, TN, district 7; district 15.

18 "Thirteenth Census of the United States, 1910, Manuscript Population Schedule," Carter County, TN, district 10; district 12. For the prevalence of women's work in preindustrial societies and for the traditional values that permitted families to send their daughters to take advantage of the new opportunities offered by industrialization, see Joan W. Scott and Louise A. Tilly, "Women's Work and the Family in Nineteenth-Century Europe," *Comparative Studies in Society and History*, 17 (January 1975): 36–64. For a somewhat different view, see Dublin, *Women at Work*, 23–57.

19 Grindstaff interview.
20 Bessie Edens interview by Mary Frederickson, 14 August 1975, transcript, p. 21, Southern Oral History Program Collection; Bessie Edens interview by Hall, 5 August 1979 (in Hall's possession); *Elizabethton Star*, 8 March 1985.
21 Nettie Reece [pseud.] interview by Hall, 18 and 19 May 1983 (in Hall's possession).
22 Grindstaff interview; *Knoxville News Sentinel*, 10 April, 27 April, 20 May 1929.
23 For men's working conditions, see Hoffmann, "Mountaineer in Industry," 3; Schuettler interview; *Elizabethton Star*, 15 August 1929; *Knoxville News Sentinel*, 10 May 1929; Duane McCracken, *Strike Injunctions in the New South* (Chapel Hill, NC: 1931), 247; Lawrence Range interview by Hall, 9 August 1979 (in Hall's possession); Thomas S. Mancuso, *Help for the Working Wounded* (Washington, DC: 1976), 75–7; Bessie Edens, "My Work in an Artificial Silk Mill," in *Scraps of Work and Play*, Southern Summer School for Women Workers in Industry, Burnsville, NC, 11 July–23 August 1929, typescript, pp. 21–2, box 111, American Labor Education Service Records, 1927–1962 (Martin P. Catherwood Library, New York State School of Industrial and Labor Relations, Cornell University, Ithaca, NY); Committee on Manufactures, *Working Conditions of the Textile Industry in North Carolina, South Carolina, and Tennessee*, 85. For women's working conditions, see Christine (Hinkle) Galliher, "Where I Work," in *Scraps of Work and Play*, 23; Ida Heaton, "Glanzstoff Silk Mill," in *Scraps of Work and Play*, 24; Edens interview, 14 August 1975, pp. 1–2, 31–2; Edens interview, 5 August 1979; Grindstaff interview; and Dorothy Conkin interview by Hall, 16 June 1982 (in Hall's possession).
24 Committee on Manufactures, *Working Conditions of the Textile Industry in North Carolina, South Carolina and Tennessee*, 83; Wilma Crowe interview by Hall, 15 July 1981 (in Hall's possession); Hoffmann, "Mountaineer in Industry," 3; Edens interview, 14 August 1975, p. 32; Grindstaff interview. See also Edens, "My Work in an Artificial Silk Mill."
25 Reece interview. See also Bowen, "Story of the Elizabethton Strike," 666.
26 *Knoxville News Sentinel*, 13 May 1929; *American Bemberg Corp. v. George Miller et al.*, East Tennessee District Supreme Court, 29 January 1930, record of evidence, typescript, box 660, Tennessee Supreme Court Records (Tennessee State Library and Archives, Nashville). See also, *Knoxville News Sentinel*, 14 May 1929; *Elizabethton Star*, 9 February 1929; Holly, "Elizabethton, Tennessee," 217; and "Synopsis of Appeal of Major George L. Berry, President of the International Printing Pressmen and Assistants' Union of North America of Pressmen's Home, Tennessee, with Relation to the Elizabethton Situation," n.d., Records of the Conciliation Service, RG 280 (National Archives). For such uses of Americanism, see Corbin, *Life, Work, and Rebellion in the Coal Fields*, 236–52.

27 Ina Nell (Hinkle) Harrison interview by Hall, 8 August 1979, transcript, p. 6, Southern Oral History Program Collection; Albert ("Red") Harrison interview by Evans, 9 August 1979 (in Hall's possession); Evelyn Hardin, written comments in *Scraps of Work and Play*, 25. Most helpful to my thinking about modes of management control were Jeremy Brecher, "Uncovering the Hidden History of the American Workplace," *Review of Radical Political Economics* 10 (Winter 1978): 1–23; and Richard Edwards, *Contested Terrain: The Transformation of the Workplace in the Twentieth Century* (New York: 1979), esp. 3–34.

28 Scraps of evidence indicate that a number of short-term walkouts occurred before the March strike, but those walkouts were not reported by the newspapers, and accounts of them differ in detail. See Hoffmann, "Mountaineer in Industry," 3–4; E. T. Willson to Secretary of Labor, 25 May, 26 June 1929, Records of the Conciliation Service; McCracken, *Strike Injunctions in the New South*, 246; *Knoxville News Sentinel*, 13 March, 15 March 1929; Holly, "Elizabethton, Tennessee," 307; and Clarence Raulston interview by Evans and Hall, 3 August 1979 (in Hall's possession).

29 *Knoxville News Sentinel*, 14 March 1929; Christine (Hinkle) Galliher and Dave Galliher interview by Hall, 8 August 1979, transcript, p. 5, Southern Oral History Program Collection; Committee on Manufactures, *Working Conditions of the Textile Industry in North Carolina, South Carolina, and Tennessee*, 79. Although interviews provided important information about the motives, actions, and reactions of individuals, they were not a reliable source of constructing a factual, chronological overview of the strike. Nor did they yield a detailed account of the inner workings of the local union. The most reliable written sources are the court records; the stories of John Moutoux, a reporter for the *Knoxville News Sentinel*; and a report commissioned by the Bemberg Corporation, Industrial Relations Counsellors, Inc., and Konsul Kummer, comps., "Bericht Uber die Striks in Johnson City (Tenn.) ausgebrochen am 12. Marz und 5. April 1929" (in Hall's possession). Gertraude Wittig supplied me with this document. For the point of view of the local management and other industrialists, see Sargent, "East Tennessee's Rayon Strikes of 1929," 7–32.

30 *Knoxville News Sentinel*, 14 March 1929. For other comments on the religious atmosphere of union meetings, see Galliher interview, 8–9; Tom Tippett, "Southern Situation," speech typescript, meeting held at the National Board, 15 May 1929, p. 3, box 25, and Tippett, "Impressions of Situation at Elizabethton, Tenn. May 10, 11, 1929," typescript, p. 1, both from Young Women's Christian Association Papers, Sophia Smith Collection (Smith College, Northampton, MA).

31 *Knoxville News Sentinel*, 20 March, 29 March 1929; "Instructions for Adjustment of Wage Scale for Girl Help," 15 March 1929; "Bemberg-Glanzstoff Strike (Counter Proposition from Workers)," 22 March 1929; "Preliminary Report of Commissioner of Conciliation," 22 March 1929, all from Records of the Conciliation Service.

32 Grindstaff interview; Committee of Striking Workers[,] Members of United Textile Workers of America to the Honorable Herbert Hoover, 16 April 1929, Records of the Conciliation Service. See also "Preliminary Report of Commissioner of Conciliation," 16 April 1929; William Kelly to James J. Davis, Secretary, US Department of Labor, 15 April 1929; "Excerpts," 16 April 1929, all from Records of the Conciliation Service; and *Elizabethton Star*, 15 April 1929.

33 Dr. J. A. Hardin to Hon. H. H. Horton, 16 May 1929, box 12, Governor Henry H. Horton Papers (Tennessee State Library and Archives); *Knoxville News Sentinel*, 6 May, 10 May, 12 May, 14 May, 19 May, 24 May 1929; Bernstein, *Lean Years*, 18.

34 Edens interview, 14 August 1975, pp. 40, 49; Galliher interview, 33; *Knoxville News Sentinel*, 15 March, 14 May, 16 May, 17 May 1929.

35 Mary Frederickson, "Citizens for Democracy: The Industrial Programs of the YWCA," in *Sisterhood and Solidarity; Workers' Education for Women, 1914–1984*, ed. Joyce L. Kornbluh and Mary Frederickson (Philadelphia: 1984), 75–106; Mary Evans Frederickson, "A Place to Speak Our Minds: The Southern School for Women Workers" (Ph.D. dissertation, University of North Carolina, Chapel Hill, 1981), 92–101; Katharine DuPre Lumpkin interview by Hall, 4 August 1974, transcript, pp. 23–65, Southern Oral History Program Collection; "Marching On," *Life and Labor Bulletin* 7 (June 1929): 2. See also Marion W. Roydhouse, "The 'Universal Sisterhood of Women': Women and Labor Reform in North Carolina, 1900–1932" (Ph.D. dissertation, Duke University, 1980).

36 Alice Henry, "Southern Impressions," 23 August 1927, box 16; and Executive Board Meeting, 30 October 1927, box 2, National Women's Trade Union League Papers (Schlesinger Library, Radcliffe College, Cambridge, MA). *Knoxville News Sentinel*, 7 May, 19 March 1929; "Marching On," 1, 3. See also Elizabeth Christman to Mrs. Howorth, 11 June 1929, box 12, Somerville-Howorth Papers (Schlesinger Library).

37 Reece interview; Galliher interview, 26; *Knoxville News Sentinel*, 14 March, 30 April, 23 May, 25 May 1929; Robert (Bob) Cole interview by Hall, 10 July 1981, transcript, p. 12, Southern Oral History Program Collection; Ina Nell (Hinkle) Harrison interview, 4; Tennessee Federation of Labor, *Proceedings of the Thirty-Third Annual Convention* (Pressmen's Home, TN: 1929), 38.

38 *Knoxville News Sentinel*, 19 March, 14 April, 27 April, 5 May, 27 May 1929; Cole interview, 6–7; Vesta Finley and Sam Finley interview by Frederickson and Marion Roydhouse, 22 July 1975, transcript, pp. 18–19, Southern Oral History Program Collection; *American Bemberg Corp. v. George Miller et al.*, East Tennessee Supreme District Court, 29 January 1930, record of evidence, typescript, box 660, Tennessee Supreme Court Records (Tennessee State Library and Archives); "Hoffman[n] Convicted on Riot Charge: To Appeal Verdict," *Hosiery Worker*, 30 November 1929, pp. 1–2; [company spy] to Horton, 14 April, 15 April 1929, box 13, Horton Papers; Mary Heaton Vorse,

"Rayon Strikers Reluctantly Accept Settlement," press release, 27 May 1929, box 156, Mary Heaton Vorse Papers, Archives of Labor and Urban Affairs (Walter P. Reuther Library, Wayne State University, Detroit, MI); "Norman Thomas Hits at Strike Efficiency," press release, 27 May 1929, ibid.; Ina Nell (Hinkle) Harrison interview, 2; *Chattanooga Times*, 26 May 1929.

39 "Rays of Sunshine in the Rayon War," *Literary Digest*, 8 June 1929, p. 12; *Charlotte Observer*, 2 June 1929; *Raleigh News and Observer*, 24 May 1929.

40 *Raleigh News and Observer*, 24 May 1929. See also, *New York Times*, 26 May 1929, sec. 3, p. 5.

41 Edens interview, 14 August 1975, pp. 43–4; Schuettler interview; Myrtle Simmerly interview by Hall, 18 May 1983 (in Hall's possession); Dugger interview, 22; Ollie Hardin interview by Hall and Evans, 9 August 1979 (in Hall's possession); Effie (Hardin) Carson interview by Hall and Evans, 6 August 1979, transcript, p. 41. Southern Oral History Program Collection. John Fred Holly, who grew up in Elizabethton and worked at the plant during the 1930s, reported that banker E. Crawford (E. C.) Alexander showed him a copy of an agreement between the company and the Elizabethton Chamber of Commerce assuring the rayon concerns that they would never have to pay weekly wages in excess of ten dollars and that no labor unions would be allowed to operate in the town. Holly, "Elizabethton, Tennessee," 306–7. For earlier manifestations of town–county tensions, see *Mountaineer*, 28 December, 31 December 1887; 2 May, 7 March 1902. A model for this community-oriented approach to labor conflict is Herbert G. Gutman, *Work, Culture, and Society in Industrializing America: Essays in American Working-Class and Social History* (New York: 1976), 234–60.

42 James Myers, "Field Notes: Textile Strikes in the South," box 374, Archive Union Files (Martin P. Catherwood Library); *Raleigh News and Observer*, 15 March 1929. See also Hoffmann, "Mountaineer in Industry," 2–5; and *Knoxville News Sentinel*, 14 March, 20 May 1929.

43 Hoffmann, "Mountaineer in Industry," 2–5; Robert (Bob) Moreland and Barbara Moreland interview by Hall, 11 July 1981 (in Hall's possession); Bertha Moreland interview by Hall, 11 July 1981, ibid.; *Chattanooga Times*, 26 May 1929; "Resolution Adopted at Citizens Meeting," 11 March 1930, Records of the Conciliation Service; *New York Times*, 22 April 1929, p. 17; *St. Louis Post Dispatch*, 26 May 1929; *Knoxville News Sentinel*, 15 March, 20 March 1929; *Elizabethton Star*, 15 March 1929; Hardin interview; *American Bemberg Corp. v. George Miller, et al.*, East Tennessee Supreme District Court, 29 January 1930, record of evidence, typescript, box 660, Tennessee Supreme Court Records (Tennessee State Library and Archives). For other support from the countryside, see *Knoxville News Sentinel*, 21 March, 10 May, 20 May 1929.

44 *Knoxville News Sentinel*, 19 March, 24 May 1929; Tippett, "Impressions of Situation at Elizabethton, Tenn.," 1; "Armed Mob in South Kidnaps Organizer Hoffmann," *Hosiery Worker*, 30 March

1929, p. 2; *American Bemberg Corp. v. George Miller et al.*, Tennessee Court of Appeals, 5 September 1930, records of evidence, typescript, box 660, Tennessee Supreme Court Records (Tennessee State Library and Archives); Honard Ward interview by Hall, n.d. [1981] (in Hall's possession).

45 *Knoxville News Sentinel*, 15 May 1929; Reece interview; McCracken, *Strike Injunctions in the New South*, 246. See also Hardin interview; and Raulston interview.

46 Christine Stansell drew my attention to the importance of generational discontinuity. For the argument that precisely because they are "left behind" by the economic developments that pull men into wage labor, woman-centered families may become repositories of alternative or oppositional values, see Mina Davis Caulfield, "Imperialism, the Family, and Cultures of Resistance," *Socialist Revolution* 4 (Oct. 1974): 67–85; and Helen Matthews Lewis, Sue Easterling Kobak, and Linda Johnson, "Family, Religion and Colonialism in Central Appalachia or Bury My Rifle at Big Stone Gap," in *Colonialism in Modern America: The Appalachian Case*, ed. Helen Matthews Lewis, Linda Johnson, and Don Askins (Boone, NC: 1978), 113–39. For a review of the literature on women and development, see Ellen Carol DuBois, Gail Paradise Kelly, Elizabeth Lapovsky Kennedy, Carolyn W. Korsmeyer, and Lillian S. Robinson, *Feminist Scholarship: Kindling in the Groves of Academe* (Urbana, IL: 1985), 135–44. For a modern example relevant to the Elizabethton case, see Elizabeth Moen, Elise Boulding, Jane Lillydahl, and Risa Palm, *Women and the Social Costs of Economic Development; Two Colorado Case Studies* (Boulder, CO: 1981), 1–16, 22–3, 171–8.

47 Bessie Edens, "Why a Married Woman Should Work," in *Scraps of Work and Play*, 30–1; Edens interview, 14 August 1975, pp. 14, 21, 34–5; Edens interview, 5 August 1975; Millie Sample, "Impressions," August 1931, box 9, American Labor Education Service Records.

48 Marion Bonner, "Behind the Southern Textile Strikes," *Nation*, 2 October 1929, pp. 351–2; "Scraps From Our Lives," in *Scraps of Work and Play*, 5–11; Raymond Williams, *The Long Revolution* (London: 1961), 48–71.

49 Corbin, *Life, Work and Rebellion in the Coal Fields*, 92–3; Jameson, "Imperfect Unions"; Nash, "Resistance as Protest"; Tilly, "Paths of Proletarianization"; Bob Korstad, "Those Who Were Not Afraid: Winston-Salem, 1943," in *Working Lives; The Southern Exposure History of Labor in the South*, ed. Marc S. Miller (New York: 1980), 184–99; Dublin, *Women at Work*; Strom, "Challenging 'Woman's Place.' " For the suggestion that female strikers could fall back on parental resources, see Alice Kessler-Harris, *Out to Work: A History of Wage-Earning Women in the United States* (New York: 1982), 160.

50 For the symbolism of female militancy in other cultures, see Shirley Ardener, "Sexual Insult and Female Militancy," in *Perceiving Women*, ed. Shirley Ardener (New York: 1975), 29–53; Caroline

Ifeka-Moller, "Female Militancy and Colonial Revolt: The Women's War of 1929, Eastern Nigeria," in *Perceiving Women*, 127–57; and Judith Van Allen, " 'Sitting on a Man': Colonialism and the Lost Political Institutions of Igbo Women," *Canadian Journal of African Studies*, 6, 2 (1972): 165–81.

51 "Thirteenth Census of the United States, 1910, Manuscript Population Schedule," Carter County, TN, district 7; *Miller's Elizabethton, Tenn.*, *City Directory*, I (Asheville, NC: April 1928); *Miller's Elizabethton, Tenn.*, *City Directory* (1930); *Elizabethton Star*, 14 November 1953, 31 January 1986; Reece interview; Carson interview, 25; Nellie Bowers interview by Hall, 15 May 1983 (in Hall's possession); *Knoxville News Sentinel*, 17 May, 18 May 1929.

52 *American Bemberg Corp. v. George Miller et al.*, East Tennessee District Supreme Court, 29 January 1930, record of evidence, typescript, box 660, Tennessee Supreme Court Records (Tennessee State Library and Archives).

53 Ibid.

54 *Knoxville News Sentinel*, 17 May 1929.

55 Ibid., *American Bemberg Corp. v. George Miller et al.*, East Tennessee District Supreme Court, 29 January 1930, record of evidence, typescript, box 660, Tennessee Supreme Court Records (Tennessee State Library and Archives).

56 *American Bemberg Corp. v. George Miller et al.*, minute books "Q" and "R", Chancery Court minutes, Carter County, TN, 22 July 1929; *American Glanzstoff Corp. v. George Miller et al.*, Court of Appeals, 1, 5 September 1930 (Tennessee Supreme Court and Court of Appeals, Knoxville). On Southern women's bawdy humor, see Rayna Green, "Magnolias Grow in Dirt: The Bawdy Lore of Southern Women," *Southern Exposure* 4, 4 (1977): 29–33.

57 Davis, *Society and Culture in Early Modern France*, 124–51; Ulrich, *Good Wives*, 191–7. For the association of men, rather than women, with individual and collective aggressiveness, see Richard A. Cloward and Frances Fox Pivan, "Hidden Protest: The Channeling of Female Innovation and Resistance," *Signs* 4 (Summer 1979): 651–69.

58 Elizabethton City Council, minutes, 23 May 1929, Minute Book, vol. 5, pp. 356–7 (City Hall, Elizabethton, TN:).

59 *Knoxville News Sentinel*, 5 May 1929; Myers, "Field Notes." For working-class standards of respectability and sexual morality, see Barbara Taylor, *Eve and the New Jerusalem: Socialism and Feminism in the Nineteenth Century* (New York: 1983), 192–205; Ellen Ross, " 'Not the Sort That Would Sit on the Doorstep': Respectability in Pre-World War I London Neighborhoods," *International Labor and Working Class History* 27 (Spring 1985): 39–59; and Kathy Peiss, *Cheap Amusements: Working Women and Leisure in Turn-of-the-Century New York* (Philadelphia: 1986), esp. 88–114.

60 See, for example, Alice Kessler-Harris, "The Autobiography of Ann Washington Craton," *Signs* 1 (Summer 1976): 1019–37.

61 *Knoxville News Sentinel*, 18 May 1929; *American Bemberg Corp. v. George Miller et al.* East Tennessee District Supreme Court, 29 January

1930, record of evidence, typescript, box 660, Tennessee Supreme Court Records (Tennessee State Library and Archives).

62 Edens interview, 5 August 1929.

63 Reece interview.

64 I am classifying as "activists" female strikers who appeared as such in newspaper stories, court records, and interviews – and for whom background information could be found.

65 Danny Miller, "The Mountain Woman in Fact and Fiction of the Early Twentieth Century, Part I," *Appalachian Heritage* 6 (Summer 1978): 48–56; Danny Miller, "The Mountain Woman in Fact and Fiction of the Early Twentieth Century, Part II," ibid., 6 (Fall 1978): 66–72; Danny Miller, "The Mountain Woman in Fact and Fiction of the Early Twentieth Century, Part III," ibid., 7 (Winter 1979): 16–21; Edward Alsworth Ross, "Pocketed Americans," *New Republic*, January 1924, pp. 170–2.

66 For colonists' views of American Indian women, see Mary E. Young, "Women, Civilization, and the Indian Question," in *Clio Was a Woman: Studies in the History of American Women*, ed. Mabel E. Deutrich and Virginia C. Purdy (Washington, DC: 1980), 98–110. For a particularly interesting account of sexual mores, see "Olive Dame Campbell Journal," vol. 4, Jan. 1900–March 1900, esp. pp. 26–7, 30, 33–4, 42–4, 61, 63–5, 67, 72, 78–80, 82, 92, 97, 102, 107–8, 115, 119–20, box 7, John C. and Olive Dame Campbell Papers, Southern Historical Collection; and Whisnant, *All That Is Native & Fine*, 103–79.

67 Charles K. Wolfe, *Tennessee Strings: The Story of Country Music in Tennessee* (Knoxville: 1977), 22–90; Barry O'Connell, "Dick Boggs, Musician and Coal Miner," *Appalachian Journal* 11 (Autumn–Winter 1983–84): 48.

68 *Miller's Elizabethton, Tenn., City Directory* (1930); Reece Interview; *American Bemberg Corp. v. George Miller et al.*, East Tennessee District Supreme Court, 29 January 1930, record of evidence, typescript, box 660, Tennessee Supreme Court Records (Tennessee State Library and Archives); *Knoxville News Sentinel*, 16 May, 17 May 1929; Kelley, "Our Newest South," 343; "Analysis of Union List," 21 October 1929, Records of the Conciliation Service.

69 Whisnant, *All That Is Native & Fine*, 48.

70 Grindstaff interview; Robert and Barbara Moreland interview.

71 Simmerly interview.

72 *Knoxville Journal*, 22 April 1929; sixteen-millimeter film (1 reel), ca. 1929, Helen Raulston Collection (Archives of Appalachia, East Tennessee State University, Johnson City); sixteen-millimeter film (20 reels), ca. 1927–28, Bemberg Industry Records (Tennessee State Library and Archives). Mimi Conway drew my attention to these films and, more important, helped prevent their loss or destruction when the Bemberg plant closed.

73 Anna Weinstock Schneider interview by Julia Blodgett Curtis, 1969, transcript, pp. 161, 166, 172–3, 177, box 1, Anna Weinstock Schneider Papers (Martin P. Catherwood Library).

74 Edens interview, 14 August 1975, p. 4; *Watauga Spinnerette* 1 (July 1930).

75 Bessie Edens, "All Quiet on the Elizabethton Front," *News of Southern Summer School for Women Workers in Industry* 1 (October 1930): 2, American Labor Education Service Records; Dugger interview, 18–19; Grindstaff interview; Charles Wolff, Plant Manager, to Employees, 25 February 1930, Records of the Conciliation Service; Willson to Secretary of Labor, 26 June 1929; "Analysis of Union List."

76 Spencer Miller, Jr., to Davis, 21 March 1930, Records of the Conciliation Service; *American Bemberg Corp. v. George Miller et al.*, East Tennessee District Supreme Court, 29 January 1930, record of evidence, typescript, box 660, Tennessee Supreme Court Records (Tennessee State Library and Archives); Holly, "Elizabethton, Tennessee," 336–68; [US National Labor Relations Board], *Decisions and Orders of the National Labor Relations Board*, vol. 23: *April 22–May 28, 1940* (Washington, DC: 1941), 623–9; ibid., vol. 24: *May 29–June 30, 1940* (Washington, DC: 1940), 727–78.

77 *Elizabethton News*, 13 August 1931; "Resolution Adopted at Citizens Meeting"; Tennessee Taxpayers Association, *A Report with Recommendations Covering a Survey of the Finances and Administrative Methods of the City of Elizabethton Tennessee*. Research Report no. 46 (Nashville: 1940); Holly, "Elizabethton, Tennessee," 179, 212–16, 279.

78 By the fall of 1929, with the rayon plants in full operation, women made up a smaller percentage of the work force than they had before the strike. Whereas they constituted 44 per cent of Glanzstoff workers before the conflict, afterward they made up only 35 per cent. Although most of that change can be accounted for by an expansion in the number of male workers, the absolute number of women employed also fell from 850 to 797, while the number of men employed rose from 1,099 to 1,507. *Knoxville News Sentinel*, 20 May 1929; RR to Willson, 9 October 1929, Records of the Conciliation Service. For Elizabethton activists returning to the work force, see *Miller's Elizabethton, Tenn., City Directory* (1930); Carson interview, 2, 35–8; Edens interview, 14 August 1975, pp. 5–7; Hazel Perry interview by Hall, 20 May 1983 (in Hall's possession); Grindstaff interview; Reece interview; Mamie Horne interview by Hall and Evans, 6 August 1979 (in Hall's possession); and Ina Nell (Hinkle) Harrison interview, pp. 9–10.

79 Bureau of the Census, *Fifteenth Census of the United States: 1930. Population*, vol. III. pt. 2, p. 909; US Department of Commerce, Bureau of the Census, *Sixteenth Census of the United States: 1940. Population*, vol. II, pt. 6 (Washington, DC: 1943), 616; Grindstaff interview.

80 See note 79 above.

81 Edens interview, 14 August 1975, p. 50.

82 For similar conclusions about first-generation immigrant workers, see Peiss, *Cheap Amusements*, 185–8; and Elizabeth Ewen, *Immigrant*

Women in the Land of Dollars; Life and Culture on the Lower East Side, 1890–1925 (New York: 1985), 264–9. For hints of sexual harassment on the job and for women's vulnerability in a marriage market that was no longer controlled by parents, see Reece interview, and Ina Nell (Hinkle) Harrison interview, pp. 18–22.

11

FAMILY VIOLENCE, FEMINISM, AND SOCIAL CONTROL

Linda Gordon

Linda Gordon maps out a new history of social welfare by bringing gender into view. This essay probes the successive frames of interpretation that have guided understandings of family violence, from the nativism of early twentieth-century reformers to the feminism of our own time. In examining historians' interpretations, Gordon comments extensively on the "social control" critique, a historiographical position that emphasizes reform as a vehicle for maintaining the dominant class and controlling those who are seen to threaten it. Gordon does not entirely reject the historiography of reform as social control, but she argues that it does not allow us a way to understand family violence from within.

Feminist views of family violence fully acknowledge conflict within the family, but they have failed to take account of women as perpetrators as well as victims of abuse. Just as men's and women's interests may diverge, Gordon reminds us, so women's and children's interests are not identical.

As she surveys the historiography and changing circumstances of family violence, Gordon suggests the outlines of a revised history of social welfare, one attentive to the complex interrelationships of gender, class, race, and state power.

* * *

In studying the history of family violence, I found myself also confronting the issue of social control, incarnated in the charitable "friendly visitors" and later professional child protection workers who composed the case records I was reading. At first I experienced these social control agents as intruding themselves unwanted into my research. My study was based on the records of Boston "child-saving" agencies, in which the oppressions of class, culture, and gender were immediately evident. The "clients" were mainly poor, Catholic, female immigrants. (It was not that women were responsible for most of the family violence but that they were more often involved with agencies for reasons we shall see below.) The social workers were exclusively well educated and male and overwhelmingly white Anglo-Saxon Protestant (WASP). These workers, authors of case records, were often disdainful, ignorant, and obtuse – at best, paternalistic – toward their clients.

Yet, ironically, these very biases created a useful discipline, showing that it was impossible to study family violence as an objective problem. Attempts at social control were part of the original definition and construction of family violence as a social issue. The very concept of family violence is a product of conflict and negotiation between people troubled by domestic violence and social control agents attempting to change their supposedly unruly and deviant behavior.

In this essay I want to argue not a defense of social control but a critique of its critiques and some thoughts about a better, feminist, framework. I would like to make my argument as it came to me, through studying child abuse and neglect. Nine years ago when I began to study the history of family violence, I assumed I would be focusing largely on wife beating because that was the target of the contemporary feminist activism which had drawn my attention to the problem. I was surprised, however, to find that violence against children represented a more complex challenge to the task of envisioning feminist family policy and a feminist theory of social control.

SOCIAL CONTROL

Many historians of women and the family have inherited a critical view of social control, as an aspect of domination and the source of decline in family and individual autonomy. In situating ourselves with respect to this tradition, it may be useful to trace very briefly the history of the concept. "Social control" is a phrase usually attributed to the sociologist E. A. Ross. He used the phrase as the title of a collection of his essays in 1901, referring to the widest range of influence and regulation socie- ties imposed upon individuals.[1] Building on a Hobbesian view of human individuals as naturally in conflict, Ross saw "social control" as inevitable. Moving beyond liberal individualism, however, he argued for social control in a more specific, American Progressive sense. Ross advocated the active, deliber- ate, expert guidance of human life not only as the source of human progress but also as the best replacement for older, familial, and communitarian forms of control, which he believed were disappearing in modern society.

Agencies attempting to control family violence are preemi- nent examples of the kind of expert social control institutions that were endorsed by Ross and other Progressive reformers. These agencies – the most typical were the Societies for the Prevention of Cruelty to Children (SPCCs) – were established in the 1870s in a decade of acute international alarm about child abuse. They began as punitive and moralistic "chari- table" endeavors, characteristic of nineteenth-century elite moral purity reforms. These societies blamed the problem of family violence on the depravity, immorality, and drunken- ness of individuals, which they often traced to the innate inferiority of the immigrants who constituted the great bulk of their targets. By the early twentieth century, the SPCCs took on a more ambitious task, hoping not merely to cure family pathology but also to reform family life and childrais- ing. Describing the change slightly differently, in the nine- teenth century, child protection agents saw themselves as paralegal, punishing specific offenses, protecting children from specific dangers; in the early twentieth century, they tried to supervise and direct the family lives of those con- sidered deviant.

The view that intervention into the family has increased and has become a characteristic feature of modern society is now often associated with Talcott Parsons's writings of the late 1940s and 1950s. Parsons proposed the "transfer of functions" thesis, the notion that professionals had taken over many family func- tions (for example, education, childcare, therapy, and medical care). Parsons's was a liberal, optimistic view; he thought this professionalization a step forward, leaving the family free to devote more of its time and energy to affective relations. There was already a contrasting, far more pessimistic, interpretation, emanating from the Frankfurt school* of German Marxists who condemned the decline of family autonomy and even attributed to it, in part, the horrors of totalitarianism.

The latter tradition, critical of social control, has conditioned most of the historical writing about social control agencies and influences. Much of the earlier work in this mid-twentieth-century revival of women's history adopted this perspective on social control, substituting gender for class or national categories in the analysis of women's subordination. In the field of child saving in particular, the most influential historical work has adopted this perspective.[2] These critiques usually distinguished an "us" and a "them," oppressed and oppressor. They tended to assume or argue that the social control practices in question served the material interests of a dominant group and hindered the interests of the subordinate. More recently, some women's historians have integrated class and gender into this model, arguing that the growth of the state in the past 150 years has increased individual rights for prosperous women but has only subjected poor women to ever greater control.[3] Alternatively, women's historians represent social control as half of a bargain in which material benefits – welfare benefits, for example – are given to those controlled in exchange for the surrender of power or autonomy.[4]

The development of women's history in the past decade has begun to correct some of the oversimplifications of this "anti-social-control" school of analysis. This work recognizes women's activity – in this case, in constructing modern forms of social control.[5] Historians of social work or other social control institutions, however, have not participated in the rethinking of the paradigm of elite domination and plebian victimization.[6]

The critique of the domination exercised by social work and human services bureaucracies and professionals is not wrong, but its incompleteness allows for some serious distortion. My own views derive from a study of the history of family violence

---

*Associated with the German Institute of Social Research, the intellectuals of the Frankfurt school produced influential social critiques that drew on the work of Sigmund Freud and Karl Marx. Major figures include Theodor W. Adorno, Walter Benjamin, Leo Lowenthal, and Max Horkheimer. Most influential from 1920 to 1950, the Frankfurt school is perhaps best known for its deep pessimism about mass culture, which these philosophers saw as a powerful vehicle of social control and totalitarianism.

and its social control in Boston from 1880 to 1960, using both the quantitative and qualitative analyses of case records from three leading child-saving agencies.[7] Looking at these records from the perspective of children and their primary caretakers (and abusers), women, reveals the impoverishment of the anti-social-control perspective sketched above and its inadequacy to the task of conceptualizing who is controlled and who is controlling in these family conflicts. A case history may suggest some of the complexities that have influenced my thinking.

In 1910 a Syrian family in Boston's South End, here called the Kashys, came to the attention of the Massachusetts Society for the Prevention of Cruelty to Children (MSPCC) because of the abuse of the mother's 13-year-old girl.[8] Mr Kashy had just died of appendicitis. The family, like so many immigrants, had moved back and forth between Syria and the United States several times; two other children had been left in Syria with their paternal grandparents. In this country, in addition to the central "victim," whom I shall call Fatima, there was a 6-year-old boy and a 3-year-old girl, and Mrs Kashy was pregnant. The complainant was the father's sister, and indeed all the paternal relatives were hostile to Mrs Kashy. The MSPCC investigation substantiated their allegations: Mrs Kashy hit Fatima with a stick and with chairs, bit her ear, kept her from school and overworked her, expecting her to do all the housework and to care for the younger children. When Fatima fell ill, her mother refused to let her go to the hospital. The hostility of the paternal relatives, however, focused not only on the mother's treatment of Fatima but mainly on her custody rights. It was their position that custody should have fallen to them after Mr Kashy's death, arguing that "in Syria a woman's rights to the care of her chn [abbreviations in original] or the control of property is not recognized." In Syrian tradition, the paternal grandfather had rights to the children, and he had delegated this control to his son, the children's paternal uncle.

The paternal kin, then, had expected Mrs Kashy to bow to their rights; certainly her difficult economic and social situation would make it understandable if she had. The complainant, the father's sister, was Mrs Kashy's landlady and was thus in a position to make her life very difficult. Mrs Kashy lived with her three children in one attic room without water; she had to go to the ground level and carry water up to her apartment. The relatives offered her no help after her bereavement and Mrs Kashy was desperate; she was trying to earn a living by continuing her husband's peddling. She needed Fatima to keep the house and care for the children.

When Mrs Kashy resisted their custody claims, the paternal relatives called in as a mediator a Syrian community leader, publisher of the *New Syria*, a Boston Arabic-language newspaper. Ultimately the case went to court, however, and here the relatives lost as their custody traditions conflicted with the new preference in the United States for women's custody. Fatima's wishes were of no help to the agency in sorting out this conflict, because throughout the struggle she was ambivalent: sometimes she begged to be kept away from her mother, yet when away, she begged to be returned to her mother. Ultimately, Mrs Kashy won custody but no material help in supporting her children by herself. As in so many child abuse cases, it was the victim who was punished: Fatima was sent to the Gwynne Home, where – at least so her relatives believed – she was treated abusively.

If the story had stopped there one might be tempted to see Mrs Kashy as relatively blameless, driven perhaps to episodes of harshness and temper by her difficult lot. But thirteen years later, in 1923, a "school visitor" brought the second daughter, now 16, to the MSPCC to complain of abuse by her mother and by her older, now married, sister Fatima. In the elapsed years, this second daughter had been sent back to Syria; perhaps Mrs Kashy had had to give up her efforts to support her children. Returning to the United States eighteen months previously, the girl had arrived to find that her mother intended to marry her involuntarily to a boarder. The daughter displayed blood on her shirt which she said came from her mother's beatings. Interviewed by an MSPCC agent, Mrs Kashy was now openly hostile and defiant, saying that she would beat her daughter as she liked.

In its very complexity, the Kashy case exemplifies certain generalizations central to my argument. One is that it is often difficult to identify a unique victim. It should not be surprising that the oppressed Mrs Kashy was angry and violent, but feminist rhetoric about family violence has often avoided this complexity. Mrs Kashy was the victim of her isolation, widow-hood, single motherhood, and patriarchal, hostile in-laws; she also exploited and abused her daughter. Indeed, Mrs Kashy's attitude to Fatima was patriarchal: she believed that children should serve parents and not vice versa. This aspect of patriar-chal tradition served Mrs Kashy. But, in other respects, the general interests of the oppressed group – here the Syrian immigrants – as expressed by its male, *petit bourgeois* leadership, were more inimical to Mrs Kashy's (and other women's) aspira-tions and "rights" than those of the elite agency, the MSPCC. Furthermore, one can reasonably surmise that the daughters were also actors in this drama, resisting their mother's expec-tations as well as those of the male-dominated community, as New World ideas of children's rights coincided with aspirations entirely their own. None of the existing social control critiques can adequately conceptualize the complex struggles in the Kashy family, nor can they propose nonoppressive ways for Fatima's "rights" to be protected.

FEMINISM AND CHILD ABUSE

Feminist theory in general and women's history in particular have moved only slowly beyond the "victimization" paradigm that dominated the rebirth of feminist scholarship. The obstacles to perceiving and describing women's own power have been particularly great in issues relating to social policy and to family violence, because of the legacy of victim blaming. Defending women against male violence is so urgent that we fear women's loss of status as deserving, political "victims" if we acknowledge women's own aggressions. These complexities are at their greatest in the situation of mothers because they are simul-taneously victims and victimizers, dependent and depended on, weak and powerful.

If feminist theory needs a new view of social control, thinking about child abuse virtually demands it. Child abuse cases reveal suffering that is incontrovertible, unnecessary, and remediable. However severe the biases of the social workers attempting to "save" the children and reform their parents – and I will have more to say about this later – one could not advocate a policy of inaction in regard to children chained to beds, left in filthy diapers for days, turned out in the cold. Children, unlike women, lack even the potential for social and economic independence. A beneficial social policy could at least partly address the problem of wife-beating by empowering women to leave abusive situations, enabling them to live in comfort and dignity without men, and encouraging them to espouse high standards in their expectations of treatment by others. It is not clear how one could empower children in analogous ways. If children are to have "rights" then some adults must be appointed and accepted, by other adults, to define and defend them.

Women, who do most of the labor of childcare and thus have the strongest emotional bonds to children, have fought for and largely won rights to child custody over the past 150 years. Yet women are often the abusers and neglecters of children. Indeed, child abuse becomes the more interesting and challenging to feminists because in it we meet women's rage and abuses of power. Furthermore, child abuse is a gendered phenomenon, related to the oppression of women, whether women or men are the culprits, because it reflects the sexual division of the labor of reproduction. Because men spend, on the whole, so much less time with children than do women, what is remarkable is not that women are violent toward children but that men are responsible for nearly half of the child abuse. But women are always implicated because even when men are the culprits, women are usually the primary caretakers who have been, by definition, unable to protect the children. When protective organizations remove children or undertake supervision of their caretakers, women often suffer greatly, for their maternal work, trying as it may be, is usually the most pleasurable part of their lives.

Yet in the past two decades of intense publicity and scholarship about child abuse, the feminist contribution has been negligible. This silence is the more striking in contrast to the legacy of the first wave of feminism, particularly in the period 1880 to 1930, in which the women's rights movement was tightly connected to child welfare reform campaigns. By contrast, the second wave of feminism, a movement heavily influenced by younger and childless women, has spent relatively little energy on children's issues. Feminist scholars have studied the social organization of mothering in theory but not the actual experiences of childraising, and the movement as a whole has not significantly influenced child welfare debates or policies. When such issues emerge publicly, feminists too often assume that women's and children's interests always coincide. The facts of child abuse and neglect challenge this assumption, as does the necessity sometimes of severing maternal custody in order to protect children.

PROTECTING CHILDREN

Child abuse was "discovered" as a social problem in the 1870s. Surely many children had been ill-treated by parents before this, but new social conditions created an increased sensitivity to the treatment of children and, possibly, actually worsened children's lot. Conditions of labor and family life under industrial capitalism may have made poverty, stress, and parental anger bear more heavily on children. The child abuse alarm also reflected growing class and cultural differences in beliefs about how children *should* be raised. The anti-cruelty-to-children movement grew out of an anti-corporal-punishment campaign, and both reflected a uniquely professional-class view that children could be disciplined by reason and with mildness. The SPCCs also grew from widespread fears among more privileged people about violence and "depravity" among the urban poor; in the United States, these fears were exacerbated by the fact that these poor were largely immigrants and Catholics, threatening the WASP domination of city culture and government.

On one level, my study of the case records of Boston child-saving agencies corroborated the anti-social-control critique: the work of the agencies did represent oppressive intervention into working-class families. The MSPCC attempted to enforce culturally specific norms of proper parenting that were not only alien to the cultural legacy of their "clients" but also flew in the face of many of the economic necessities of the clients' lives. Thus, MSPCC agents prosecuted cases in which cruelty to children was caused, in their view, by children's labor: girls doing housework and childcare, often staying home from school because their parents required it; girls and boys working in shops, peddling on the streets; boys working for organ grinders and lying about their ages to enlist in the navy. Before the First World War, the enemies of the truant officers were usually parents, not children. To immigrants from peasant backgrounds it seemed irrational and blasphemous that adult women should work while able-bodied children remained idle. Similarly, the MSPCC was opposed to the common immigrant practice of leaving children unattended and allowing them to play and wander in the streets. Both violated the MSPCC's norm of domesticity for women and children; proper middle-class children in those days did not – at least not in the cities – play outside on their own.

The child savers were attempting to impose a new, middle-class urban style of mothering and fathering. Mothers were supposed to be tender and gentle and above all, to protect their children from immoral influences; the child savers considered yelling, rude language, or sexually explicit talk to be forms of cruelty to children. Fathers were to provide models of emotional containment, to be relatively uninvolved with children; their failure to provide adequate economic support was often interpreted as a character flaw, no matter what the evidence of widespread, structural unemployment.

MSPCC agents in practice and in rhetoric expressed disdain for immigrant cultures. They hated the garlic and olive oil smells of Italian cooking and considered this food unhealthy (over-stimulating, aphrodisiac). The agents were unable to distinguish alcoholics and heavy drinkers from moderate wine and beer drinkers, and they believed that women who took spirits were degenerate and unfit as mothers. They associated many of these forms of depravity with Catholicism. Agents were also convinced of the subnormal intelligence of most non-WASP and especially non-English-speaking clients; indeed, the agents' comments and expectations in this early period were similar to social workers' views of black clients in the mid-twentieth century. These child welfare specialists were particularly befuddled by and disapproving of non-nuclear childraising patterns: children raised by grandmothers, complex households composed of children from several different marriages (or, worse, out-of-wedlock relationships), children sent temporarily to other households.

The peasant backgrounds of so many of the "hyphenated" Americans created a situation in which ethnic bias could not easily be separated from class bias. Class misunderstanding, moreover, took a form specific to urban capitalism: a failure to grasp the actual economic and physical circumstances of this immigrant proletariat and subproletariat. Unemployment was not yet understood to be a structural characteristic of industrial capitalism. Disease, overcrowding, crime, and – above all – dependence were also not understood to be part of the system, but, rather, were seen as personal failings.

This line of criticism, however, only partially uncovers the significance of child protection. Another dimension and a great deal more complexity are revealed by considering the feminist aspect of the movement. Much of the child welfare reform energy of the nineteenth century came from women and was organized by the "woman movement."[9] The campaign against corporal punishment, from which the anti-child-abuse movement grew, depended upon a critique of violence rooted in feminist thought and in women's reform activity. Women's reform influence was largely responsible for the softening of childraising norms.[10] The delegitimation of corporal punishment, noticeable among the prosperous classes by mid-century, was associated with exclusive female responsibility for childraising, with women's victories in child custody cases, even with women's criticisms of traditionally paternal discipline.[11]

Feminist thinking exerted an important influence on the agencies' original formulations of the problem of family violence. Most MSPCC spokesmen (and those who represented the agency in public were men) viewed men as aggressors and women and children, jointly, as blameless victims. However simplistic, this was a feminist attitude. It was also, of course, saturated with class and cultural elitism: these "brutal" and "depraved" men were of a different class and ethnicity than the MSPCC agents, and the language of victimization applied to women and children was also one of condescension. Nevertheless, despite the definition of the "crime" as cruelty to children, MSPCC agents soon included wife beating in their agenda of reform.

Even more fundamentally, the very undertaking of child protection was a challenge to patriarchal relations. A pause to look at my definition of "patriarchy" is necessary here. In the 1970s a new definition of that term came into use, first proposed by Kate Millett but quickly adopted by the US feminist movement: patriarchy became a synonym for male supremacy, for "sexism." I use the term in its earlier, historical, and more specific sense, referring to a family form in which fathers had control over all other family members – children, women, and servants.

This concept of a patriarchal family is an abstraction, postulating common features among family forms that differed widely across geography and time. If there was a common material base supporting this patriarchal family norm (a question requiring a great deal more study before it can be answered decisively), it was an economic system in which the family was the unit of production. Most of the MSPCC's early clients came from peasant societies in which this kind of family economy prevailed. In these families, fathers maintained control not only over property and tools but also, above all, over the labor power of family members. Historical patriarchy defined a set of parent–child relations as much as it did relations between the sexes, for children rarely had opportunities for economic independence except by inheriting the family property, trade, or craft. In some ways mothers, too, benefited from patriarchal parent–child relations. Their authority over daughters and young sons was important when they lacked other kinds of authority and independence, and in old age they gained respect, help, and consideration from younger kinfolk.

The claim of an organization such as an SPCC to speak on behalf of children's rights, its claim to the license to intervene in parental treatment of children, was an attack on patriarchal power. At the same time, the new sensibility about children's rights and the concern about child abuse were symptoms of a weakening of patriarchal family expectations and realities that had already taken place, particularly during the eighteenth and early nineteenth centuries in the United States. In this weakening, father–child relations had changed more than husband–wife relations. Children had, for example, gained the power to arrange their own betrothals and marriages and to embark on wage work independent of their fathers' occupations (of course, children's options remained determined by class and cultural privileges or the lack of them, inherited from fathers). In contrast, however, wage labor and long-distance mobility often made women, on balance, more dependent on husbands for sustenance and less able to deploy kinfolk and neighbors to defend their interests against husbands.

Early child protection work did not, of course, envision a general liberation of children from arbitrary parental control or from the responsibility of filial obedience. On the contrary, the SPCCs aimed as much to reinforce a failing parental/paternal authority as to limit it. Indeed, the SPCC spokemen often criticized excessive physical violence against children as a symptom of inadequate parental authority. Assaults on children were provoked by children's insubordination; in the interpretation of nineteenth-century child protectors, this showed that parental weakness, children's disobedience, and child abuse were mutually reinforcing. Furthermore, by the turn of the century, the SPCCs discovered that the majority of their cases concerned neglect, not assault, and neglect exemplified to them the problems created by the withdrawal, albeit not always conscious or deliberate, of parental supervision and authority (among the poor who formed the agency clientele there were many fathers who deserted and many more who were inadequate providers). Many neglect and abuse cases ended with *children* being punished, sent to reform schools on "stubborn child" charges.

In sum, the SPCCs sought to reconstruct the family along lines that altered the old patriarchy, already economically unviable, and to replace it with a modern version of male supremacy. The SPCCs' rhetoric about children's rights did not extend to a parallel articulation of women's rights; their condemnation of wife beating did not include endorsement of the kind of marriage later called "companionate," implying equality between wife and husband. Their new family and childraising norms included the conviction that children's respect for parents needed to be inculcated ideologically, moralistically, and psychologically because it no longer rested on an economic dependence lasting beyond childhood. Fathers, now as wage laborers rather than as slaves, artisans, peasants, or entrepreneurs, were to have single-handed responsibility for economic support of their families; women and children should not contribute to the family economy, at least not monetarily. Children instead should be occupied full-time in learning cognitive lessons from professional teachers, psychological and moral lessons from the full-time attention of a mother. In turn, women should devote themselves to mothering and domesticity.

FEMINISM, MOTHERING, AND INDUSTRIAL CAPITALISM

This childraising program points to a larger irony – that the "modernization" of male domination, its adaptation to new economic and social conditions, was partly a result of the influence of the first wave of feminism. These first "feminists" rarely advocated full equality between women and men and never promoted the abolition of traditional gender relations or the sexual division of labor. Allowing for differences of emphasis, the program just defined constituted a feminist as well as a liberal family reform program in the 1870s. Indeed, organized feminism *was* in part such a liberal reform program, a program to adapt the family and the civil society to the new economic conditions of industrial capitalism, for consciously or not, feminists felt that these new conditions provided greater possibilities for the freedom and empowerment of women.

To recapitulate, child protection work was an integral part of the feminist as well as the bourgeois program for modernizing the family. Child saving had gender as well as class and ethnic content, but in none of these aspects did it simply or homogeneously represent the interests of a dominant group. The antipatriarchalism of the child protection agencies was an unstable product of several conflicting interests. Understanding this illuminates the influence of feminism on the development of a capitalist industrial culture even as feminists criticized the new privileges it bestowed on men and its degradation of women's traditional work. Historians have often relied on one of these oversimplified views of the relation of feminism to capitalism and industrialism: either feminism is the expression of bourgeois woman's aspirations, an ultimate individualism that tears apart the remaining noninstrumental bonds in a capitalist society; *or*, feminism is inherently anticapitalist, deepening and extending the critique of domination to show its penetration even of personal life and the allegedly "natural." Although there is a little truth in both versions, at least one central aspect of feminism's significance for capitalism has been omitted in these formulations – its role in redefining family norms and particularly norms of mothering.

Changes in the conditions of motherhood in an industrializing society were an important part of the experiences that drew women to the postbellum feminist movement. For most women, and particularly for urban poor women, motherhood became more difficult in wage labor conditions. Mothers were more isolated from support networks of kin, and mothering furthered that isolation, often requiring that women remain out of public space. The potential dangers from which children needed protection multiplied, and the increasing cultural demands for a "psychological parenting" increased the potential for maternal "failure."[12] These changes affected women of all classes, while, at the same time, motherhood remained the central identity for women of all classes. Childbirth and child-raising, the most universal parts of female experience, were the common referents – the metaphoric base of political language – by which feminist ideas were communicated.

As industrial capitalism changed the conditions of motherhood, so women began to redefine motherhood in ways that would influence the entire culture. They "used" motherhood simultaneously to increase their own status, to promote greater social expenditure on children, and to loosen their dependence on men, just as capitalists "used" motherhood as a form of unpaid labor. The working-class and even sub-working-class women of the child abuse case records drew "feminist" conclusions – that is, they diagnosed their problems in terms of male supremacy – in their efforts to improve their own conditions of mothering. In their experiences, men's greater power (economic and social), in combination with men's lesser sense of responsibility toward children, kept these women from being as good at mothering as they wanted. They responded by trying to rid themselves of those forms of male domination that impinged most directly on their identity and work as mothers and on children's needs as they interpreted those needs.

But if child protection work may have represented *all* mothers' demands, it made *some* mothers – poor urban mothers – extremely vulnerable by calling into question the quality of their mothering, already made more problematic by urban wage-labor living conditions, and by threatening them with the loss of their children. Poor women had less privacy and therefore less impunity in their deviance from the new childraising norms, but their poverty often led them to ask for help from relief agencies, therefore calling themselves to the attention of the child-saving networks. Yet poor women did not by any means figure only on the victim side, for they were also often enthusiastic about defending children's "rights" and correcting cruel or neglectful parents. Furthermore, they used an eclectic variety of arguments and devices to defend their control of their children. At times they mobilized liberal premises and rhetoric to escape from patriarchal households and to defend their custody rights; they were quick to learn the right terms in which to criticize their husbands and relatives and to manipulate social workers to side with them against patriarchal controls of other family members. Yet at other times they called upon traditional relations when community and kinfolk could help them retain control or defend children. Poor women often denounced the "intervention" of outside social control agencies like the SPCCs but only when it suited them, and at other times they eagerly used and asked such agencies for help.

Let me offer another case history to illustrate this opportunistic and resourceful approach to social control agencies. An Italian immigrant family, which I will call the Amatos, were "clients" of the MSPCC from 1910 to 1916.[13] They had five young children from the current marriage and Mrs Amato had three from a previous marriage, two of them still in Italy and one daughter in Boston. Mrs Amato kept that daughter at home to do housework and look after the younger children while she earned money doing piece-rate sewing at home. This got the family in trouble with a truant officer, and they were also accused, in court, of lying to Associated Charities (a consortium of private relief agencies), saying that the father had deserted them when he was in fact living at home. Furthermore, once while left alone, probably in the charge of a sibling, one of the younger children fell out of a window and had to be hospitalized. This incident provoked agency suspicions that the mother was negligent.

Despite her awareness of these suspicions against her, Mrs Amato sought help from many different organizations, starting with those of the Italian immigrant community and then reaching out to elite social work agencies, reporting that her husband was a drunkard, a gambler, a nonsupporter, and a wife beater. The MSPCC agents at first doubted her claims because Mr Amato impressed them as a "good and sober man," and they blamed the neglect of the children on his wife's incompetence in managing the wages he gave her. The MSPCC ultimately became convinced of Mrs Amato's story because of her repeated appearances with severe bruises and the corroboration of the husband's father, who was intimately involved in the family troubles and took responsibility for attempting to control his son. Once the father came to the house and gave his son "a warning and a couple of slaps," after which he improved for a while. Another time the father extracted from him a pledge not to beat his wife for two years!

Mrs Amato wanted none of this. She begged the MSPCC agent to help her get a divorce; later she claimed that she had not dared take this step because her husband's relatives threatened to beat her if she tried it. Then Mrs Amato's daughter (from her previous marriage) took action, coming independently to the MSPCC to bring an agent to the house to help her mother. As a result of this complaint, Mr Amato was convicted of assault once and sentenced to six months. During that time Mrs Amato survived by "a little work and. . .Italian friends have helped her." Her husband returned, more violent than before: he went at her with an axe, beat the children so much on the head that their "eyes wabbled [sic]" permanently, and supported his family so poorly that the children went out begging. This case closed, like so many, without a resolution.

The Amatos' case will not support the usual anti-social-control interpretation of the relation between oppressed clients and social agencies. There was no unity among the client family and none among the professional intervenors. Furthermore, the intervenors were often dragged into the case and by individuals with conflicting points of view. Mrs Amato and Mrs Kashy were not atypical in their attempts to use "social control" agencies in their own interests. Clients frequently initiated agency intervention; even in family violence cases, where the stakes were high – losing one's children – the majority of complaints in this study came from parents or close relatives who believed that their own standards of childraising were being violated.[14]

In their sparring with social work agencies, clients did not usually or collectively win because the professionals had more resources. Usually no one decisively "won." Considering these cases collectively, professional social work overrode working-class or poor people's interests, but in specific cases the professionals did not always formulate definite goals, let alone achieve them. Indeed, the bewilderment of the social workers (something usually overlooked because most scholarship about social work is based on policy statements, not on actual case records) frequently enabled the clients to go some distance toward achieving their own goals.

The social control experience was not a simple two-sided

trade-off in which the client sacrificed autonomy and control in return for some material help. Rather, the clients helped shape the nature of the social control itself. Formulating these criticisms about the inadequacy of simple anti-social-control explanations in some analytic order, I would make four general points.

First, the condemnation of agency intervention into the family, and the condemnation of social control itself as something automatically evil, usually assumes that there can be, and once was, an autonomous family. On the contrary, no family relations have been immune from social regulation.[15] Certainly the forms of social control I examine here are qualitatively and quantitatively different, based on regulation from "outside," by those without a legitimate claim to caring about local, individual values and traditions. Contrasting the experience of social control to a hypothetical era of autonomy, however, distorts both traditional and modern forms of social regulation.

The tendency to consider social control as unprecedented, invasive regulation is not only an academic mistake. It grew from nineteenth-century emotional and political responses to social change. Family autonomy became a symbol of patriarchy only in its era of decline (as in 1980s' New Right* rhetoric). Family "autonomy" was an oppositional concept in the nineteenth century, expressing a liberal ideal of home as a private and caring space in contrast to the public realm of increasingly instrumental relations. This symbolic cluster surrounding the family contained both critical and legitimating responses to industrial capitalist society. But as urban society created more individual opportunities for women, the defense of family autonomy came to stand against women's autonomy in a conservative opposition to women's demands for individual freedoms. (The concept of family autonomy today, as it is manipulated in political discourse, mainly has the latter function, suggesting that women's individual rights to autonomous citizenship will make the family more vulnerable to outside

*Gaining influence in the 1980s, the New Right promoted a conservative agenda that sought to use state power to strengthen its version of social and family values – for example, by seeking to reinstate prayer in public schools and censoring pornography. The New Right's most prominent success has been in its efforts to restrict abortion. The term "New Right" signals a departure from traditional American conservatism, which has been more libertarian – that is, opposed to government intervention.

intervention.) The Amatos' pattern, a more patriarchal pattern, of turning to relatives, friends, and, when they could not help, Italian-American organizations (no doubt the closest analogue to a "community" in the New World), was not adequate to the urban problems they now encountered. Even the violent and defensive Mr Amato did not question the right of his father, relatives, and friends to intervene forcibly, and Mrs Amato did not appear shocked that her husband's relatives tried, perhaps successfully, to hold her forcibly in her marriage. Family autonomy was not an expectation of the Amatos.

Second, the social control explanation sees the flow of initiative going in only one direction: from top to bottom, from professionals to clients, from elite to subordinate. The power of this interpretation of social work comes from the large proportion of truth it holds and also from the influence of scholars of poor people's movements who have denounced elite attempts to blame "the victims." The case records show, however, that clients were not passive but, rather, active negotiators in a complex bargaining. Textbooks of casework recognize the intense interactions and relationships that develop between social worker and client and often counsel the social worker to examine her or his participation in that relationship.[16] This sense of mutuality, power struggle, and interrelationship, however, has not penetrated historical accounts of social work/social control encounters.

Third, critics of social control often fail to recognize the active role of agency clients because they conceive of the family as a homogeneous unit. This notion of the family as a unified entity is revealed in sentence structure, particularly in academic language: "The family is in decline," "threats to the family," "the family responds to industrialization." These usages often express particular cultural norms about what "the family" is and does, and they mask intrafamily differences and conflicts of interest. Usually "the family" becomes a representation of the interests of the family head, if it is a man, carrying an assumption that all family members share his interests. (Families without a married male head, such as single-parent or grandparent-headed families, are in the common usage broken, deformed, or incomplete families, and thus do not qualify for these assumptions regarding family unity.) Among the clients in family violence cases, outrage over the intervention into the family was frequently anger over a territorial violation, a challenge to male authority; expressed differently, it was a reaction to the exposure to others of intrafamily conflict and of the family head's lack of control. Indeed, the interventions actually *were* more substantive, more invasive, when their purpose was to change the status quo than if they had been designed to reinforce it. The effect of social workers' involvement was often to change existing family power relations, usually in the interest of the weaker family members.

Social work interventions were often invited by family members; the inviters, however, were usually the weaker members of a family power structure, women and children. These invitations were made despite the fact, well known to clients, that women and children usually had the most to lose (despite fathers' frequent outrage at their loss of face) from MSPCC intervention because by far the most common outcome of agency action was not prosecution and jail sentences but the removal of children, an action fathers dreaded less than mothers. In the immigrant working-class neighborhoods of Boston the MSPCC became known as "the Cruelty," eloquently suggesting poor people's recognition and fear of its power. But these fears did not stop poor people from initiating contact with the organization. After the MSPCC had been in operation ten years, 60 per cent of the complaints of known origin (excluding anonymous accusations) came from family members, the overwhelming majority of these from women with children following second. These requests for help came not only from victims but also from mothers distressed that they were not able to raise their children according to their own standards of good parenting. Women also maneuvered to bring child welfare agencies into family struggles on their sides. There was no Society for the Prevention of Cruelty to Women, but in fact women like Mrs Amato were trying to turn the SPCC into just that. A frequent tactic of beaten, deserted, or unsupported wives was to report their husbands as child abusers; even when investigations found no evidence of child abuse, social workers came into their homes offering, at best, help in getting other things women wanted – such as support payments, separation and maintenance agreements, relief – and, at least, moral support to the women and condemnation of the men.[17]

A fourth problem is that simple social control explanations

often imply that the clients' problems are only figments of social workers' biases. One culture's neglect may be another culture's norm, and in such cultural clashes, one group usually has more power than the other. In many immigrant families, for example, 5-year-olds were expected to care for babies and toddlers; to middle-class reformers, 5-year-olds left alone were neglected, and their infant charges deserted. Social control critiques are right to call attention to the power of experts not only to "treat" social deviance but also to define problems in the first place. But the power of labeling, the representation of poor people's behavior by experts whose status is defined through their critique of the problematic behavior of others, coexists with real family oppressions. In one case an immigrant father, who sexually molested his 13-year-old daughter, told a social worker that that was the way it was done in the old country. He was not only lying but also trying to manipulate a social worker, perhaps one he had recognized as guilt-ridden over her privileged role, using his own fictitious cultural relativism. His daughter's victimization by incest was not the result of oppression by professionals.

FEMINISM AND LIBERALISM

The overall problem with virtually all existing critiques of social control is that they remain liberal and have in particular neglected what feminists have shown to be the limits of liberalism. Liberalism is commonly conceived as a political and economic theory without social content. In fact, liberal political and economic theory rests on assumptions about the sexual division of labor and on notions of citizens as heads of families.[18] The currently dominant left-wing tradition of anti-social-control critique, that of the Frankfurt school, merely restates these assumptions, identifying the sphere of the "private" as somehow natural, productive of strong egos and inner direction, in contrast to the sphere of the public as invasive, productive of conformity and passivity. If we reject the social premises of liberalism (and of Marx), that gender and the sexual division of labor are natural, then we can hardly maintain the premise that familial forms of social control are inherently benign and public forms are malignant.

Certainly class relations and domination are involved in social control. Child protection work developed and still functions in class society, and the critique of bureaucracies and professionalism has shown the inevitable deformation of attempts to "help" in a society of inequality, where only a few have the power to define what social order should be. But this critique of certain kinds of domination often serves to mask other kinds, particularly those between women and men and between adults and children.

Social work, and, more generally, aspects of the welfare state have a unique bearing on gender conflicts. Women's subordination in the family, and their struggle against it, not only affected the construction of the welfare state but also the operations of social control bureaucracies. In fact, social control agencies such as the MSPCC and, more often, individual social workers, did sometimes help poor and working-class people. They aided the weaker against the stronger and not merely by rendering clients passive. Social work interventions rarely changed assailants' behavior, but they had a greater impact on victims. Ironically, the MSPCC thereby contributed more to help battered women, defined as outside its jurisdiction, than it did abused children. Industrial capitalist society gave women some opportunity to leave abusive men because they could earn their own livings. In these circumstances even a tiny bit of material help, a mere hint as to how to "work" the relief agencies, could turn these women's aspirations for autonomy into reality. Women could sometimes get this help despite class and ethnic prejudices against them. Italian-American women might reap this benefit even from social workers who held derogatory views of Italians; single mothers might be able to get help in establishing independent households despite charity workers' suspicions of the immorality of their intentions. Just as in diplomacy the enemy of one's enemy may be *ipso facto* a friend, in these domestic dramas the enemy of one's oppressor could be an ally.

These immigrant clients – victims of racism, sexism, and poverty, perhaps occasional beneficiaries of child welfare work – were also part of the creation of modern child welfare standards and institutions. The welfare state was not a bargain in which the poor got material help by giving up control. The control itself was invented and structured out of these interactions. Because many of the MSPPC's early "interventions" were in fact invitations by family members, the latter were in some ways teaching the agents what were appropriate and enforceable standards of childcare. A more institutional example is the mothers' pension legislation developed in most of the United States between 1910 and 1920. As I have argued elsewhere, the feminist reformers who campaigned for that reform were influenced by the unending demands of single mothers, abounding in the records of child neglect, for support in raising their children without the benefit of men's wages.[19]

The entire Progressive era's child welfare reform package, the social program of the women's rights movement, and the reforms that accumulated to form the "welfare state" need to be reconceived as not only a campaign spearheaded by elites. They resulted also from a powerful if unsteady pressure for economic and domestic power from poor and working-class women. For them, social work agencies were a resource in their struggle to change the terms of their continuing, traditional, social control, which included but was not limited to the familial. The issues involved in an anti-family-violence campaign were fundamental to poor women: the right to immunity from physical attack at home, the power to protect their children from abuse, the right to keep their children – not merely the legal right to custody but the actual power to support their children – and the power to provide a standard of care for those children that met their own standards and aspirations. That family violence became a social problem at all, that charities and professional agencies were drawn into attempts to control it, were as much a product of the demands of those at the bottom as of those at the top.

Still, if these family and child welfare agencies contributed to women's options, they had a constricting impact too. I do not wish to discard the cumulative insights offered by many critiques of social control. The discrimination and victim blaming that women encountered from professionals were considerable, the more so because they were proffered by those defined as "helping." Often the main beneficiaries of professionals' intervention hated them most, because in wrestling with them one rarely gets what one really wants but rather another interpretation of one's needs. An accurate view of the meanings of this "outside" intervention into the family must maintain in its analysis, as the women clients did in their strategic decisions, awareness of a tension between various forms of social control and the variety of factors that might contribute to improvements in personal life. This is a contradiction that women particularly face, and there is no easy resolution of it. There is no returning to an old or newly romanticized "community control" when the remnants of community rest on a patriarchal power structure hostile to women's aspirations. A feminist critique of social control must contain and wrestle with, not seek to eradicate, this tension.

NOTES

First published in *Feminist Studies* 12 (Fall 1986): 453–78. Used by permission.

Because this paper distills material I have been musing on throughout my work on my book about family violence, *Heroes of Their Own Lives: The Politics and History of Family Violence* (New York: 1988), my intellectual debts are vast. Several friends took the time to read and help me with versions of this essay, including Ros Baxandall, Sara Bershtel, Susan Stanford Friedman, Allen Hunter, Judith Leavitt, Ann Stoler, Susan Schechter, Pauline Terrelonge, Barrie Thorne; I am extremely grateful. Elizabeth Pleck took time out from her own book on the history of family violence to give me the benefit of her detailed critique. I had help in doing this research from Anne Doyle Kenney, Paul O'Keefe, and Jan Lambertz in particular. Discussions with Ellen Bassuk, Wini Breines, Caroline Bynum, Elizabeth Ewen, Stuart Ewen, Marilyn Chapin Massey, and Eve Kosofsky Sedgewick helped me clarify my thoughts.

1 E. A. Ross, *Social Control* (New York: 1901).
2 A few examples follow: Anthony M. Platt, *The Child Savers: The Invention of Delinquency* (Chicago: 1969); Barbara Ehrenreich and Deirdre English, *For Her Own Good: One Hundred and Fifty Years of the Experts' Advice to Women* (Garden City, NY: 1978); Christopher Lasch, *Haven in a Heartless World: The Family Besieged* (New York: 1977); and his *The Culture of Narcissism: American Life in an Age of Diminishing Expectations* (New York: 1979); Jacques Donzelot, *The Policing of Families*, trans. Hurley (New York: 1979); Barbara M. Brenzel, *Daughters of the State: A Social Portrait of the First Reform School for Girls in North America, 1856–1905* (Cambridge: 1983); Stuart Ewen, *Captains of Consciousness: Advertising and the Social Roots of the Consumer Culture* (New York: 1976); Daniel T. Rodgers, *The Work Ethic in Industrial America, 1850–1920* (Chicago: 1974); and Nigel Parton, *The Politics of Child Abuse* (New York: 1985).
3 Eileen Boris and Peter Bardaglio, "The Transformation of Patriarchy: The Historic Role of the State," in *Families, Politics, and Public Policy: A Feminist Dialogue on Women and the State*, ed. Irene Diamond (New York: 1983), 70–93; Judith Areen, "Intervention between Parent and Child: A Reappraisal of the State's Role in Child Neglect and Abuse Cases," *Georgetown Law Journal* 63 (March 1975): 899–902; Mason P.

Thomas, Jr., "Child Abuse and Neglect, pt. 1: Historical Overview, Legal Matrix, and Social Perspectives," *North Carolina Law Review* 50 (February 1972): 299–303.

4 John H. Ehrenreich, *The Altruistic Imagination: A History of Social Work and Social Policy in the United States* (Ithaca, NY: 1985).

5 Alice Kessler-Harris, *Out to Work: A History of Wage-Earning Women in the United States* (New York: 1982), esp. chap. 7; Gwendolyn Wright, *Moralism and the Modern Home: Domestic Architecture and Cultural Conflict in Chicago, 1873–1913* (Chicago: 1980); Kathryn Sklar, "Hull House As a Community of Women in the 1890s," *Signs* 10 (Summer 1985): 658–77; Susan Ware, *Beyond Suffrage: Women in the New Deal* (Cambridge, MA: 1981).

6 Exceptions include Michael C. Grossberg, "Law and the Family in Nineteenth-Century America" (Ph.D. dissertation, Brandeis University, 1979); Boris and Bardaglio, "The Transformation of Patriarchy."

7 The agencies were the Boston Children's Service Association, the Massachusetts Society for the Prevention of Cruelty to Children, and the Judge Baker Guidance Center. A random sample of cases from every tenth year was coded and analyzed. A summary of the methodology and a sampling of findings can be found in my "Single Mothers and Child Neglect, 1880–1920," *American Quarterly* 37 (Summer 1985): 173–92.

8 Case code no. 2044.

9 In Boston the MSPCC was called into being largely by Kate Gannett Wells, a moral reformer, along with other members of the New England Women's Club and the Moral Education Association. These women were united as much by class as by gender unity. Wells, for example, was an antisuffragist, yet in her club work she cooperated with suffrage militants such as Lucy Stone and Harriet Robinson, for they considered themselves all members of a larger, loosely defined but nonetheless coherent community of prosperous, respectable women reformers. This unity of class and gender purpose *was* organized feminism at this time. See New England Women's Club Papers, Schlesinger Library; MSPCC Correspondence Files, University of Massachusetts/Boston Archives, folder 1; Arthur Mann, *Yankee Reformers in the Urban Age* (Cambridge, MA: 1954), 208.

10 Ann Douglas, *The Feminization of American Culture* (New York: 1977).

11 For examples of the growing anti-corporal-punishment campaign, see Lyman Cobb, *The Evil Tendencies of Corporal Punishment As a Means of Moral Discipline in Families and School* (New York: 1847); Mrs. C.A. Hopkinson, *Hints for the Nursery* (Boston: 1863); Mary Blake, *Twenty-Six Hours a Day* (Boston: 1883); Bolton Hall, "Education by Assault and Battery," *Arena* 39 (June 1908): 466–7. For historical commentary, see N. Ray Hiner, "Children's Rights, Corporal Punishment, and Child Abuse: Changing American Attitudes, 1870–1920," *Bulletin of the Menninger Clinic* 43, 3 (1979): 233–48; Carl F. Kaestle, "Social Change, Discipline, and the Common School in Early Nineteenth-Century America," *Journal of Interdisciplinary*

History 9 (Summer 1978): 1–17; Myra C. Glenn, "The Naval Reform Campaign against Flogging: A Case Study in Changing Attitudes toward Corporal Punishment, 1830–1850," *American Quarterly* 35 (Fall 1983): 408–25; Robert Elno McGlone, "Suffer the Children: The Emergence of Modern Middle-Class Family Life in America, 1820–1870" (Ph.D. dissertation, University of California at Los Angeles, 1971).

12 Nancy Chodorow and Susan Contratto, "The Fantasy of the Perfect Mother," in *Rethinking the Family: Some Feminist Questions*, ed. Barrie Thorne and Marilyn Yalom (New York: 1982); Joseph Goldstein, Anna Freud, and Albert J. Solnit, *Beyond the Best Interests of the Child* (New York: 1973); and *Before the Best Interests of the Child* (New York: 1979).

13 Case code no. 2042.

14 To this argument it could be responded that it is difficult to define what would be a parent's "own" standards of childraising. In heterogeneous urban situations, childraising patterns change rather quickly, and new patterns become normative. Certainly the child welfare agencies were part of a "modernization" (in the United States called Americanization) effort, attempting to present new family norms as objectively right. However, in the poor neighborhoods, poverty, crowding, and the structure of housing allowed very little privacy, and the largely immigrant clients resisted these attempts and retained autonomous family patterns, often for several generations. Moreover, my own clinical and research experience suggests that even "anomic" parents, or mothers, to be precise, tend to have extremely firm convictions about right and wrong childraising methods.

15 Nancy Cott, for example, has identified some of the processes of community involvement in family life in eighteenth-century Massachusetts, in her "Eighteenth-Century Family and Social Life Revealed in Massachusetts Divorce Records," *Journal of Social History* 10 (Fall 1976): 20–43; Ann Whitehead has described the informal regulation of marital relations that occurred in pub conversations in her "Sexual Antagonism in Herefordshire," in Diana Leonard Barker and Sheila Allen, *Dependence and Exploitation in Work and Marriage* (London: 1976), 169–203.

16 For example, see William Jordan, *The Social Worker in Family Situations* (London: 1972); James W. Green, *Cultural Awareness in the Human Services* (Englewood Cliffs, NJ: 1982); Alfred Kadushin, *Child Welfare Services* (New York: 1980), chap. 13.

17 Indeed, so widespread were these attempts to enmesh social workers in intrafamily feuds that they were responsible for a high proportion of the many unfounded complaints the MSPCC always met. Rejected men, then as now, often fought for the custody of children they did not really want as a means of hurting their wives. One way of doing this was to bring complaints against their wives of cruel treatment of children, or the men charged wives with child neglect when their main desire was to force the women to live with them again. Embittered, deserted wives might arrange to have their

husbands caught with other women.

18 Zillah Eisenstein, *The Radical Future of Liberal Feminism* (New York: 1981); Joan B. Landes, "Hegel's Conception of the Family" (125–44); and Mary Lyndon Shanley, "Marriage Contract and Social Contract in Seventeenth-Century English Political Thought" (80–95), both in Jean Bethke Elshtain, ed., *The Family in Political Thought* (Amherst: 1982).

19 See my "Single Mothers and Child Neglect."